# The Metrics Manifesto

# The Metrics Manifesto

## Confronting Security with Data

**RICHARD SEIERSEN**

WILEY

Published by John Wiley & Sons, Inc., Hoboken, New Jersey.
Published simultaneously in Canada.

For general information on our other products and services or for technical support,
please contact our Customer Care Department within the United States at (800)
762-2974, outside the United States at (317) 572-3993 or fax (317) 572-4002.

Wiley also publishes its books in a variety of electronic formats. Some content that
appears in print may not be available in electronic formats. For more information about
Wiley products, visit our website at www.wiley.com.

*Library of Congress Cataloging-in-Publication Data*

Names: Seiersen, Richard, author.
Title: The metrics manifesto : confronting security with data / Richard
    Seiersen.
Description: First edition. | Hoboken, New Jersey : Wiley, [2022] |
    Includes index.
Identifiers: LCCN 2021062802 (print) | LCCN 2021062803 (ebook) | ISBN
    9781119515364 (cloth) | ISBN 9781119515401 (adobe pdf) | ISBN
    9781119515418 (epub)
Subjects: LCSH: Risk assessment—Data processing. |
    Performance—Measurement—Data processing. | Quantitative research—Data
    processing. | Security systems—Data processing. | Hazard
    mitigation—Data processing.
Classification: LCC TA169.55.R57 S45 2022 (print) | LCC TA169.55.R57
    (ebook) | DDC 363.1/02—dc23/eng/20220302
LC record available at https://lccn.loc.gov/2021062802
LC ebook record available at https://lccn.loc.gov/2021062803

Cover Design: Wiley
Cover Image: © Sandipkumar Patel/Getty Images
SKY10033129_032422

To Helena. If patience is a virtue, then you are the most virtuous person I know. Thank you for your unending support, understanding, caring, and occasionally awe-inspiring motivation. I love you.

—Richard

# Contents

# Foreword

*By Doug Hubbard*

When Richard and I co-authored *How to Measure Anything in Cybersecurity Risk*, I saw firsthand how he applies his energy, wit, and real-world experience to one of the most important issues in twenty-first-century management. Now, he has brought his insights and style of delivery to this critical issue again in *The Metrics Manifesto*.

At one point in this book, Richard suggests that *The Metrics Manifesto* may be a lofty title, but he does everything an author could do to justify the name. It is an ambitious book in the breadth of solutions described in comprehensive examples. The chapters of his book avoid the hand-waving common to so many books for managers and, instead, focus on delivering understanding as well as the details of doing real-world risk analysis. Whether the reader is just starting to explore these topics or is already an expert looking for the finer points of risk analysis, this book has the goods.

He starts with primers on basic subjects like the logic of uncertainty. The reader gets plenty of help with numerous illustrations and examples throughout the book. He includes extensive discussions of everything needed to apply these ideas, including hundreds of lines of R code for those who want to be more hands-on. The book could even be a standalone explanation of Monte Carlo simulations and Bayesian methods by itself.

Like me, Richard is a skeptic by habit. He questions many common assumptions about what works and what doesn't in cybersecurity. After we implement cybersecurity capabilities, he challenges us to ask, "*What would I see occurring that would let me know if it does (work)?*" He refers to this as *productive skepticism* (a term I think I will use more often). While his professional experience – as both a hands-on cybersecurity expert and a CISO – is an excellent basis for accepting many of his claims, he doesn't ask the reader to rely entirely on that. He supports his claims with numerous specific references in each chapter.

As a cybersecurity professional who rose through the ranks, Richard has direct experience with what data should inform the decision-making in cyber.

He introduces the reader to a set of critical "rate" metrics: burndown, arrival, wait-time, and escape rates. Each has a dedicated chapter where he justifies the need for such measurements, as well as giving complete instructions and code that is nearly "copy/paste" ready. These metrics and others are combined into a dashboard that actually supports decisions, which is refreshing compared to so many that I see.

Richard Seiersen has a knack for entertaining delivery while never compromising on practical, useful information. The balance he has found ensures that he covers basic concepts without fluff while managing to cover detail with context. Rarely will a professional in any field find a book that combines textbook-like examples, detailed code like a how-to manual, the extensive citations of a scientific publication, easy-to-understand illustrations for the visually oriented, interesting historical backgrounds for the methods, and the humor and excitement of a passionate writer. *The Metrics Manifesto* should be on the short list of required reading for cybersecurity professionals everywhere.

# Preface: How This Book Came to Be

*"Retain uncertainty without obscuring certainty."*

A lot has changed since the publication of *How to Measure Anything in Cybersecurity Risk*. At the time, I was getting pulled into consulting side hustles, keynotes, and numerous meetups, on top of my former day gig as a serial CISO. It seemed that Fortune-level enterprises, leading startups, and nonprofits had a growing interest in quantitatively measuring risk. In the span of a year, what started out as informally helping a few fellow CISOs grew into what I call *speed consulting*.

In the last year alone, I have had about 50 of these "hot dates." Initially, engagements were framed as recovery from "stoplight" risk management. You likely know what I am talking about. It's the risk register that is made of red, yellow, and green colors. And if you throw in a couple of fancy heatmaps, you have the state of the art in risk management. These customers wanted to move beyond that.

As I met with more quant sojourners, I started to notice a different and more fundamental problem: metrics. Thus, my focus shifted from the ivory tower of quantitative risk management to the rubber-meets-the-road of operational metrics.

The first step in helping customers was identifying where they were on their metrics journey. From there, paving the way to the next destination. As I listened and learned, a common pattern of questions emerged:

- Am I covering all my assets?
- Am I remediating my security backlog fast enough?
- Am I creating more or less attack surface?
- Am I reducing the time to live of threats and vulnerabilities?
- Am I getting a good return on my security investments?

All of the above can be summarized as *"Can I prove I am getting better?"* I ran with this question and started to evolve a simple approach around these five things. It needed to be delivered in an initial one-hour engagement. And I wanted something applicable to both legacy and digitally elite players alike. So I created a framework and started using it religiously on all my engagements.

I am pleased this framework-based approach received "10 out of 10" scores with my customers (most of them). I always received an email just after a consultation with scores and comments. And the follow-up notes often consisted of, *"Can I get more, is there a book on this? What's next?"* I sensed there might be more to explore here. That sense led to the book you are reading.

I think a big contributor to the positive feedback was a simple, but contagious, measurement point of view. At the root of that point of view is one sentiment, *confrontation.* Those who have worked with me have likely heard me quip, *"What would I see occurring specifically, unambiguously, empirically that would let me know we are getting better?"* This is a confrontational question. It's also a data-driven question. It asks, *"Where are the countable things that tell me how we are doing?"*

My other favorite thing to say is, *"Retain uncertainty without obscuring certainty."* All I am saying is this: If we are going to measure things, leave room for the unknown. Don't throw your hands up and rub a red, yellow, green, or high, medium, low over your data. (Colors are fine, they just need to be undergirded with unambiguously counting.) Let's learn how to make the best bets we can, given our data and our uncertainty.

This book aims to bring this all together for you. It starts with the point-of-view material – what I call the manifesto – and then follows through with a framework and quantitative methods. Hanging off of all of that is some code – occasionally a lot of code.

This is the book I would give to all my speed consulting dates. It's all here and then some. Thanks to them – you can have it too. I hope it helps you in your metrics journey as you begin to confront security with data.

# About the Technical Review Team

I would like to thank my technical review team for the insights they provided.

## Robert D. Brown III

Robert D. Brown III is a senior decision and risk analyst supporting executives facing complex, high-risk strategic planning opportunities, and project and portfolio evaluation and risk management problems. As a practitioner of decision analysis, Robert helps decision makers measure the value and risk associated with the important decisions they face in order to make informed trade-offs and choices. His experience spans diverse industrial and commercial fields, including petroleum and chemicals, energy, utilities, supply chain and logistics, pharmaceuticals, electronics manufacturing, telecommunications, IT, commercial real estate, federal agencies, insurance, and project finance. He currently serves as a senior strategy analyst with Novelis Inc., the world's largest manufacturer of flat-rolled aluminum products.

Robert has been an avid promoter of escaping "spreadsheet hell" using superior quantitative tools like Analytica (since 1996) and the R language for statistical computing. He is the author of *Business Case Analysis with R – Simulation Tutorials to Support Complex Business Decisions* (March 2018), a collection of tutorials intended to help analysts perform business case analyses and communicate their results with better tools than error-prone spreadsheets.

Robert graduated from the Georgia Institute of Technology with a Bachelor of Science in Mechanical Engineering.

## Anuj Gargeya Malkapuram

Anuj Gargeya Malkapuram is a security engineer supporting and leading cross-functional teams and enterprise-level security initiatives. As an expert and practitioner in security detection and incident response, threat intelligence and security engineering, Anuj evangelizes information security across organizations. He is currently working as a lead security engineer with Salesforce. Prior to that, he worked in FinTech, e-commerce, and SaaS organizations such as Amazon and LendingClub Corporation.

Anuj has filed multiple patents with the United States Patent and Trademark Office. He was named first Inventor in detecting active security threats using innovative methods such as data science, machine learning, and statistical methods. His work was also published in multiple international journals. Anuj is working with nonprofit organizations, such as the Council for Emerging National Security Affairs (CENSA), to identify and study future national security challenges and improve long-term policy making; Cloud Security Alliance; and various other recognized internet security organizations.

Anuj graduated from San Jose State University with a Master of Science in Electrical Engineering, specializing in Computer Networking and Security.

## Kaela Seiersen

Kaela Seiersen's editing experience spans breadth of both genre and size. Her past work includes technical nonfiction on both a large and small scale, scientific articles, personal statements, academic essays, and creative pieces, among others. Past editing works have been published by *Forbes* and Wiley, as well as many smaller tech and collegiate publications.

Kaela honed her editing skills during her time at University of California–Berkeley, where she studied Cognitive Science. She is currently based out of Salt Lake City, Utah, and is focused on expanding her technical and editorial skills. She hopes that her skillset will soon include both web design and bluegrass banjo.

# CHAPTER 1

# Introduction: The Manifesto and the BOOM! Framework

*I don't believe in astrology; I'm a Sagittarius and we're skeptical.*

— Arthur C. Clarke

*We are scientists. We don't blog. We don't twitter. We take our time... bear with us while we think.* Comical words found in *The Slow Science Manifesto*[1] written by none other than The Slow Science Academy. Their manifesto serves first and foremost as a reminder to themselves. It defines who they are and aspire to be. It also serves to set public expectations. In this case, "don't expect much, and certainly not via Twitter." And yet they humbly advocate for a point of view, *"Science needs time to think. Science needs time to read, and time to fail. Science does not always know what it might be at right now."* A good manifesto does all these things. It creates identity for its signees, it sets expectations for its audience, and it advocates for a point of view without being too much of a bully.

The Metrics Manifesto strives to do all those things, particularly the last one – a point of view without too much tyranny. It endeavors to be a framework for creating simple security metrics and advanced ones for those who need them. Lastly, this book serves as a guide for making a complete enterprise security metrics program – a program that is grounded in the principle of confronting security with data.

One caveat before you start: A manifesto typically outlines a minority position. You wouldn't need a manifesto if everyone already agreed with you. And while this is a minority position relative to security, it's likely a majority position with measurement professionals at large. The term *measurement professionals* includes scientists, actuaries, statisticians, engineers, and others. This is the group of people who seemed to align with our previous book titled *How to Measure Anything in Cybersecurity Risk*

(Wiley 2016). The actuaries really liked it! In 2018, it was required reading for The Society of Actuaries exam prep. While the Manifesto is quite different from that work, it fully aligns in measurement spirit. Be forewarned: The methods herein may be foreign and at times challenging. When you feel unsure, just imagine measurement experts past and present cheering you on!

Lastly, I do hope "The Manifesto" produces *productive skepticism* about security. It should come naturally to us. After all, security professionals poke and prod to discover why someone else's digital ideas are risky. Shouldn't a true skeptic turn that same confrontational mindset on themselves and muse, *"This security capability I've deployed may not work. What would I see occurring that would let me know if it does?"* That's the first step in confronting security. It's the first step in designing a powerful security metrics system that makes a significant difference in our battle against our adversaries.

## What's Next: Caveats and Epiphanies

The next section covers the manifesto and the BOOM Framework. The manifesto is built around four key observations. Each observation, in turn, has one or more supporting beliefs. You don't need to become a convert to those beliefs. In fact, you should maintain doubt. That would line up with the theme of "confronting security with data."

The BOOM Framework is built around five key baselines. And these five baselines each get hefty chapters dedicated to them. Now for some caveats.

**The first caveat** is that skipping chapters will be rough without the right background. That's why I recommend reading the whole book.

**My next caveat** is the same one Doug Hubbard and I made in our last book: *This is not a statistics book.* What is it then? It's a metrics book. I know it seems obvious to say that – but I think certain readers appreciate being forewarned. If you are coming here looking for the latest, greatest, in-depth quantitative stuff, then this may not be the book for you. That being said, there may be some perspectives that even seasoned data scientists, statisticians, and others may find of interest.

**Next to the last caveat:** This book has code. The good news is that much of the code is in the form of one-liners (some lines might be quite long due to clever tricks of the trade). It's not my plan to turn you into a data scientist. First, I don't think I am qualified. Second, it's completely unnecessary. Why become a carpenter when you only need to use a hammer?

**Last caveat:** This one is on my qualifications to write a book with such a lofty title. My qualifications are that I am well acquainted with operational sadness. I've spent most of my career in the foxhole – both on the vendor side and in operations at varying organizational levels. The whole time, I couldn't shake the feeling that there must be a better way to manage operations – particularly security. Dissatisfied, and prone to wander, I started to look outside of security and even technology. My question was, *"Who else was solving big problems where uncertainty abounds and the risks are real?"* This is when I started running across people I will refer to as *measurement experts.*

Measurement experts are the humble statisticians, natural scientists, decision analysts, and other folks tackling seemingly impossible-to-measure problems. They are all decidedly more educated than me, and a few can sling code really well. But what I bring to the kitchen table, and you do too, is operational experience within a problem domain. Once I relaxed my prejudices about my lack of quantitative savvy, I started to become productive – dare I say creative. This newfound freedom led to the following "epiphanies of the obvious."

Epiphanies of the Obvious

- **Computers are very good at math.** So good at it, in fact, that you don't need to be. Understanding calculus has great utility, but your computers often know enough for most of your problems.
- **Measurement experts create their wares for other people to use.** This is similar to the cobbler who makes shoes for others to wear – just not for himself. There is a vast array of freely available analytic tools made for people like you and me.
- **Problem understanding is job #1, not quantitative skills.** My favorite quote by Charles Kettering reads, *"A problem well defined is a problem half solved."* Once you have framed your problem well, you can usually pull down the code you need from the spice rack of analytics to start baking. If you happen to have a problem that is out of reach, call an expert – 99% of the problems you have are likely in reach if you spend enough time framing your problem and being resourceful.
- **The last epiphany (which we covered in the first book) was that our goal should be to "beat the competing model."** I just need to be slightly better than the competition, not perfect. In short, when you think you must have perfect math, code, statistics, i.e. "metrics" then you are bound to the fate of Sisyphus. He was the king cursed to push a boulder up a hill for all eternity. I think this mindset may be the blocker that prevents security teams from taking things to the next level in operational excellence, I am very sad to say.

Thus, my ambitions for this book, and for you, remain humble. I merely want to beat the competing model for security metrics. That model is typically just a list of basic counts of things and not much more. Don't get me wrong – lists of metrics and counts are not necessarily bad. In fact, they are necessary. I just know we can do better together.

Next up is "The Manifesto" and the BOOM! Metrics Framework.

## The Metrics Manifesto and BOOM!

*A lot of people have problems with public confrontation, but it doesn't worry me at all. I can handle myself. I know my martial arts.* – Pink

This section presents the pithy "Metrics Manifesto." It's less than a page in length. Think of it as the ethos, or spirit, behind the book. I encourage re-reading it from time to time.

The rest of the chapter outlines the BOOM! Framework. It's the metrics framework that evolved out of the aforementioned speed consulting. It also provides an outline for the book. With BOOM, you will encounter interesting measurement methods like survival analysis, burndown rates, arrival analysis, interarrival analysis, escape rate, Bayesian data analysis, and more. Each method is designed to help you confront your security program with data. Taken as a whole, these methods embody the Metrics Manifesto.

## The (Modern) Metrics Manifesto

**Observation:** Most metrics count; the best ones confront.

*Belief: "We believe shrinking attack surface, while not slowing value exposure, is the new job #1 for security."*
*Belief: "We also believe not doing this gives advantage to our adversaries and reduces business opportunity."*

**Observation:** Most metrics reveal what is certain; the best ones also retain what is uncertain.

*Belief: "We believe metrics that ignore our uncertainty ignore our adversaries."*

**Observation:** Most metrics focus on beating benchmarks; the best ones focus on beating the competing model.

*Belief: "We don't believe in benchmarks (for the most part), and neither do our adversaries."*
*Belief: "We believe in continuous improvement because our adversaries attack, and our business expose value…continuously."*

**Observation:** Most metrics require data; the best ones can start with little or none.

*Belief:* *"We believe resourcefulness with small data is always better than complexity with big data."*
*Belief:* *"We also believe expertise can be turned into data when you have none – data, that is."*

## BOOM: Baseline Objectives and Optimization Measurements

*The winners are usually the guys who get 5% fewer of their planes shot down, or use 5% less fuel, or get 5% more nutrition into their infantry at 95% of the cost.* – How Not to Be Wrong[2]

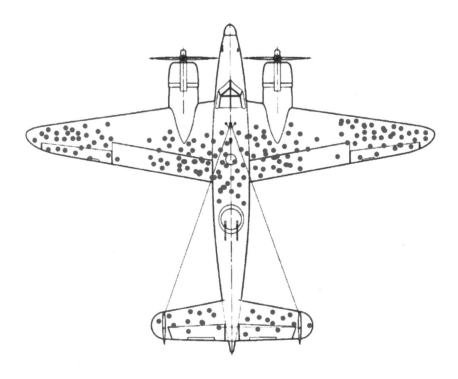

## Bullet Holes and Bombers

During WWII, the US Navy continually lost bombers to anti-aircraft artillery. In hopes of building a more resilient aircraft, officers suggested they examine all planes returning from battle. They came to the conclusion that reinforcements should go above the wings and tailpiece, where there were more bullet holes (see image above).

That approach seemed reasonable to everyone … except for one statistician by the name of Abraham Wald. Wald believed that the secret to building a more anti-aircraft-proof bomber lay in the planes that *didn't* make it back. It turns out Wald was right. Planes that had damage in low-impact areas (as seen in the figure) survived. Planes that didn't make it back had bullet holes in critical areas, where pilots sat and where the engines were located.

What was the problem here? The Navy officers were using the wrong object of measurement. If they had followed through with their plans, armor would have gone everywhere but where it was needed. The engines and cockpit would have stayed exposed, leading to a colossal waste of life and money.

We discuss the problems of having the wrong object of measurement in our first book. It is a frequent and costly error that can plague whole industries. How could battle-hardened military experts be so wrong about something so important?

### The Ease of Self-Deception

We confuse what's *easy to measure*, like bullet holes in returned planes, with what is *important to measure*, like bullet holes in downed planes. We deceive ourselves by measuring only what is obvious, forgetting the goal of our measurement. Wald's statistics training prepared him to catch this form of self-deception.

As security people, the question we have to ask is, *"Are we measuring the right things?"* Or, have we been deceived? If we only count security events without considering our objectives, then the answer is likely, "Yes we have been deceived!" The next section introduces BOOM – a framework to help you avoid deception and focus on capability measurement and objectives for betterment.

## BOOM Defined

BOOM stands for Baseline Objectives and Optimization Measurements. Its ingredients include:

- Five baseline measurements
- A KPI-based scoring system

- Reusable data structures
- Simple dashboard objects

The first component of **B**OOM is **B**aselines – the fundamental measurements behind the BOOM framework. These metrics baseline your capabilities over time. They reveal if your capabilities are optimizing (improving), scaling (keeping up), or degrading.

The second concept in **BO**OM is **O**bjectives. Objectives define the capability "outcome" and its goal for improvement. An objective is similar to key performance indicators (KPIs). An example objective might be: *Reduce the time to live of customer facing exploitable vulnerabilities by 80% by the end of Q4.* You would use one or more baselines to measure this objective.

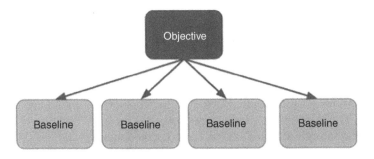

The next section defines each of the five baselines starting with survival analysis.

## Survival Analysis

Survival analysis, TTL analysis, and engineering failure analysis are all related analytics for measurement of event survival times. In this case, they measure the complete range of survival times as a curve (seen below). As you will learn in Chapter 2, survival analysis dates back 400-plus years. Today it's used prominently in epidemiology and actuarial sciences.

The goal is a more complete and data-rich answer to how long risk survives. For example: "50% of critical vulnerabilities live for 48 hours or longer, 10% live for two weeks or longer, and 1% live for one year or longer." You may have an improvement in the average TTL of critical vulnerabilities while seeing those at the 1% ranges growing in age.

Plain averages obscure your capabilities' true performance. That's why not measuring this way leads to uncertainty that gives advantage to the bad guys.

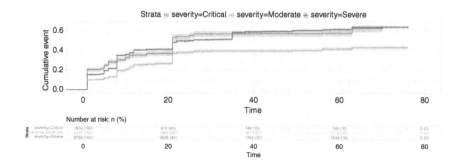

## Burndown Metrics

Burndowns are a ratio of risk removed over total risk. Imagine in January you had 100 new critical vulnerabilities added and 50 removed. That is a 50% burndown rate. Next month, there are 10 new and 25 fixed. The overall, or cumulative, burndown for the two months is 68% (75/110) with a positive trend of 18%.

The following graph is an example of BOOM at work. It's one of many visualizations for measuring quarterly KPIs. The vertical dotted lines are KPI targets. The distributions (bell-shaped objects) show our uncertainty.

If the far-right distribution for Team B could talk, it would say, *"The real burndown rate is around 85% but it may be closer to 75% or 90% . . . if you want more certainty I need more data!"* Don't worry if this seems a bit Greek to you. By the end of the book, and particularly Chapter 3, it will seem normal.

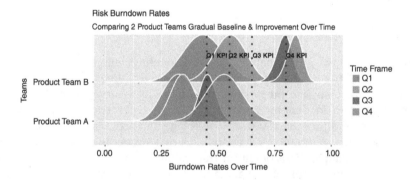

Measuring our uncertainty about meeting KPIs reflects the second manifesto observation, *"Most metrics reveal what is certain, the best ones also retain what is uncertain."* When you are measuring capabilities, you are measuring rates over time.

There will always be some uncertainty when it comes to rates. Consider batting averages. Batting averages are based on an accumulation of data over a time frame. In five games, you may bat .400. Over the last three years, you batted .270. Without a broader time frame, you can get fooled due to small data.

In the graph above, Product Team B is largely meeting their Q4 objective. I say "largely" because the distribution is ~20% to the left of the last KPI line. Team B clearly met their Q3 KPI. We know this because there is zero overlap of the Q3 distribution with the third KPI line.

Note how Team B's Q3 and Q4 distributions overlap. The fact is, Q3 and Q4 may be nearly identical, given our uncertainty. Does that mean burndown rates haven't moved much in the last six months? Perhaps. The big gains were between Q2 and Q3.

One last observation. It is entirely possible that Product Team A (row below B) made no real progress the whole year. Look at how much the distributions overlap. You will be introduced to methods to help you credibly gauge the differences in data rates.

## Arrival Rates

Burndown rates measure your capabilities for getting rid of risk. It's considered a "right of boom," or shift right, measurement – meaning, burndown measures processes that occur after a bad thing has happened.

Arrival rates are "left of boom" – or "shift left." You are baselining the rate with which risk materializes, with the idea being that you can implement risk-prevention capabilities.

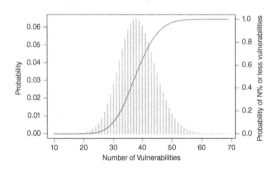

It may seem counterintuitive, but things like vulnerabilities tend to have consistent arrival rates over time. In Chapter 6, which focuses on interarrivals, you will apply "Open Source Intelligence" (OSINT) on the National Vulnerability Database (NVD). Spoiler, what we also learn is that the arrival rates for extreme vulnerabilities do not fluctuate wildly year over year.

Arrivals have an impact on your organization. You have to respond to the rate with which risk materializes – be it third- or first-party sourced.

You will learn how to create and interpret graphs like this one that measure the probability of vulnerability arrivals. Based on the data, there is a 60% chance of 40 extreme vulnerabilities (or less) showing up over the next 365 days. It is retaining our uncertainty without obscuring our certainty.

## Wait-Times (Interarrival Time)

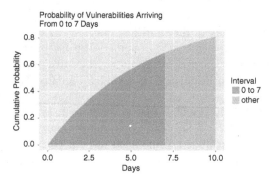

Arrivals measure how much risk shows up in a given time frame. A related measure is the time between arrivals, called interarrival times (aka wait-times). This is the focus of Chapter 6.

Interarrival time is a common measure in operations management. It is used for queue measurement and optimization. The "things" in our queue are threats and vulnerabilities. If we are going to effectively manage the queue, we need to measure what's in it.

A leading risk indicator would be a decrease in wait-times. This graph shows a predicted wait-time between extreme vulnerabilities. It is forecasting the probability of one event in seven days or less. It's roughly 70%. This could also be applied to any type of threat – phishing, ransomware, or any myriad of event types you are looking to control. In a sense, you have queues for each of these risks.

## Escape Rates

There is a rate with which risk moves from a state of control to a lesser state of control. A canonical use case is software bugs. Bugs that move from development to production have escaped. While this is a fairly common software measure, it has not been applied broadly to security. Chapter 7 focuses on escape rates.

Modern software development is predicated on speed of release. Being able to reduce escapes without impacting velocity would be an important asset in such environments. (Consider Spotify. It deploys upwards of 20,000 times a day.)[3]

There is a rate at which risk escapes. How might you measure that?

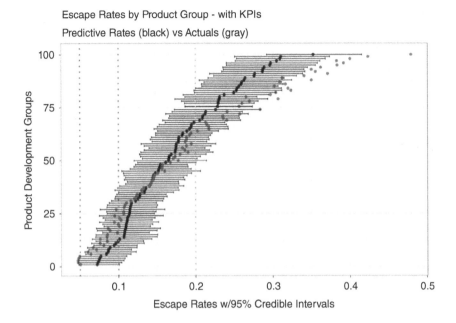

Escape Rates by Product Group - with KPIs

Predictive Rates (black) vs Actuals (gray)

A reasonable place to start would be with naive escape rates. That is a simple cumulative ratio of vulnerabilities found in stage over those found in production. At first, there would not be a one-to-one correlation between vulnerabilities found in development to those later discovered in production, of course. The law of large numbers would soon produce stable rates. As correlative capabilities improve, one-to-one symmetry could be achieved. That is just not the place to start for 99% of teams.

## Next Steps

This chapter sets both the ethos and direction for what is to come. The next section of the book focuses almost exclusively on the five BOOM baselines. Along the way, you will get exposed to Bayesian data analysis.

The goal is not a cookie-cutter approach to metrics. Rather, it is a model-based approach. The intent is to expose security practitioners to new ideas – to bring more into the measurement fold, and to help lift security up as a practice and career through better measurement.

## Administrivia and Sundry Items

### *Book Site*

All code will be hosted on the book's site: www.themetricsmanifesto.com. As is only natural for books with lots of code – there will be updates. Thus, I will publish bug fixes along with new and interesting tools with regularity.

### *Getting R*

You can download R at https://cran.r-project.org/mirrors.html. CRAN stands for Comprehensive R Archive Network. Select the CRAN mirror site closest to you, then use the box labeled "Download and Install R." Or, you can use one of these two options based on your operating system:

- https://cloud.r-project.org/bin/macosx/
- https://cloud.r-project.org/bin/windows/

### *Getting RStudio*

RStudio is an "integrated development environment," or IDE. While you likely only copy and paste code in this book, RStudio can be a convenience for running R applications. You can download and install it from the links found here:

- https://www.rstudio.com/products/rstudio/download/#download
  - Windows 10
  - Mac

### *Learning R*

There are hundreds if not thousands of freely available resources for learning R. Here are a few you may want to consider. I frankly have not tried them. Google seemed to like them:

- Free Code Camp: https://www.youtube.com/watch?v=_V8eKsto3Ug
- Tutorial Point: https://www.tutorialspoint.com/r/index.htm
- Code Academy: https://www.codecademy.com/learn/learn-r

## *How I Learned R*

My learning path on R started about 10 years ago. I used books, Google, and coffee. I rarely if ever read plain-ol'-coding books. My favorite materials are from people dealing with small and messy data sets. This includes research psychologists, cognitive scientists, evolutionary biologists, and such. Many of them are instructors who had to learn stats to do their jobs, as opposed to being statisticians already. Perhaps that makes them better explainers.

## Notes

1. Slow Science Academy. (2021). The Slow Science Manifesto. http://slow-science.org/
2. Ellenberg, J. (2015). *How Not to Be Wrong: The Power of Mathematical Thinking* (Illustrated ed.). Penguin Books.
3. Nelson, D. (2020, November 20). Spotify scales its infrastructure with thousands of microservices, open source, and "fail faster" approach. SiliconANGLE. https://siliconangle.com/2020/11/20/spotify-scales-infrastructure-thousands-microservices-open-source-fail-faster-approach-kubecon/#:%7E:text=With%20thousands%20of%20data%20pipelines,today%2C%20if%20not%20more%20so

# CHAPTER 2

# Time to Event Metrics

*Ticking away the moments that make up a dull day*
*You fritter and waste the hours in an offhand way*

— Pink Floyd, *Time*

Plague Doctor

**This chapter introduces basic time-to-event metrics.** We start with historical background and motivation for improvement. We will borrow heavily from a class of threat hunters called *epidemiologists*. We also introduce a 400-year-old risk management tool called the *life table* – a tool still in use by actuaries and epidemiologists. Next, we present the tiniest amount of code (five lines or less), and we will explain what each line does. Useful visualizations are also presented.

Chapter Contents:

- **Threat Hunting with Dr. Snow:** Historical motivation for our methods
- **A Haberdasher's Life Tables:** A 400-year-old reusable data structure for time to live metrics – created by the first data scientist
- **Measuring Time to Events in R!:** A detailed explanation of a tiny amount of code for the novice analyst
- **Life Table Metrics:** Basic metrics that are very useful
- **Visualizing Survival:** Standard visualization

## Threat Hunting with Dr. Snow

Dr. Thomas Snow is the father of modern epidemiology. He led a data science battle on cholera, a deadly threat ravaging 1850s London. His data-driven methods traced the source of the disease so it could be mitigated. Despite having scientifically sound data (even by today's standards), he faced fierce opposition from a gang of scientists called *miasmists*.

> *In Snow's day most physicians believed that cholera was caused by "miasmas" – poisonous gases that were thought to arise from sewers, swamps, garbage pits, open graves, and other foul-smelling sites of organic decay.*[1]

In contrast, Snow was convinced cholera was a waterborne disease. He came to this conclusion through tallying up the frequencies of deaths combined with patterns like location and time. You can see a data visualization (map) in Figure 2.1. It shows his analysis as a rudimentary but useful data visualization. Black marks represent frequency and location of deaths within a given time frame.

He then pinpointed commonalities in these locations – likely causes and interventions. His analysis led him to dig up sewage lines in specific spots. At first digging proved fruitless – to the applause of the miasmists. Unphased, Snow pushed on, emboldened by the results coming from his data modeling.

Eventually, he discovered the leaky culprit. It was a sewage cistern spewing disease into a major water pump's well. This led to the now-famous removal of the handle from the Broad Street pump.[2] You can see the pump in Figure 2.1. It's the one center in the cluster or data. Deaths in the pump's area quickly waned.

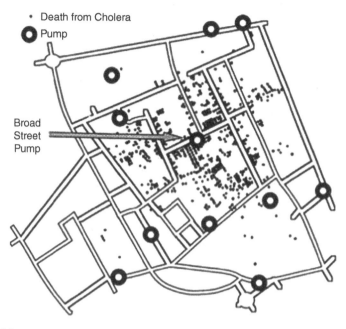

FIGURE 2.1

Despite his success, Snow's nemeses persisted in mocking his anti-miasmatic ways. The thought of waterborne organisms causing gruesome deaths was more than their gentlemanly minds could bear. The good news is that the weight of evidence in favor of Snow's theories soon pummeled the miasmists into submission. But unfortunately, Snow did not live to see his own vindication.

Epidemiologists have since produced many wonderful methods of measuring time-to-event processes. A critical one for security is Survival Analysis, which measures the probability of experiencing a hazard by a certain time. While the hazard measured is often death, it has less morbid applications, too. This is where security comes in.

# From Cholera to Security

Security measurements of interest include things like time to discover, time to respond, time to recover, time to deploy, time to patch, time to block, and many more. These are all classes of metrics common to defenders.

You may already measure many of these, but likely not in the way an epidemiologist would. Survival analysis compares the probability of an event occurring *to a process* within a given time. Or conversely, the probability of a process surviving until an event occurs. Advanced methods measure (weigh) the effect of environmental factors on those probabilities:

- What's the probability of services getting patched within SLA?
- What factors account for the largest differences in incident response times between teams?
- Do development teams who manage their own infrastructure patch faster than those who don't – and by how much?
- How long do cloud misconfiguration errors, like open buckets, go undetected?
- What percentage of successful phishing attempts are responded to under 1 hour, 4 hours, 8 hours, 1 day, 1 week … What is the change from last quarter?

Survival analysis lives for this (pun intended). Yet it's little used within security circles. It's a matter of exposure and explanation. The methods aren't hard. If they were, I likely wouldn't be the one exposing them to you.

We start our exploration of survival analysis with a simple invention that predates Snow (by 200 years) called the *life table*. It's a *data structure* you will use repeatedly in survival analysis. You can generate these structures with data you already have – with minimal effort. In our case, with only five lines of R.

## Life Tables

As stated, the life table is one of our main survival analysis tools. It was invented by John Graunt, a seventeenth-century haberdasher and amateur demographer.[3] (See Figure 2.2)

Graunt may have also been the first data scientist. He accumulated 70 years of seventeenth-century "big data" from *The Bills of Mortality*.[4] *The Bills of Mortality* was a weekly magazine started in the sixteenth century to keep score of deaths. It sounds morbid, but this was a big deal in plague-ridden London. People relied on *The Bills of Mortality* to see if there were increases in deaths in their area so they could take protective measures.

Graunt's genius was in structuring the data into the following life table. Using this new format, he was able to ask questions of the data that others couldn't. It was so impactful that it won him a spot in the prestigious Royal Society of London – an invitation you could only get from the king!

**Inspiring side note:** Graunt was not a mathematician nor a man of society, but he was intuitive, resourceful, and persistent. He would need persistence to pull together 70 years of mortality data by hand!

| John Graunt's Life Table (Updated) | | |
|---|---|---|
| Age Interval | Prop. Deaths in Interval | Prop. Surviving Til Start of Interval |
| 0–6 | 0.36 | 1.00 |
| 7–16 | 0.24 | 0.64 |
| 17–26 | 0.15 | 0.40 |
| 27–36 | 0.09 | 0.25 |
| 37–46 | 0.06 | 0.16 |
| 47–56 | 0.04 | 0.10 |
| 57–66 | 0.03 | 0.06 |
| 67–76 | 0.02 | 0.03 |
| 77–86 | 0.01 | 0.01 |

FIGURE 2.2

*Life Table Purpose*

All life tables measure the duration of a process. In the simple case shown in Figure 2.2, we are taking a page from John Graunt's book, measuring thousands of individual life spans aggregated together. The objective is measuring the probability of dying within a certain interval of time. It also measures the probability of surviving until the start of that interval.

In 17th century plague-ridden London, if you are between the ages of 7 and 16 years old, you have a 24% chance of dying. Not great. You also have a 64% chance of living until the age of 7. To our modern minds, this is not earth-shattering mathematics, but this was cutting edge in 17th century England. This basic life table remains in use today by epidemiologists, actuaries, and more. It should become commonplace in security.

## Life Table Structure

In the life table, there are two types of events we care about. The first event is a form of process termination called a *hazard*. Any event that stops a process is a hazard. By this definition, a patch for a vulnerability is a hazard. The approval of a ticket is a hazard. Blocking an attack is also a hazard. Think of it this way: If the process is a vulnerability, then a patch is a hazard, since it terminates the life of the vulnerability.

> **Think About It:** What other important security processes can you think of? What are their terminating events (hazards)? Do they have specific start- and end-dates? Many processes are made up of several sub-processes. As a metrician, your job is to be resourceful in identifying and measuring the ones that matter. Strictly speaking, if you aren't measuring the life-of-security processes, then the process is unmanaged. It may be performing well. It may not be. You don't know.

I said there are two types of events. The second type is called *censoring*. Censoring is fancy talk for *stopped measuring the processes for one reason or another*. If I discovered a vulnerability last week that is still alive today, we say it's censored. What does that mean? It means we have no idea how much longer said vulnerability will live, only that it's still alive when we last measured it. While there are other forms of censoring, we focus only on the "still alive" type.

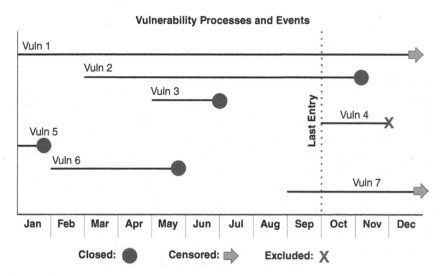

FIGURE 2.3

Figure 2.3 represents data before it is formatted as a life table. It tracks seven vulnerabilities, each starting on or after January 1, 2020.

Four of the vulnerabilities were patched. They are marked with the circle. Two vulnerabilities are not patched. They live past December 31. We aren't measuring past that date. They are marked with the arrows. Those two vulnerabilities are censored, but they are not rejected. As you will learn, they still play a role in our survival analysis.

The last entry line (vertical dotted line) is set for October 1. Any new vulnerabilities found at that date or later are excluded. That's why vuln 4 is excluded. We still measure the vulnerabilities that start before, and cross, the last entry line. Vuln 2 is an example of this.

The last entry line ensures at least a quarter's worth of data is available for measurement. If you had a lot of vulnerabilities that entered a week before the end of the year (December 31), you would get a lot of censoring. That would negatively impact your survival analysis. I will demonstrate this in more detail as we build our own data set below.

Figure 2.4 has the same data as Figure 2.3. It's arranged from the perspective of a life table. This is how we are going to format our data using R. This table mimics what Graunt did with ink and paper. Note that the x-axis is now an index of months by number. Once the data is in this format, it becomes trivial to do simple yet powerful analysis that reveals trends – using arithmetic.

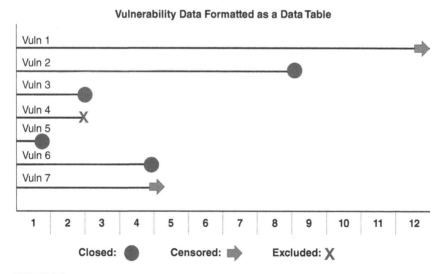

FIGURE 2.4

## Making a Life Table in R

**Concept over Code:** I expect many readers will start with this chapter. That's because time-to-live measurements are so needed in security. I also expect most of these readers will be new to R, and to analytics in general. *The good news is that this is my target demographic.*

I also know many readers will have little interest in mastering R. Your interests lie in understanding measurement concepts first. At the same time, you are also looking for something practical that you can use on the job now. Thus, I will do my best to explain the code *conceptually* over *technically* – that is to say, emphasizing the "why" over the "how."

Have no fear, you can copy and paste what you need without having to master R at all. That being said, I do hope the code explanations are enlightening. The purpose is to teach rudimentary survival analysis and a small amount of R – so you can use both for your own analysis and metrics.

Let's cook up our life table from scratch. You can see the code in Figure 2.5. Have no fear! If it's scary, just look away for now.

The first step requires loading the libraries we need. The tidyverse library includes fundamental data-wrangling capabilities. Think of the tidyverse as an API (application programming interface) that treats data frames like mini databases. You can also think of data frames as spreadsheets if that makes you more comfortable – since data frames have columns and rows.

The tidyverse supports a useful capability called data pipelines. Piping is represented by this symbol: %>%. You will see it a lot. The %>% takes the data output flowing in from the left and "pipes" it to data-wrangling functions to the right. I use it below as we manipulate our data into a life table format. Pipes keep our code short – five lines of R in our first-use case (albeit there are some long lines).

The next library is lubridate. It simplifies doing math with dates. The last two libraries, survival and survminer, are for survival analysis. They have helper functions for making life tables, graphing, and much more. Don't be overwhelmed by the following code. I am about to talk through it. In fact, you only need to copy and paste – or just use the code right from the website.

```
# Code available at www.themetricsmanifesto.com

library(tidyverse)
library(lubridate)
library(survival)
library(survminer)

# Step 1: Get Data
tmm <-read.csv(
  "https://raw.githubusercontent.com/ribsy/mdata/main/tmm_start_small.csv")

# Step 2: Tidy Data
tmm <- tmm %>% mutate(status = ifelse(last.seen > "2020-12-31", 0, 1),
                      time.diff = ymd(last.seen) - ymd(first.seen) + 1)  %>%
                # filter(first.seen <= ymd("2020-10-01") &
                #        group == 1 & idTeam %in% 1 ) %>%
                select(time.diff, status)

# Step 3: Execute Survival Functions
t_surv <- survfit(data = tmm,
                  Surv(time.diff, status) ~ 1)

# Step 4a: Make Life Table
ltable <-
  tibble(day = t_surv$time) %>%
  mutate(time_int    = str_c("[", day, ", ", day + 1, ")"),
         n_opened    = t_surv$n.risk,
         n_closed    = t_surv$n.event) %>%
  mutate(n_censored  = n_opened - n_closed - lead(n_opened, default = 0),
         hazard_fun  = n_closed / n_opened,
         survivor_fun = t_surv$surv,
         cum_hazard  = t_surv$cumhaz)

# Step 4b: Update Life Table - Add First Row
ltable <- bind_rows(tibble(day      = 0,
                    time_int     = "[0, 1)",
                    n_opened     = t_surv$n.risk[1],
                    n_closed     = 0,
                    n_censored   = 0,
                    hazard_fun   = 0,
                    survivor_fun = 1,
                    cum_hazard   = 0), ltable)
```

**FIGURE 2.5**

The data source for this type of analysis could come from just about any security domain: threat, vulnerability, identity, and access management, etc. In this use case, I am imagining data coming from an enterprise vulnerability management tool, ticketing system, log management solution, etc. Nearly all enterprise security solutions record some concept of first and last seen. In the broad domain of vulnerability management (my focus for now), I would include network scanners, appsec scanners, static analysis security testing (SAST), dynamic analysis security testing (DAST), and Bug Bounty services.

In this exercise, you will (minimally) extract two columns of data from your system of choice: first.seen and last.seen. Most security solutions will allow you to download what you need as a CSV. For the programmatically savvy among you, most allow for api-based data extraction.

For the data sample used here, I picture a large global enterprise with hundreds or thousands of developers bucketed into product groups. Each group is responsible for revenue-generating products. A group may have hundreds of developers in it. Developers within these groups are further bucketed into small teams. You can think of a small team as a scrum team or squad – aka two-pizza teams.[5]

Next, we walk through each line of the code above in some detail. Think of it less as code and more as a tutorial on analytics concepts. It is a good way to start understanding how survival analysis works. If what you see below doesn't make sense at first glance, then rest assured you are reading the right book. It's for beginners – not experts – so not getting it at first is normal. If tempted to run for the hills, allow me to redirect you to the "concept over code" box above.

## Code Explained in Detail

We start by loading tmm_start_small.csv into a data frame:

```
# Load tmm_start_small.csv into the tmm data frame
tmm <- read.csv("https://raw.githubusercontent.com/ribsy/mdata/main/tmm_start_small.csv")
```

Let's take a quick peek at the tmm data frame. We can look at the first 10 rows by typing in the head() function as seen below. Your data should look something like this once printed to the RStudio screen:

```
> head(tmm,10)
   idTeam group first.seen  last.seen
1       2     1 2020-01-04 2020-01-23
2       2     1 2020-01-18 2020-01-19
3       2     1 2020-07-18 2020-07-19
4       3     1 2020-03-29 2020-04-29
5       3     1 2020-04-23 2020-05-07
6       3     1 2020-04-23 2020-05-01
7       3     1 2020-07-10 2020-07-30
8       3     1 2020-09-24 2020-10-02
9       3     1 2020-10-11 2020-10-12
10      3     1 2020-10-11 2020-10-24
```

We have four columns, excluding the row IDs on the left: idTeam, group, first.seen, last.seen. Again, you only need the two date columns to make this all work. Each row represents a process with a start time and end time. It can be any security process related to threats or vulnerabilities. It could even be provisioning and deprovisioning of access within our IAM program. Or, it could be the arrival and elimination of malware, etc. The particular process I am imagining here is appsec vulnerabilities, for no other reason than it's a vexing issue I continue to deal with as a CISO.

This second line of code below prepares the raw tmm data for survival analysis. The first thing you see is the tmm data frame. It's getting piped %>% into a function called "mutate()." Mutate is used to create and or update data frame columns. It mutates the data frame. In this case, we use mutate to create two columns: status and time.diff.

We will look at the status column first. Status tells us if the record being processed is censored. If the last.seen date is past the end of the year "2020-12-31" then we mark the status as censored with a 0. If it's not censored, we mark it with a 1. You can see Figure 2.4, the far right side, to get a visual example. The following ifelse() function inputs the "0" or "1" based on date evaluation.

> **Note:** There are other reasons for censoring to occur. We will limit our focus to the type of censoring associated with a process that passes the end of the measurement period.

```
# Make data ready for the survival function
tmm <- tmm %>% mutate( status = ifelse(last.seen > "2020-12-31", 0, 1),
```

The next column created by mutate() is time.diff. It's the difference in days between the last.seen date and the first.seen date. You can look at the data in Figure 2.6 to see what this looks like visually. The ymd() function comes from the lubridate library. It makes it easy to add and subtract dates. In this case, we simply subtract first.seen from last.seen. It returns a count of days. The +1 adds a day to time.diff. This is necessary for the life table format, which will be explained shortly.

```
time.diff = ymd(last.seen) - ymd(first.seen) + 1)  %>%
```

Here is what a subset of the data looks like at this stage in the pipeline. Note the addition of two new columns to the right. Now we know how long each vulnerability has lived. We also know its status in terms of censoring:

```
> tmm
  idTeam group first.seen  last.seen status time.diff
1      2     1 2020-01-04 2020-01-23      1   20 days
2      2     1 2020-01-18 2020-01-19      1    2 days
3      2     1 2020-07-18 2020-07-19      1    2 days
4      3     1 2020-03-29 2020-04-29      1   32 days
5      3     1 2020-04-23 2020-05-07      1   15 days
```

FIGURE 2.6

The next portion of code filters our data set. First, we filter to include records that start three months or more before the year's end. I explained this in Figure 2.3 with the "last entry line." You use it to avoid biasing your data with excess censoring. The optional group and team filters subset the data to a specific group and team. If you left this filter out, you would get all teams and groups – which we did in the original code sample.

```
filter(first.seen <= ymd("2020-10-01") &
       group == "Test Team 1" & team == 1) %>%
```

The data is then piped to the following final tidying step. In this case, I am removing columns I no longer need. I do that by calling select().

```
select(time.diff, status)
```

You may recall that the beginning of this line points back to the tmm data frame. All this means is that we are overwriting the original tmm data frame with the results of all the operations we just performed.

```
tmm <- tmm %>% mutate…
```

Here is what our new tmm data frame looks like. It's nice and tidy. Notice that first.seen and last.seen are gone and replaced with status and time.diff.

```
> head(tmm)
  time.diff status
1    20 days      1
2     2 days      1
3     2 days      1
4    32 days      1
5    15 days      1
6     9 days      1
```

## The Survival Functions

Two lines of code later and our data is tidy and ready for survival analysis. There are two functions at work here. The first is Surv() and the second is survfit(). I will explain each briefly.

First, let's look at some data that results from calling these two functions. If we print out t_surv from our survival analysis functions, we get our first set of useful metrics. If the following result could speak, it would say, "*Roughly 50% of the vulnerabilities expire within 53 days, give or take.*"

```
t_surv <- survfit(data = tmm,
       Surv(time.diff, status) ~ 1)

       n  events  median 0.95LCL 0.95UCL
   21354   19040      53      52      53
```

FIGURE 2.7

To see what Surv() is doing by itself, we can call it directly. We do that by inputting our two new columns of data for time.diff and status. I am only asking for a subset of results – hence the "[65:80]" below.

What we get back is a vector of time.diff results that represent a particular vulns time to live in days. The first one lived for 18 days before experiencing a hazard event (i.e., patching).

The "+" sign means the vulnerability is censored. For example, the twelfth record is "26+". It may live to be 27 or 455 days, we don't know. It's similar to Vuln 1 in Figure 2.4. Vuln 1 was marked green because it is censored, which in this case means that it lived beyond the point of measurement.

```
> Surv(tmm$time.diff, tmm$status)[65:80]
 [1] 18   12   15   28   26   15   20   26   27    7   28   26+   7   16+ 15   20
```

Now let's look at the last 15 records. Note the use of nrow(). That returns the count of records in the tmm data frame. One of the main things you see in this data set is many censored items. That's because these records start closer to the "Last Entry Line" in Figure 2.3. In short, these vulnerabilities likely started their lives in the September time frame and haven't lived long enough to get patched. Again, *censored* means we don't really know if/when these vulnerabilities will be patched.

```
> Surv(tmm$time.diff, tmm$status)[(nrow(tmm)-15):nrow(tmm)]
56   100+  60    91+  74    67+ 111+  89+ 122+  74+ 106+ 101+  71+  76+ 94+ 101+
```

You may be wondering what the ~1 means in Figure 2.7. It tells the function to return (or group by) the overall average. We will revisit the grouping parameter later in the chapter.

## Life Table Detail

Next we use data from t_surv to make a nice and tidy life table. Before I go over the code, let's look at our soon-to-be life table's output. Can you see some similarities between this and Graunt's table in Figure 2.2?

```
> head(ltable, 10)
# A tibble: 10 x 8
      day time_int n_opened n_closed n_censored hazard_fun survivor_fun cum_hazard
    <dbl> <chr>       <dbl>    <dbl>      <dbl>      <dbl>        <dbl>      <dbl>
1       0 [0, 1)       4404        0          0   0                   1          0
2       1 [1, 2)       4404      140          0   0.0318          0.968     0.0318
3       2 [2, 3)       4264       74          0   0.0174          0.951     0.0491
4       3 [3, 4)       4190       38          0   0.00907         0.943     0.0582
5       4 [4, 5)       4152        8          0   0.00193         0.941     0.0601
6       5 [5, 6)       4144        1          0   0.000241        0.941     0.0604
7       6 [6, 7)       4143        7          0   0.00169         0.939     0.0621
8       7 [7, 8)       4136       15          0   0.00363         0.936     0.0657
9       8 [8, 9)       4121      111          0   0.0269          0.911     0.0926
10      9 [9, 10)      4010       35          0   0.00873         0.903     0.101
```

FIGURE 2.8

Here is how each column works:

- **day:** The day number. We start with day zero. It holds the total counts of things alive (vulns in this case) and the percentage still surviving, which is 1, or 100%. Day increment by one for each record.
- **time_int:** This stands for time interval. The bracket on the left means "include this day" and the parens on the right mean "up to, but excluding this day." Some intervals are in years, some in quarters, some in seconds or less.
- **n_opened:** The *total* number remaining open.
- **n_closed:** The number closed on that day. Strictly speaking, the number that experienced the hazard on that day.
- **n_censored:** The number of processes (vulns) that are still alive (open) after we stopped measuring at the end of the year.
- **hazard_fun:** This stands for hazard function. It's simply **n_closed / n_opened**. Or, the percentage closed that day proportional to what is still open.
- **survivor_fun:** This is the percentage of processes still surviving.
- **cum_hazard:** Mostly used with graphing to create a curve.

Now that we know where we are going data-wise, let's assemble the life table piece by piece using data from t_surv. Our first step is making a new data frame called "ltable" to hold our data (ltable standard for "life table").

Next, we call tibble(). It's used to create our first column in ltable called "day." It's the same "day" column in the raw t_surv output in Figure 2.8. We pipe day to mutate. In this case, mutate adds three additional columns to ltable: time_int, n_opened, and n_closed. The tricky portion below is the str_c() function. It is simply concatenating text together with "day" data to create the time_int column. Note the "[" and the ")".

```
ltable <-
  tibble(day = t_surv$time) %>%
  mutate(time_int  = str_c("[", day, ", ", day + 1, ")"),
         n_opened  = t_surv$n.risk,
         n_closed  = t_surv$n.event) %>%
```

We continue making more columns by piping along our four-columned tibble named ltable. There is one small trick of the trade being used below – lead(). It's key in building our n_censored column. I'm going to unpack how this works, as it's insightful to understanding survival analysis and the life table.

```
  mutate(n_censored  = n_opened - n_closed - lead(n_opened, default = 0),
         hazard_fun   = n_closed / n_opened,
         survivor_fun = t_surv$surv,
         cum_hazard   = t_surv$cumhaz)
```

To explain how lead works, I'm going to replace the line of code high-lighted above. I will do this by starting with the second and third values seen in the two lists in Figure 2.9 below. The first list holds n_opened values and the second list holds n_closed values. I sub in the second value from each list: 21354 – 362 – 20989 = 3. So what does lead() do? It looks ahead one record in n_opened and grabs it. In the n_opened column, the next value after 21354 is 20989. Can you see how I substituted it above?

Think about it this way. If you subtract 21354 – 20989, you get 365. That equals the number of closed items on day two. The change be-tween one day and the next is clearly accounted for. But, if you look at the n_closed for the first day, it's equal to 362. Where did the three vulnerabilities go if it was not closed? They were censored. Meaning, they are still alive and kicking. It doesn't have a closed date – just a last scanned date. It aged out of this analysis. You can see that in the third row of output below.

```
> head(ltable$n_opened,10)
 [1] 21354 21354 20989 20919 20856 20766 20682 20597 20514 20406
> head(ltable$n_closed,10)
 [1]   0 362  70  63  89  84  83  82 107 106
> head(ltable$n_censored,10)
 [1] 0 3 0 0 1 0 2 1 1 2
```

FIGURE 2.9

The last two columns (hazard_fun, survivor_fun) are straightforward and documented at the beginning of this section. That leaves us with our last line of code in Figure 2.5. It looks more complicated than it is. In short, it adds a new first row to the life table. It's just for completeness, as it relates to creating a formal life table.

## Basic Life Table Metrics

Now the real fun begins … Metrics! Let's start by asking a metrics question, "How many days does it take on average (or less) for vulnerabilities to close?" Again, a vulnerability is the process and the hazard is something that stops it – like a patch. Based on the data we have, including censored data (stuff that overran our time frame), the answer is about 52 days.

```
> max(ltable$day[(1 - ltable$survivor_fun) <= .5])
1    52
```

You see standard R subsetting in action above. In comprehending subsetting it's good to work from the inside out. What we see first is the subtraction of the survivor_fun column from the number 1. It just creates the inverse of those values – think of it as flipping that column on its head. I then ask for all the values less than or equal to 50%.

You can think of the process as creating a virtual table like below, and querying it once it's created for everything in the inv_sur_fun column that is under 50%.

```
     day inv_surv_fun
    <dbl>       <dbl>
1      0    0  ·
2      2    0.0170
3      3    0.0202
...
...
50    50    0.471
51    51    0.484
52    52    0.497
53    53    0.510
```

We then ask for the maximum day value. What I get back is day 52. If you were to just ask for the mean() of the ltable days column, you would get ~84. That would be wrong.

This small one line of code is the start of a very useful metric tool. I can use this tool to start comparing two types of processes. The first is comparing a process to itself over time. The second is comparing it to other processes over time. For example, *How is team 1 doing over time? Is the survival rate better this quarter than last quarter for critical vulnerabilities?* I can also ask, *How are various groups comparing one to another now and over time?*

The good news is that there are visualizations built into R that make answering questions like these very simple. I will run a quick example here using the tools you have just learned:

```
# Another downloadable data set with vuln severity
tmm <-read.csv(
  "https://raw.githubusercontent.com/ribsy/mdata/main/tmm_start.csv")

# Step 2: Tidy Data
tmm <- tmm %>%

  # Add two new columns
  mutate(status = ifelse(last.seen > "2020-12-31", 0, 1),
         time.diff = ymd(last.seen) - ymd(first.seen) + 1)   %>%

  # Subset data - look for crit and high only
  filter(first.seen <= ymd("2020-10-01") &
         group == 1 &
         idTeam == 1 ) %>%

  # Keep these three colums
  select(time.diff,status,severity)
```

This is what our data looks like after the various manipulations:

```
> head(tmm,10)
      time.diff status severity
1      25 days       1 critical
2      25 days       1 critical
3      28 days       1 critical
4      30 days       1 critical
5      22 days       1 critical
6      45 days       1 critical
7      26 days       1 critical
8      18 days       1 critical
9      28 days       1 critical
10     30 days       1 critical
```

Now we can create a very simple graph using default graphing functions. This is just scraping the surface of visualization capabilities for survival analysis. You will see a slightly more advanced version in the chapter on dashboarding.

```
t_surv <- survfit(data = tmm,
          Surv(time.diff, status) ~ severity)

ggsurvplot(t_surv,
      conf.int = TRUE,
      risk.table.col = "strata", # Change risk table color by groups
      ggtheme = theme_light(), # Change ggplot2 theme
      palette = c("coral3", "darkorange"),
      risk.table = "abs_pct",
      risk.table.y.text.col = T,
      fun = "event")
```

And here is what our visualization looks like. Note that the graph includes both trends for forecasting and empirical counts, too. A lot of information is packed into this graph:

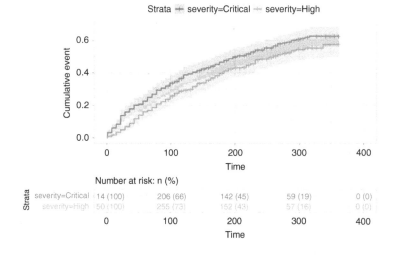

## Conclusion

This has been a relatively gentle introduction to survival analysis. It is one of the largest gaps in security measurement. That is why I put it here first.

Ultimately, I wanted to whet your appetite for survival analysis – to get you started. And it was easy. Our analysis only required five (long) lines of code – including a useful graph.

What is ahead? More code, more history, and more theory. Our next chapter starts to introduce Bayesian data analysis. It starts simply – but progresses steadily.

## Notes

1. Vachon, D. (2005). *Father of Modern Epidemiology*. UCLA Department of Epidemiology. https://www.ph.ucla.edu/epi/snow/fatherofepidemiology.html

2. UCLA Department of Epidemiology. (2005). *John Snow and the Removal of the Broad Street Pump Handle*. Removal. https://www.ph.ucla.edu/epi/snow/removal.html

3. Wikipedia contributors. (2021a, July 22). *John Graunt*. Wikipedia. https://en.wikipedia.org/wiki/John_Graunt

4. Eschner, K. (2017, April 24). *People Have Been Using Big Data Since the 1600s*. *Smithsonian Magazine*. https://www.smithsonianmag.com/smart-news/people-have-been-using-big-data-1600s-180962949/

5. Choi, J. (2020, August 21). *Why Jeff Bezos' Two-Pizza Team Rule Still Holds True in 2018*. I Done This Blog. http://blog.idonethis.com/two-pizza-team/

# CHAPTER 3

# Counting on Uncertainty

## *Preparing for Burndown, Arrival, Wait-Times, and Escape Rates*

*Probability does not exist.*

— Bruno de Finetti

## Gamblers, Scientists, and a Theologian

We owe a debt to gamblers and gambling. Or, should I say, to theory-driven cheating.

A dice player by the name of Antoine Gombaud, Chevalier de Méré, wanted an edge over the house. He believed his current approach to beating the odds was flawed. He needed help. So, he called in the big guns.

Blaise Pascal, one of history's most famous mathematicians, answered Chevalier de Méré's call. Pascal then pulled in Pierre de Fermat, an equally famous mathematician, and a long-distance correspondence on gambling ensued. The fruit of Pascal's and Fermant's penpalship led to early advancements in modern probability. It also led to a string of additional scholars exploring the intersection of probability and gambling.

Fast forward 100 years. Gambling is still the dominant use case in probability scholarship – until Pierre de Laplace (pictured on the left above) shows up. He broadened the application of probability well beyond games of chance.

It is a subset of Laplace's work (a theory he later abandoned) that set the stage for this chapter. Given the volume of Laplace's total work, the probability theory used in this book and many others should have been called "Laplace's theorem." That credit went to another.

The Reverend Thomas Bayes (pictured on the right above) beat Laplace to both develop and then to also abandon his theory – Bayes' theorem. He authored one paper on it. It was his only mathematical publication, published posthumously. Yet, Bayes gets all the glory for this theorem with abandonment issues. The good news for Laplace is that he published a large body of groundbreaking work on a variety of scientific topics. Many consider him to be one of the greatest scientists of all time.

## The Persistence and Dominance of Bayes

The fortune-cookie description of Bayes' theorem (Bayes) says that you can update your beliefs about probable future events as you get more data. Earth shattering? No. Our intuition lines up with this. Despite its common sense appeal, Bayes has been a source of deep controversy in the sciences.

Bayes is like the Rasputin of theories. Over its 200-plus years, many have tried to strangle it. Yet Bayes persists. Today, it holds an increasingly dominant place in the sciences and even in popular topics like artificial intelligence.

Many of the applications that inform this book come from Bayesian practitioners. This includes authors who work in the natural sciences,[1] psychology,[2] and some sports analytics.[3] The former two deal with chaotic and messy systems with sparse data. The latter emerged from the need to win (think *Moneyball*[4]) and gambling.

Yet, many of these scientists and sports enthusiasts are not statisticians by trade. They've struggled to learn and apply Bayesian methods to solve their problems. Their struggles have made my learning easier. And I hope it will have the same impact for you. I will endeavor to give them ample credit throughout this chapter and beyond.

The reality is that we all stand on the shoulders of giants. It's Bayesian turtles all the way down.

# A Bayesian Primer

The Reverend's Gambling Game

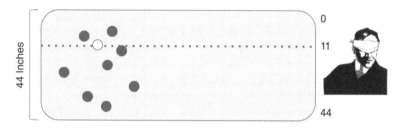

Let's play a gambling game. It will set the stage for the security metrics use cases that follow.

First, we sit you down in front of a pool table – blindfolded. A friend then tosses a white ball on the table and marks its position. (It's at 11 inches in the image above.)

Next, he starts randomly tossing red balls onto the table. After each toss, he lets you know if a red ball lands to the left or right of the white ball – but nothing more.

Your job is to infer the location of the white ball. All you know is a series of left, right, left, left, right, etc.

## *The Gamble*

You start out with a $100 credit. Each red ball costs you $5 to toss.

If you toss 8 red balls prior to guessing, then you've spent $40. 8 × $5 = $40.

You can toss more or less. You just can't exceed $100 in tosses.

Your goal is to approximately guess the white ball's location in inches. Each inch off of the white ball costs you $5.

Let's say you guess 17 inches. That is 6 inches away from 11. You just lost $30 more in credits. 6 × $5 = $30.

If you had guessed 5 instead of 17 (which would be odd, given the data in the image above), you would have still lost $30 in credits. 11 – 5 = 6 and $5 × 6 = $30.

All told, you spent $70 of your $100 in credits: $40 for the tossed red balls and $30 for your guess. That leaves $30. $100 – ($30 + $40).

In other words, **you just won $30!**

*Note:* If your guess was really off, you could have exceeded your $100 credit. For example, if you guessed 40 inches, you would be off by 21 inches: 40 – 11 = 21. That is $105 in credits. 21 × $5 = $105. You had already tossed forty dollars' worth of red balls. $105 + $40 = $145.

That means you pay $45! $145 – $100 (in credits) = $45.

## *Bayesian Thinking*

That game is loosely based on the origin story of Bayesian reasoning. The Reverend Thomas Bayes' posthumously published paper included a billiards example similar to this.[5]

At the time of publication, his billiards example would have been considered radical. It stated that as you incrementally get more information, you can incrementally reduce your uncertainty. What you are uncertain about is the probability of some unseen event represented by the probable location of the white ball.

In the field of security metrics, we are making inferences about rates. Rates come from data-generating processes – processes that are on the move. (It's as if the white ball was on the move over time.) This means you are never perfectly certain about a given rate. You are also not "perfectly uncertain."

Of course, if our metrics say a process is too random, then we have still learned something. We learned, "*I can't measure this process, given this data, given these algorithms, and with these tools…at this moment.*"

What we have not learned is that a given process is not measurable because it's too chaotic. That is a scientific statement. It presupposes you have done some sort of measurement of entropy – of information value and utility. Making immeasurability claims prior to actual measurement is a stumbling block that can lead us to stop measuring before we start. It is a risk-inducing mistake.

In the chapters to follow, you will get exposure to security examples that resemble our billiards betting game. After all, we are blindfolded in security. We get signals from various data-generating processes. We use those signals to make inferences about underlying patterns. Our job is to be resourceful with that data to better understand these patterns. Ultimately, our job is to use those inferences to optimize processes that are underperforming.

Before moving on, let's walk through a couple of simple metrics examples. They will help you get the right mindset – the Bayesian mindset. You will need it for what is to come. These examples will also give you an opportunity to warm up to R.

**Note:** I'm going to assume you don't know R. And indeed, you might not be looking to know much beyond cutting and pasting. Because I want this book to work for everyone, I have taken this into account in my **"concept over code"** approach – which you might remember from earlier. I will explain what we are trying to get done, with only occasionally explaining the nitty-gritty details of how R is doing it.

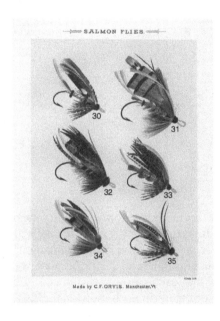

SALMON FLIES.

Made by C.F.ORVIS. Manchester,Vt

## Metrics Example: Phishing for Improvement

Phishing is a problem. That's why most security leaders have programs in place to curb it. Let's assume for the moment that you're in the market for a phishing solution. Before you buy, you want to baseline phishing click rates. Long term, you want to measure the impact of training and other activities on reducing phishing.

You start by bringing in a phishing simulation vendor for a proof of concept. They run a test. The test sends phishing emails to 100 recipients. And over the next 48 hours you get *five clicks*. Is this bad? What should you expect in the future? Let's do some quick analysis to find out how we should react to this data.

### Learning Your ABCs

The approach we will use for this analysis is called "Approximate Bayesian Computation," or ABC.[6] If you find this approach interesting, then check out Rasmus Bååth's entertaining three-part video series on ABC.[7] Alan Downing, the author of *Think Bayes*, also has a chapter on ABC. It's Python based, as opposed to R.[8] The chapter is freely available.

**ABC** is typically used for computationally complex and seemingly messy problems. This includes areas like ecology, genetics, and epidemiology. Yet, ABC in concept is fairly straightforward. It's a great way to start understanding data-generating processes and modeling. That's why I am introducing it now, as a conceptual steppingstone to the Bayesian concepts that follow.

## Phish in 15 Lines of Code

Each piece of code gets an explanation. At the end, I will provide the code in its entirety.

```
######
## Simple ABCs of Phishing

# Make lots of phish
sim_phish <- 1000000

# Count of phishing emails
campaign_size <- 100

# Make no assumptions about click rates
prior_rate <- runif(sim_phish, 0, 1)
```

The sim_phish variable tells our ABC scenario to run one million times. (You could get by with one hundred thousand.) Recall, we ran one real phishing campaign. Using that data, we create one million virtual campaigns. Each of the one million campaigns is slightly different. That's because we infuse some uncertainty, or randomness, into each run.

Campaign size represents the count of emails in each individual phishing campaign. In this case, it is always 100 emails. Some portion of those will get clicks.

Next comes the "prior_rate" variable. It's the rate of clicks we believe will occur. It is called the "prior" because it represents what we believe about clicking *prior* to seeing any data. Our current prior is formally called an "uninformative prior." That is a fancy name for a simple concept.

Look at the graph of prior_rate below. Is it clear why it's called an uninformative prior?

```
hist(prior_rate)
```

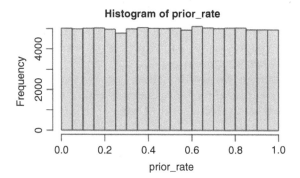

If our prior_rate could speak, it would say, "*All phishing click rates are equally plausible to me. 1% is just as likely as 82%.*"

Many metrics assume all things are equally likely prior to seeing data. We assume that too, for the moment. Yet, this is not the Bayesian way. Bayesian methods allow you to incorporate information before seeing data. These are called *informative priors*. We will make an informative prior shortly. First, let's make some phish.

```
# Make Phish Data - by looping 1 Million times
phish_chance <- rep(NA, sim_phish)
for(i in 1:sim_phish) {
   phish_chance[i] <- rbinom(1, size = campaign_size, prob = prior_rate[i])
}
```

The first line of code creates one million buckets. Each bucket gets filled with some phish (clicks). Below you see the first 20 buckets prior to filling:

```
> head(phish_chance, 20)
 [1] NA NA NA NA NA NA NA NA NA NA NA NA NA NA NA NA NA NA NA NA
```

The next three lines make phish. And it inserts them into the one million phish_chance buckets – one bucket at a time. Here are the first 20 values (buckets) after the loop:

```
> head(phish_chance, 20)
 [1] 97 11 97 97 99 40 34 23 72 95 10 41 55 73 43  4  5 69 14 59
```

Each one of those 20 values represents a phishing campaign. The first campaign got 97 clicks out of 100 possible. That's a bad day indeed! Why such a high number? Our prior rates are to blame. Let's look at the first 20 rates. You can visually compare the phish_chance with prior_rates to see what is going on. When a rate is high, phish counts are high:

```
> head(prior_rate,20)
0.97377145 0.08826468 0.97616615 0.98081863 0.98809544 0.32797767
0.44447221 0.25451132 0.75460889 0.92358140 0.14762888 0.39875616
0.57030234 0.74610149 0.45552747 0.04343707 0.04592483 0.62585542
0.14940299 0.61159701
```

The workhorse of our loop is a function called rbinom(). For now, think of it as a configurable count generator. You can see an example of it at work below. You tell it how many buckets you want. We ask for 20 in the example here. Next, you give it the max size of phish counts it should consider for each bucket. We say 100. That's because we sent out 100 phishing emails. Lastly, you bias the count generator with a rate – our rate is 10%. Note how the counts hover around 10, plus or minus.

```
> rbinom(20,100,.10)
 [1] 12  8 16  7  9  8  6 10  7  9 11  7 10 11 16 13 15 10 10 14
```

The graph below shows what phish_chance looks like after all its buckets are filled. The shape of this graph should not be surprising. After all, we stated that our prior was "everything is equally probable."

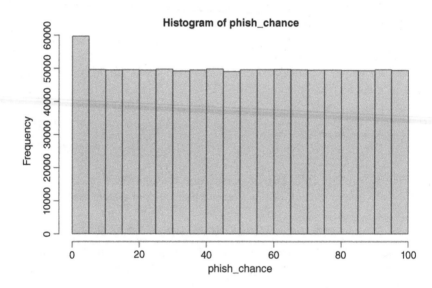

The following graph shows the relationship of phish_chance to prior_rate. There's many millions of phish in this graph. The results are highly correlated, with some wiggle. *Wiggle* is a nonfancy word for spread, or variance, of the data. The random noise in our data makes the data cigar shaped. If the data were perfectly correlated, you would have a straight black line.

The vertical line is the five phish region. We are about to collect all the prior_rates associated with the five phish region. Can you eyeball what the range of rates might be? Look to the *y*-axis.

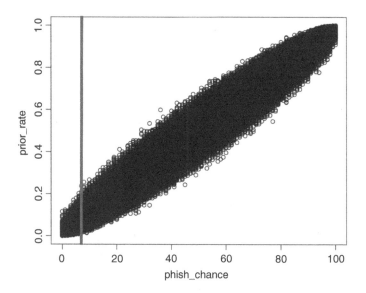

## Posterior Phish

Now we see ABC in action. Take a moment to look at the code below. Even if you don't know R, what do you think we are asking for?

```
posterior_phish <- prior_rate[phish_chance == 5]
```

The line above is subsetting our data. When you ask "phish_chance == 5" you get back a list of binary results – true and false indicators:

```
head(phish_chance == 5,20)
FALSE FALSE FALSE FALSE FALSE FALSE FALSE FALSE FALSE FALSE FALSE FALSE FALSE
FALSE FALSE FALSE TRUE  FALSE FALSE FALSE
```

The "TRUE" above is at index 17 in phish_chance. Just count from left to right. Let's see what happens when we put index 17 into prior_rate:

```
prior_rate[17]
[1] 0.06310795
```

We got back a value of ~6%. It's fair to assume that most of the values in posterior_phish will hover around 0.05. As stated, the vertical line in the cigar image above is located at five clicks. Just eyeballing it (*y*-axis), it looks like the range of prior_rates is somewhere between 0% and 18%. The majority will hover around 5%. We would say the rates are densely packed around 5%.

How many phish buckets did we collect? Meaning, the buckets with five phish in them?

```
> length(posterior_phish)
[1] 9930
```

Here's what a small sample of those nearly 10,000 rates look like. Meaning, these are the prior_rates that produced five phish. You can see there is some variability in rates. Yet, 5% will roughly be the central tendency of the data.

```
> head(posterior_phish, 20)
0.08334629 0.10153545 0.06138274 0.04524812 0.05271519 0.07290784
0.03596845 0.06424234 0.02847536 0.04846621 0.02571574 0.06864208
0.09599454 0.08432168 0.08441290 0.01957235 0.06310795 0.09179207
0.02557073 0.05275284
```

Here is the graph, which we will use to check the spread and density of our data.

```
# Histogram of final results
hist(posterior_phish, xlim = c(0, .2))
```

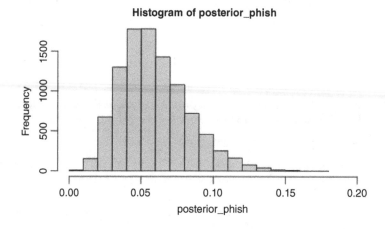

**Histogram of posterior_phish**

We can also see where 95% of our data tends to live using the quantile function.

```
quantile(posterior_phish, c(0.025, 0.975))
      2.5%        97.5%
0.02236482 0.11250259
```

Our phish click baseline rate lives somewhere between 2% and 11%. That's somewhere between 2 and 11 clicks in 100 emails.

We are getting useful analysis from the posterior_phish object. It's formally called the posterior distribution. It's what we believe after (posterior to) having seen the data. *The posterior is a compromise between the data and our prior beliefs.* The posterior is an approximation (a model) of the underlying data-generating process.

The ABC approach gets to the posterior in a simple to understand, but computationally expensive, manner. You will experience a more traditional approach to Bayesian analysis in the next section. But first, let's run our analysis by the CISO to see what she thinks.

## *Informative Prior Phish*

You share your results with your CISO, saying, *"We are looking at anywhere from a 2% to 11% phish rate. That was based on 100 phishing emails. Imagine that across 10,000 employees!"*

Your CISO says, *"I would be truly shocked if our rate was much higher than 5%. I have been here for 3 years and we haven't seen nearly that many events. I think it's much closer to 1%. And, in the worst-case scenario I'd say 5%."*

Let's make a prior that reflects her expert beliefs. This is one of the Bayesian superpowers – incorporating data to update the model's beliefs.

```
# CISO's Informative Prior
shape_vals <- GetBeliefsEvents(.01,.04)
prior_rate <- rbeta(sim_phish, shape_vals[1], shape_vals[2])
```

Her beliefs are very specific. It's almost the opposite of our uninformative prior. If our new prior could speak, it would say, *"I'm pretty sure the click rate is equally above or below 1%. I am 90% confident it's at or below 4%."*

The GetBeliefsEvents() function takes her beliefs and spits out shape parameters. Shape parameters "shape data" in terms of central location and spread. Here is what our "shaped" informative prior looks like. Compare it to the uninformative prior above.

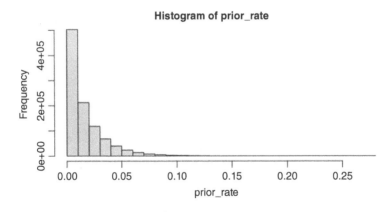

The GetBeliefsEvents() function is a wrapper around a set of functions from the ProbBayes library.[9] The author, Jim Albert, is a professor of statistics and a serious baseball fan. He has several books on Bayesian analytics. His most recent book, *Probability and Bayesian Modeling*, is great![10]

Let's run our code with our new prior and analyze the results. Note, results are incorporated directly in the following code. Again, we are focusing on concept over code:

```
# Make highly informed phish
phish_chance <- rep(NA, sim_phish)
for(i in 1:sim_phish) {
    phish_chance[i] <- rbinom(1, size = campaign_size,
                              prob = prior_rate[i])
}

# Extract rates based on the 5 we observed
posterior_phish <- prior_rate[phish_chance == 5]

# Count up posterior results - bigger result. Data is denser near 5%
length(posterior_phish)
[1] 34426

# Get the mean
mean(posterior_phish)
[1] 0.03930213

# Get the 95% interval
quantile(posterior_phish, c(0.025, 0.975))
     2.5%       97.5%
0.01434550 0.07645691

# Get the 95% Highest Density Interval
ci(posterior_phish,method="HDI", ci = 0.95, verbose = FALSE)
# Highest Density Interval
95% HDI
------------
[0.01, 0.07]

# Create a histogram of the results
hist(posterior_phish, xlim = c(0, .2))

# What's the chance of of phishing being over 5%
sum(posterior_phish > 0.05) / length(posterior_phish)
[1] 0.2263115
```

The CISO said she would be shocked if the rate was much higher than 5%. Our new (biased) analysis would largely agree with her. After all, we encoded her beliefs into our analysis. Here is what the new histogram looks like:

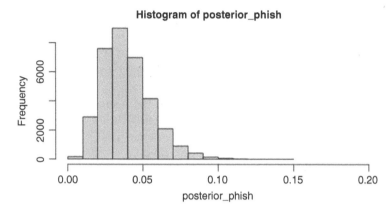

The results seem to make it clear that the rate lives in the 1% to 7% range. That is, given our data and the model we are using.

We also see that there is a ~23% chance of the rate being greater than 5%. Let's see what the click rates are for the next few posterior rates:

```
> round(sum(posterior_phish > .06) / length(posterior_phish),3)
[1] 0.106
> round(sum(posterior_phish > .07) / length(posterior_phish),3)
[1] 0.045
> round(sum(posterior_phish > .08) / length(posterior_phish),3)
[1] 0.018
> round(sum(posterior_phish > .09) / length(posterior_phish),3)
[1] 0.006
```

## ABC Conclusions and Complete Code

We wanted a baseline. We were able to produce one with small (some would say tiny) data. We also updated our baseline with a belief about the underlying process. It took minutes to produce a conservative (read defensible) range of plausible rates.

Is it the best, most accurate model of phishing? Yes and no. No, in that you can always find better and more sophisticated analytic techniques. Is it adequate for creating a baseline that *"retains our uncertainty without obscuring our certainty?"* Yes.

The question to ask is whether a 2% to 7% click rate is okay. This invariably leads to benchmarking questions. And as you may recall, one of the manifesto observations is:

**Observation:** Most metrics focus on beating benchmark; the best ones focus on beating the competing model.

*Belief:* *"We don't believe in benchmarks (for the most part), and neither do our adversaries."*
*Belief:* *"We believe in continuous improvement because our adversaries attack, and our business is exposed ... continuously."*

**A baseline is an internal benchmark, as opposed to an external one.** You use it to set goals and to measure change. As your business grows, adds more people, and exposes more value – are your phishing rates scaling? Meaning, are your rates staying the same or changing for the worse? Likewise, as bad guys create innovative phishing techniques to attack your people, are your mitigating controls and training having an impact? Do your rates reflect your investments?

These are the types of questions we will address in further chapters on objectives and optimization. We will also revisit Approximate Bayesian Computation in our chapter on A/B testing.

In the next section of this chapter, I want to introduce you to a canonical approach to Bayesian modeling. It's the approach we will be using for the remaining chapters in this section. But first, here is all the ABC code for our "toy" phishing example:

```
source("manifesto_functions.R")   #book functions
######
## Simple ABC

# Make lots of phish
sim_phish <- 1000000
campaign_size <- 100

# Make no assumptions about click rates
# Un-comment if you want an uninformative prior
#prior_rate <- runif(sim_phish, 0, 1)

# CISO's Informative Prior
shape_vals <- GetBeliefsEvents(.01,.04)   #Book Function
prior_rate <- rbeta(sim_phish, shape_vals[1], shape_vals[2])

hist(prior_rate)

# Make Phish Data
phish_chance <- rep(NA, sim_phish)
for(i in 1:sim_phish) {
  phish_chance[i] <- rbinom(1, size = campaign_size, prob = prior_rate[i])
}
```

```
# Extract rates based on the 5 we observed
posterior_phish <- prior_rate[phish_chance == 5]

# Quick Checks
length(posterior_phish)
mean(posterior_phish)

# Credible Ranges
quantile(posterior_phish, c(0.025, 0.975))
# ci(posterior_phish,method="HDI", verbose = FALSE) # Optional

# CISO 5% or greater question
sum(posterior_phish > 0.05) / length(posterior_phish)

# Histogram of final results
hist(posterior_phish, xlim = c(0, .2))
```

## From ABC to Canonical Bayes

Why did we start with ABC? It allowed me to start gently. I only had to introduce two of our three main characters, the first being the prior. The second is the posterior. The third is about to emerge.

Along the way, we met two types of priors. The first was the uninformative prior. Think of it as flat data. When you know nothing, use that. We also met the informative prior. It encodes prior data, including beliefs. The CISO's beliefs about phishing rates became our informative prior.

In this section, we meet the third Bayesian cast member. Its name is *the likelihood*. In layman's terms, the likelihood scores your data. It says, "*What is the likelihood of this phish count, given what we believe about plausible phishing click rates?*" Said more succinctly, "*What is the likelihood of the data, given our hypothesis?*"

The likelihood and the prior get multiplied together to form the posterior. It truly is that simple. And the results are largely identical to ABC.

Here is a pithy example using an uninformed prior. This is a default approach to Bayesian analysis. It's computationally heavy if your data and models are large and complex. Fortunately, our data and models are still simple. Don't sweat the nitty-gritty of the code yet:

```
# Results from POC with vendor
phish <- 5; attempts <- 100;

# Parameter Grid
phish_grid <- seq(from=0,to=1,length.out=1000)

# Posterior - multiplies likelihood times prior
posterior_phish <- dbinom(phish, attempts,
                    phish_grid)*dunif(phish_grid,0,1)
```

```
# Normalized Posterior - sums to 1
posterior_phish <- posterior_phish/sum(posterior_phish)
```

Four lines of code later, you have a posterior. Here is what the posterior phish rate looks like, using a nonfancy graph. Does it look vaguely similar to our previous histogram?

```
plot(phish_grid, posterior_phish, type='l', col='black')
```

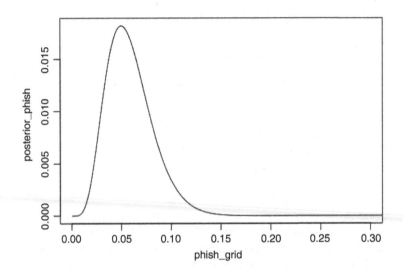

Let's bring back our CISO's informed prior. Along the way, I will add a few more tricks of the trade to better explain how Bayes works under the hood.

```
#####
## Normal Bayes Compact

# Clicks on Phish
phish <- 5;

# Emails Sent
attempts <- 100;

# Create Phish Grid, avoid 0...clashes with our prior
phish_grid <- seq(0.0001, 1, 0.0001)

# Informative Prior Shape Values - CISOs beliefs
shape_vals <- GetBeliefsEvents(.01,.04)
```

```
# Informative Prior Distribution
prior <- dbeta(phish_grid, shape_vals[1], shape_vals[2])

# Likelihood of the Data
likelihood <- dbinom(phish, attempts,phish_grid)

# Product of Likelihood and Prior
product <- likelihood * prior

# Scaled to sum to one
posterior <- product/sum(product)

# A table of data for pedagogical purposes
bayes_table <- tibble(theta = phish_grid, prior, likelihood,
           product, posterior)
```

Let's take a quick look at the "bayes_table." It holds all our computations. Only third-grade math here. Don't let the scientific notation burst any bubbles.

```
head(bayes_table, 10)
# A tibble: 10 x 5
     theta prior likelihood   product posterior
     <dbl> <dbl>      <dbl>     <dbl>     <dbl>
 1  0.0001 143.    7.46e-13 1.06e-10  3.10e-13
 2  0.0002 119.    2.36e-11 2.82e- 9  8.23e-12
 3  0.0003 107.    1.78e-10 1.91e- 8  5.57e-11
 4  0.0004  99.4   7.42e-10 7.38e- 8  2.15e-10
 5  0.0005  93.6   2.24e- 9 2.10e- 7  6.13e-10
 6  0.0006  89.0   5.53e- 9 4.92e- 7  1.44e- 9
 7  0.0007  85.3   1.18e- 8 1.01e- 6  2.95e- 9
 8  0.0008  82.1   2.29e- 8 1.88e- 6  5.48e- 9
 9  0.0009  79.4   4.08e- 8 3.24e- 6  9.46e- 9
10  0.001   77.0   6.85e- 8 5.27e- 6  1.54e- 8
```

Let's review each column:

**Theta:** It's just a shortened name for our phish_grid. Think of theta as our $x$ values on a graph. It's a fine-grained ruler that runs along the bottom of the graph.

**Prior:** The prior scores our beliefs. Each value of theta is compared to our beliefs and scored. Or if you prefer – weighted. The weights returned are called *densities*.

**Likelihood:** The likelihood scores our data. Each value of theta is compared to the data. The result is a score (weight) in the form of a density. It's asking, "How likely is five clicks in 100 emails, given each value of theta?"

**Product:** Multiply the prior with the likelihood.

**Posterior:** We make the product sum to one.

Here is how this all works together graphically:

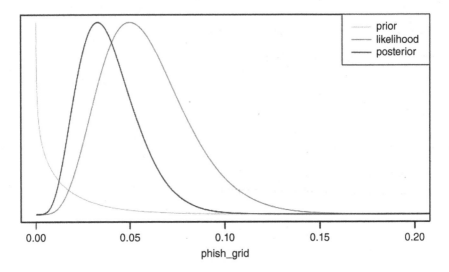

Can you see how the posterior is simply a compromise between the prior and the likelihood? The prior (line to the far left) is pulling on the posterior. It is biasing the posterior toward the CISO's beliefs about click rates. With more data, the prior loses its gravitational power. It becomes overwhelmed with data.

Here is the code for creating the graph. It will play prominently in the next few chapters. This is old-school R. You will get exposed to more advanced graphing methods as we progress.

```
# Plot Prior
plot(phish_grid, prior, type='l', col='orange', xlim=c(0, .2),
    ylab='', yaxt='n')

# Plot Likelihood
par(new=T)
plot(phish_grid, likelihood, type='l', col='skyblue', xlim=c(0, .2),
    ylab='', yaxt='n')

# Plot Posterior
par(new=T)
plot(phish_grid, product, type='l', col='seagreen', xlim=c(0, .2),
    ylab='', yaxt='n')

# Legend
legend("topright", c("prior", "likelihood", "posterior"), lty=1,
    col=c("orange", "skyblue", "seagreen"))
```

The plot() function takes in *x*-axis and *y*-axis values. Phish_grid is the *x*-axis value for each call to plot(). Phish_grid works as a ruler that runs along the bottom of the graph. The *y*-axis values are the prior, likelihood, and product, respectively. Those values make the curves go up and down. They function as scores on the phish_grid values on the *x*-axis. Higher areas on the curve mean the *x*-axis values are more plausible relative to other values.

I hope the phishing use case has warmed you up to Bayesian baselining. Our goal was to take small data and get a baseline rate. We wanted that rate to reflect both our certainty and our uncertainty.

I imagine this type of analysis being done on the fly. I imagine literally sitting across from my peers, the CISO (or being the CISO), and creating metrics like this in minutes. Security is fast moving; shouldn't your metrics be as well?

## The Following Chapters' Metrics and Model

The following chapters cover four metrics. Each follows a Bayesian approach. And our implementation roughly follows this workflow:

**Modern (Bayesian) Security Metrics Flow**

The four metrics, one per chapter, are: Burndown Rates, Arrival Rates, Wait, Times, and Escape Rates. They are four of the five baselines found in the BOOM framework. Being that these are baselines, they are designed to get a single rate. And being that they are Bayesian in nature, they also include uncertainty about those rates.

## Notes

1. McElreath, R. (2020). *Statistical Rethinking: A Bayesian Course with Examples in R and STAN (Chapman & Hall/CRC Texts in Statistical Science)* (2nd ed.). Chapman and Hall/CRC.
2. Kruschke, J. (2014). *Doing Bayesian Data Analysis: A Tutorial with R, JAGS, and Stan* (2nd ed.). Academic Press.
3. Jingchen Hu, J. A. A. (2020, July 30). *Probability and Bayesian Modeling*. Probability and Bayesian Modeling. https://bayesball.github.io/BOOK/probability-a-measurement-of-uncertainty.html
4. Wikipedia contributors. (2021c, September 25). *Moneyball*. Wikipedia. https://en.wikipedia.org/wiki/Moneyball
5. Bayes, R. B. (1763). *An Essay towards Solving a Problem in the Doctrine of Chances*. Https://Web.Archive.Org/Web/20110410085940/Http://Www.Stat.Ucla.Edu/History/Essay.Pdf. https://web.archive.org/web/20110410085940/http://www.stat.ucla.edu/history/essay.pdf
6. *Approximate Bayesian Computation*. (2013, January 1). PubMed Central (PMC). https://www.ncbi.nlm.nih.gov/pmc/articles/PMC3547661/
7. rasmusab (2017, February 12). Introduction to Bayesian data analysis – part 1: What is Bayes? YouTube. https://www.youtube.com/watch?v=3OJEae7Qb_o&t=670s
8. *Approximate Bayesian Computation — Think Bayes*. (2021). Think Bayes. http://allendowney.github.io/ThinkBayes2/chap20.html
9. Albert, J. (2020). Intro to the ProbBayes Package. https://bayesball.github.io/Intro_ProbBayes.html
10. Albert, Jim and Hu, Jingchen. *Probability and Bayesian Modeling*. Boca Raton, FL: CRS Press, 2020.

# CHAPTER 4

# Burndown Rates: Shifting Right the Bayesian Way

*It is utterly implausible that a mathematical formula should make the future known to us, and those who think it can would once have believed in witchcraft.*

— Jacob Bernoulli

$T$*he Art of Conjecturing.* What a great title. Jacob Bernoulli is the author, and is also the guy striking a pose in our picture above. We add his book to our list of posthumously published statistical hits – right alongside Bayes' theorem.

Bernoulli summarized *The Art of Conjecturing* as follows:

> *The art of measuring, as precisely as possible, probabilities of things, with the goal that we would be able always to choose or follow in our judgments and actions that course, which will have been determined to be better, more satisfactory, safer or more advantageous.*[1]

Sounds like security to me.

Bernoulli sought broader, more scientific uses for probability, as opposed to the gambling focus the theory had in his day. Gambling has constraints. For example, a die has six sides. A deck has 52 cards. You can count up all the ways (combinatorics) different outcomes can show up. Conversely, natural phenomena tend to be unbounded and squishy – yet still contain countable events. This goes for security as well.

Based on observation, you can count up how many people are born with one eye color versus others, and can start to make inferences about broader populations using local proportions. We can count up security events that happen in a given time frame and make broader inferences as well.

Bernoulli questioned whether there was a limit to how much uncertainty reduction one can glean from observing more data. You can count up all the ways certain combinations of dice or cards will fall, he considered. But, you can't do this with nature, where the vast combinations stretch out infinitely. Gambling has finite combinations. Nature is seemingly infinite.

This leads to a practical question. Is there a point where counting's value deteriorates or loses utility? And, how much data do you really need to meet your inferential needs? Is it possible to overcount for the task (decision) at hand?

This line of inquiry led to his most popular conjecture and his namesake theorem, "The (weak) Law of Large Numbers," aka Bernoulli's theorem.[2] It was central to *The Art of Conjecturing*.

## *Urns, Pool Tables, Precision, and Accuracy*

To illustrate his theory, Bernoulli used an example of pulling colored stones out of an urn. You don't know the contents of the urn. You reach your hand in, and find one stone. You start pulling more and more stones out, one at a time. Some are colored, others are plain. Your job is to infer the proportion of colored stones. As you pull more stones, your inference about the ratio of colored stones strengthens. More data, here in the form of observed stones, reduces uncertainty.

This is not all that different from our Bayesian pool table example from the previous chapter. You might be okay with a wide guess on the white ball's location. Approximately right and winning small is better than being exactly wrong and losing big.

These are the tradeoffs in data analysis and decision-making. Risk drives the tradeoff. In our pool example, money was at risk. Tosses of balls onto the table cost money. And how far off your guess was from the true location costs money. If you are flush with dough (and you aren't greedy), approximate accuracy works.

This is a great metaphor for security – where we spend millions on threat intelligence, vulnerability management, and more in an effort to be *precise*. It is all done with the hopes of getting an edge on the bad guys.

Knowing the difference between precision and accuracy is critically important. It can save you time, money, and falling prey to risks. Yet, it cuts both ways. Too little precision, and you get owned repeatedly. Too much precision, you break the bank. Also, you may still get owned.

I have put together an infographic below to explain the differences between precision and accuracy.

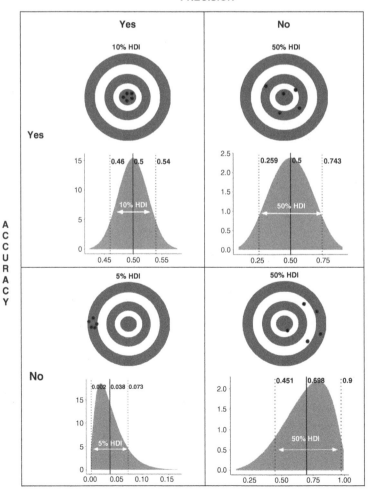

Knowing when measurements are accurate and precise enough is an important, often context-driven question. That means you need to decide. In this chapter, you will learn simple methods for determining if you have enough information to have confidence in your measurements. At the very least, you will get a sense for when you don't have what you need to be confident in your assertions.

Let's start with our next BOOM metric – burndown rates. Burndown rates are rooted in the Bernoulli distribution. Many measurements are.

## The Day 1 Metric

Imagine it is your first day as a brand-new CISO. You work for a software as a service (SaaS) company. Your company has hundreds of developers and numerous devops engineers deploying to the cloud daily. You, in contrast, have a small team consisting of yourself and two engineers.

You want to get a quick feel for the state of security – quantitatively. At the same time, you don't want to put your small, two-person team on a metrics death march. That's no way to win over new friends. You decide to start small.

**You select the following metric:** Rapidly determine the "within SLA remediation rate" for extreme, customer facing vulnerabilities.

You want to understand the rates at which risk is created and eliminated. As an SaaS company with numerous externally facing services, this seems like a reasonable starting point.

The good news is that assessments are occurring. This includes tools the team runs and third-party assessments like bug bounties.

You start by asking for a list of critical (exploitable) vulnerabilities discovered in the last quarter. These are the ones that would have been put into a ticketing system and prioritized. Some call these "break the glass" vulnerabilities – i.e., vulnerabilities ideally fixed within a week or less (if not 24 hours).

You say to your two security engineers, *"Just give me timestamps. Meaning, when we first became aware of the vulnerability and when (and if) they were fixed."*

### Get SME Beliefs

Before they run off, you also ask the following: *"Just curious, what do you believe the remediation rate is for these types of vulnerabilities? Meaning, of all the critical ones submitted for the last quarter, what percentage is fixed within a one-week SLA?"*

They respond, "*We don't know. Could be anything.*"

You ask, "*Well, is it 100%? Meaning, they always meet the SLA?*"

"*No, not even close! Never seen that anywhere ... ,*" they respond.

"*Is it zero? Meaning, they absolutely <u>never</u> meet SLA?*"

They say, "*No, we occasionally get same-day fixes.*"

"*Let's make it easy. If 10 extreme vulnerabilities are discovered in a quarter, how many get fixed within a week? If it's not a lot, you would likely say something well below 5 ... right?*"

One engineer says, "*I would bet on four...ish.*"

The second engineer exclaims, "*You're literally high! I run appsec ... so I'm going with two.*"

You then ask, "*I also want your stretch number. This is the best-case remediation count in 10. Meaning, you are 90% sure the true rate is below this number.*"

They respond with seven and four, respectively. Here are their rates in terms of expected rate and 90% stretch.

```
Security Engineer One: 4,7
Security Engineer Two: 2,4
```

## Get Small Data

This is what you got back from them for actual vulnerability data:

```
#Extreme Vulnerabilities Opened in Q3
"2020-07-25","2020-08-01","2020-08-03","2020-08-03","2020-08-03", "2020-08-
05","2020-08-05","2020-08-30","2020-09-12","2020-09-20", "2020-09-23"

#Extreme Vulnerabilities Closed Within 1 Week in Q3
"2020-07-29","2020-08-05","2020-08-06","2020-08-06","2020-09-03", "2020-09-
13","2020-09-25"
```

We now have open and closed extreme vulnerability date stamps for Q3, as well as subject matter expert (SME) beliefs about remediation rates. We are going to use all of this to get a feel for where things stand externally.

---

### Why do we use beliefs?

Because, small data can be biased. Small data may point to an average rate that doesn't reflect the underlying data generating process. So we use expert beliefs.

*(continued)*

## What is a data-generating process?

A data-generating process is the confluence of people, process, and technology that emits telemetry that we are interested in. In our case, we are interested because we want to baseline it and optimize it.

This particular data-generating process has many inputs that influence it. Here are just a few:

- Vulnerability research
- Bad guys
- Security solutions (that turn research into detections)
- Security teams (operating solutions)
- Systems (applications and infrastructure)

Those sub-processes ultimately impact our process. Beliefs can balance out overly certain data coming from uncertain processes. Meaning, it balances biased random samples.

## Also, small data may be too uncertain.

There might not be enough data to get a feel for the underlying rate tendency. Expert beliefs can bring a small amount of certainty where there is none.

## In short, beliefs can have a regulating effect on small, messy, and uncertain data.

Let's cache our beliefs before we mix them up with our data.

```
# Code available on www.themetricsmanifesto.com

source("manifesto_functions.R")   #book functions

#Extreme Vulnerabilities Closed Within 1 Week in Q3
eng_one <- c(4,7) #Median and 90% Stretch
eng_two <- c(2,4)
eng_two
[1] 2 4
```

We created two vectors of data above. I printed one out so you could see that it's just a simple list. We will need those vectors in a moment. In the meantime, let's graph our first engineer's beliefs.

It may not be obvious, but he gave us a broad range of beliefs. I am going to use a couple of simplifying functions to visualize the most probable burndown rate beliefs.

## *Seeing Is Believing: Graphing Beliefs*

The first function below takes in beliefs about hit-and-miss events. It returns shape parameters. You were introduced to GetBeliefsHits() in the previous chapter. Shape parameters "shape data." You can think of them as dials on an Etch-A-Sketch. In the following graph, the first parameter moves the graph left to right. It defines where the middle of the data tends to be. The second parameter deals with the spread of the data – is it wide or is it pointy?

```
# 4 fix, 7 stretch fix, out of 10
GetBeliefsHits(eng_one[1], eng_one[2],10)
[1] 1.96 2.78
```

Let's put these into a function that makes a graph. I will explain the inner workings of the graph function momentarily.

```
MakeBetaGraph(1.96,2.78,"Vuln Fix Rate","Plausibility",
             "Sec Eng Beliefs","4 Fix, 7 Max, out of 10")
```

Figure 4.1 is the resulting graph from those inputs:

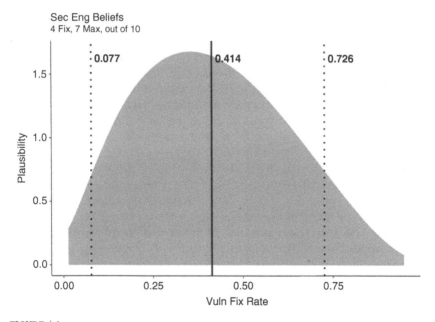

FIGURE 4.1

Let's do the same for the second engineer:

```
# 2 Fixes, 4 Stretch Fixes, out of 10
GetBeliefsHits(eng_two[1], eng_two[2],10)
[1] 2.07 7.32
MakeBetaGraph(2.07,7.32,"Vuln Fix Rate","Plausibility",
              "Sec Eng 2's Beliefs","2 Fix, 4 Max, out of 10")
```

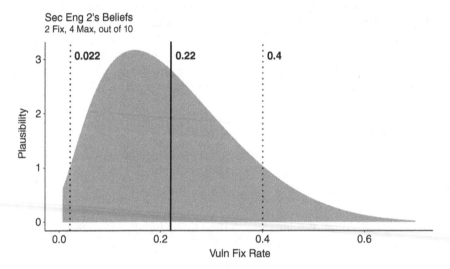

FIGURE 4.2

Figures 4.1 and 4.2 show the central tendencies of SME beliefs about vulnerability burndown and its spread. The spread is scored here by a Bayesian approach called the *highest density interval*, or HDI. We introduced the HDI (lightly) in the previous chapter. The HDI is the 89% portion of the curve that most plausibly holds the rate of interest. Think of the HDI as the best betting region. Note, you can choose alternatives to 89%, such as 95%.

On the first graph, the HDI is quite wide: 8% to 73%. It is very uncertain. The second graph's HDI is denser: 2% to 40%. After all, the second engineer claims to be on point for appsec. Maybe she knows something about vulnerability remediation, or maybe her experience is biasing her?

**Next, you can see a portion of what our graph function does on the inside.** The MakeBetaGraph() function generates data given shape parameters. (My approach in MakeBetaGraph() and a handful of other graphing functions is somewhat pedagogical. There are other more efficient ways to generate curves you will encounter later in the book.) That data is then put into a graphing function. This is the statistical stuff that makes our curves:

```
### Data Functions for MakeBetaGraph() ###

# Generate prior distribution data using SME shape parameters
prior <- distribution_beta(1000,2.07,7.32)

# Look at first 20 results
head(prior, 20)
0.006632192 0.009319321 0.011383280 0.013127152 0.014667573 0.016064094
0.017351967 0.018554094 0.019686345 0.020760249 0.021784493 0.022765814
0.023709560 0.024620063 0.025500886 0.026355005 0.027184933 0.027992815
0.028780502 0.029549602

# Get 89% Credible Interval
ci(prior, method="HDI")
# Highest Density Interval
89% HDI
------------
[0.02, 0.40]

# Add density for graphing
prior <- prior %>% estimate_density()

# Print out some results
head(prior, 5)
            x          y
1   0.006632192 0.6190828
2   0.007310269 0.6355207
3   0.007988346 0.6521709
4   0.008666424 0.6690102
5   0.009344501 0.6860361
```

The distribution_beta(), ci(), and estimate_density() functions come from the bayestestR library.[3] And bayestestR is part of a larger project called EasyStats. There are great tutorials and inspiration in the bayestestR project. It is suitable for Bayesian beginners.

## Scoring Beliefs with Data

Let's see which belief is most aligned with the data and by how much. I also consider this more pedagogical than operational.

To start, we need to load our dates into vectors, just like we did with our SME beliefs. Dates are our data, and we are being resourceful with tiny data. Imagine we queried data from the third quarter and got the following results.

```
opened_dates <- c("2020-07-25","2020-08-01","2020-08-03","2020-08-03",
                  "2020-08-03","2020-08-05","2020-08-05","2020-08-30",
                  "2020-09-12","2020-09-20","2020-09-23")
closed_dates <- c("2020-07-29","2020-08-05","2020-08-06","2020-08-06",
                  "2020-09-03","2020-09-13","2020-09-25")
```

We are going to do two things. First, we are going to use another helper function to score which engineers' beliefs seem to fit this data best. Then we run the test again, but this time we influence the algorithm to trust the appsec engineer more than the other security engineer. Why? Because, we assume rightly or wrongly, the appsec engineer is closer to the data generating process. Again, this is more pedagogical than anything else.

We will use the scoring results to select the SME belief that fits best. We then mesh that belief with our data to make a new graph. This is called Bayesian updating. We introduced Bayesian updating in the previous chapter.

```
#Get Shape Parameters For Each Engineer
eng_one <- GetBeliefsHits(4,7,10)
eng_two <- GetBeliefsHits(2,4,10)

#Get counts of opened and closed dates and their delta
opened <- length(opened_dates)
closed <- length(closed_dates)
delta <- opened - closed

# Compare each engineer's belief to the vulnerability data - no bias
raw_score <- ScoreBetaBeliefs(bias = c(.5,.5), first_belief = eng_one,
            second_belief = eng_two, hits = closed, misses = delta )

# Compare again, but bias the data toward the second engineer: .3, .7
favor_eng2_score <- ScoreBetaBeliefs(bias = c(.3,.7),
                    first_belief = eng_one, second_belief = eng_two,
                    hits = closed, misses = delta )

# Print out the unbiased Score
raw_score
first_belief
    4.334805

# Print out the biased score
favor_eng2_score
first_belief
    1.857773
```

Read the comments for the code above. It explains the flow of ideas without having to get bogged down in details. The output of the function prints out a number called an *odds*. It's just like in betting, where you place odds on a horse race. This particular odds is called a *Bayes factor*.

The odds favor the first engineer's forecast (beliefs) four times as much as the second engineer's beliefs. Even after influencing the algorithm toward the appsec engineer, it still favors our first engineer. That's because first engineer's beliefs have a central tendency and spread much closer to the data's central tendency:

```
# Vuln Data Central Tendency - date ratios
closed/opened
[1] 0.6363636
```

Look at the graph (Figure 4.1) of the first engineer's beliefs. Where does 64% sit on that graph? Is it within the 89% highest density interval? Meaning, is it within the two dotted lines marked .077 and .726? The answer is yes. It is so wide, it would be difficult not to fit into it.

Despite this, 64% is still way outside the second engineer's interval of .02–0.4 in Figure 4.2. You could likely figure this out without having to algorithmically score the data.

## Graph the Updated Model

Let's use engineer 1's beliefs combined with the data to get a new updated graph. Our Bayesian update creates a posterior distribution. The posterior combines beliefs with data:

```
# Bayesian Updating - Data + Beliefs
updated_hits <- eng_one[1] + closed    #update
updated_misses <- eng_one[2] + delta   #update
MakeBetaGraph(hit = updated_hits, miss = updated_misses,
             "Vuln Fix Rate","Plausibility","Bayesian Updating Example",
             "Eng 1 Beliefs + Data")
```

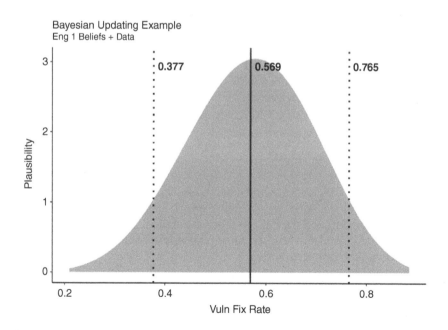

## Optional: But Where's the Likelihood!?

If you were paying close attention, you likely saw that we did not compute a likelihood like we did in the previous chapter. If you flip back a few pages to the previous chapter, you will see this:

# Product of Likelihood and Prior
product <- likelihood * prior

# Scaled to sum to one
posterior <- product/sum(product)

In our burndown model, we update engineer 1's prior with data directly – with addition. And we used that to create our posterior:

updated_hits <- eng_one[1] + closed
updated_misses <- eng_one[2] + delta

This is a short cut. Theoretically, we are using what is called a *conjugate prior*. I think of it as a process of making conjoined twins. The conjoined twins are the prior and the posterior.

Because of that relationship, you only need to use simple addition to make your posterior.

Now, when you see the likelihood disappear, you know why. Logically, it is still there, but in actual application, it is skipped (or replaced) with simple posterior addition.

There are several resources online that detail various conjugate relationships.[4]

### Predicting the Future?

We now have a rough (wide and uncertain) idea of extreme remediation rates. We combined what we thought were best-guess SME beliefs with empirical data. We used the data to score our beliefs. We used those scores to choose the beliefs that seemed most plausible. Now we want to use this model to think about the future.

What might happen if we had twice as many extreme vulnerabilities? We had 11 for Q3. So, let's double up to 22.

```
# What's A Plausible Remediation Rate For 22 Extreme Vulns?
future_count <- 22
vpred <- GetVulnPredictions(updated_hits, updated_misses, future_count)
```

This codes shows the inner workings of GetVulnPredictions(). As you can see, we have Bayesian updating at work again. This particular approach came from a book called *Hurricane Climatology*.[5] The authors are big users of LearnBayes (alternatively called ProbBayes[6]).

```
# Priors + Data
beta_vals = c(updated_hits, updated_misses)      ·

# Future count of vulnerabilities
future_count = 22;

# Store as list from 0 to 22
future_list = 0:future_count

# LearnBayes predictive function: uses beta prior and binomial data output
prob_future = pbetap(beta_vals, future_count, future_list)

# This call produces the list seen below.
round(cbind(future_list, prob_future), digits=3)
```

If we look at the results, we can get a feel for what to expect. I only share the central 10 to save on space.

```
        future_list vuln_predictions
 ....
 [8,]           7              0.035
 [9,]           8              0.051
[10,]           9              0.068
[11,]          10              0.084
[12,]          11              0.098
[13,]          12              0.107
[14,]          13              0.109
[15,]          14              0.104
[16,]          15              0.092
[17,]          16              0.076
[18,]          17              0.057
 ....
```

We can do this to find the 90% most plausible results – don't mind the code yet. Just know that it is showing the most probable remediation counts. Meaning, the counts that fit into a 90% credible interval:

```
discint(cbind(vpred[,1], vpred[,2]), .9)
$prob
[1] 0.919

$set
 [1]  7  8  9 10 11 12 13 14 15 16 17 18
```

Just to be thorough, let's run 1,000 simulations. Note how the counts ranging from 7 to 18 align with our prediction above?

```
beta_probs = rbeta(n=1000, updated_hits, updated_misses)
closed_counts = rbinom(n=1000, size=22, prob=beta_probs)
table(closed_counts)
closed_counts
    2    3    4    5    6    7    8    9   10   11   12   13   14   15   16   17   18   19   20   21
    2    1   10   16   19   32   49   69   80  102  113  105   97   91   86   54   39   20   11    4
```

If we want to view this data as a quick graph, this is all we need. This is called the posterior predictive distribution, something we touch on in the arrival metrics coming up.

```
closed_freq = table(closed_counts)
closed_props = closed_freq/sum(closed_freq)
plot(closed_props, type="h", xlab="Number Closed",
     las=1, lwd=3, ylab="Probability Closed")
```

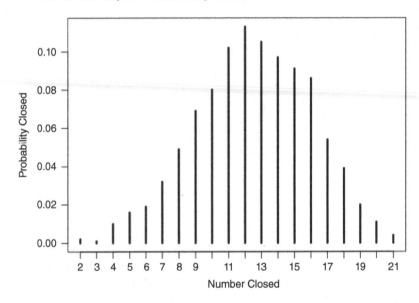

Out of 22 extreme vulnerabilities in a quarter, you can credibly believe (90% CI) that anywhere between 7 and 18 will be fixed within SLA. You should expect that the most likely value will be somewhere close to 13.

## *Wrapping Up Basic Burndown*

Did that seem like a lot of work? It's not. You can do this over lunch in under 10 lines of R. And that is the idea with metrics. When you know your target metric, the methods come easily. You should be able to move quickly on analysis and decision-making without a lot of fuss.

The only math is adding and subtracting. First, we count up date stamps. We add those counts with our beliefs. Our use of conjugate priors made the math simple (see "But Where's the Likelihood!?" box on page 64).

Below you see the core of the code for basic Bayesian burndown rates. It has eight lines.

```
# Get prior beliefs in shape parameter form
eng_one <- GetBeliefsHits(4,7,10)

# Raw Data
opened_dates <- c("2020-07-25","2020-08-01","2020-08-03","2020-08-03",
                  "2020-08-03","2020-08-05","2020-08-05","2020-08-30",
                  "2020-09-12","2020-09-20","2020-09-23")
closed_dates <- c("2020-07-29","2020-08-05","2020-08-06","2020-08-06",
                  "2020-09-03","2020-09-13","2020-09-25")

# Count Closed
closed <- length(closed_dates)

# Count left opened
delta <- length(opened_dates) - closed

# Bayesian Update, beliefs + data
updated_hits <- eng_one[1] + closed
updated_misses <- eng_one[2] + delta

# Create a graph that is a mesh of the above
MakeBetaGraph(hit = updated_hits, miss = updated_misses,
              "Vuln Fix Rate","Plausibility","Bayesian Updating Example",
              "Eng 1 Beliefs + Data")
```

**Figuring out what to measure is half the battle.** That is what this book aims to help with. The five baselines make defining your objects of measurement much easier. 99% of the time it will be: Survival, Burndown, Arrival, Wait Time, and/or Escapes.

Clarity about your baseline measurement is key. We chose burndown rates. We also had a specific policy analysis goal. I wanted to know the within-SLA remediation rate. This is a very useful metric. When in doubt where to start, start here.

**The methods of measurement come second to clear objectives.** All the methods in this section are Bayesian. And as you will see, each uses a conjugate prior. When you see the "conjugate" word, just think "easy." The optimization chapter moves beyond conjugate relationships.

Once you have a sense for the critical remediation rate, you can propose actions. Here is an example summary statement:

*The extreme vulnerability burndown rate is ~60%. Best-case scenario is ~77% and worst is ~38%. Because the data is very small, we need more time to get a better baseline. We would be shocked if the rate is anywhere close to the 90% SLA requirement. We are putting a plan in place to reduce both the occurrence and time to live of extreme vulnerabilities. We will be reporting on this rate quarterly but tracking daily.*

— CISO & Team

As you get more data you can update your metrics. The following graph demonstrates what updating looks like given all the data to date. As stated earlier, this process is formally called Bayesian updating.

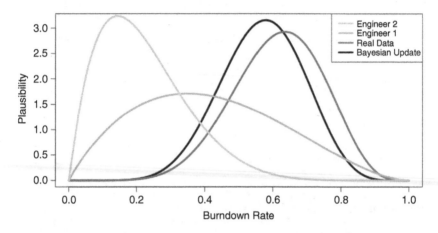

Here is the code used to make this graph. I will explain it briefly below. It is a canonical form used for understanding Bayesian updating from the prior, likelihood to posterior. We explore many alternative graphing scenarios in the chapters ahead.

```
# Bayes Burndown Curve (bold black): Eng1 Beliefs + Data
curve(dbeta(x, closed + eng_one[1], delta + eng_one[2]), from=0, to=1,
      xlab="Burndown Rate", ylab="Plausibility",col=1, lwd=4, las=1)

# Actual Vuln Data (Dates) Curve (dark gray)
curve(dbeta(x, closed + 1, delta + 1), add=TRUE, col=2,lwd=4)

# Engineer 1 Beliefs (gray)
curve(dbeta(x, eng_one[1], eng_one[2]), add=TRUE, col=3, lwd=4)

# Engineer 2 Beliefs (lite gray)
curve(dbeta(x, eng_two[1], eng_two[2]), add=TRUE, col=4, lwd=4)

#Legend
legend("topright", c("Engineer 2","Engineer 1", "Real Data",
      "Bayesian Update"), col=c(4,3, 2, 1), lwd=c(3,3, 3, 3))
```

In the graph above, you can see each engineer's beliefs about the rate. It should be pretty clear why our scoring algorithm said engineer 1's forecast was much better. This was true even after we significantly biased the data in our prior scoring test. Note how much the likelihood (data) and engineer 1's curves overlap. It's approximately 50%.

Engineer 2 was relatively confident. We know that because her beliefs are less spread out and more pointy around 20%. Given the height of the curve we would say that she believed a ~20% burndown rate was most plausible. Maybe if we get more data, her forecast might be closer to the data? Note how much her curve overlaps with the likelihood. It's small – 20% at best.

Engineer 1 was less confident – more spread. But, his central tendency was much closer to the vulnerability data's central tendency. The central tendency of the real data was within the HDI of engineer 1's beliefs.

The Bayesian Update curve (the black one, called the posterior) becomes the compromise between engineer 1's beliefs and the data. Of course, as you get more empirical data, beliefs matter less. They become overwhelmed with reality.

Lastly, as the fictional CISO, **what do you do with your day one discovery**? For me, the vulnerability elimination rate makes me curious, if not very concerned. I want to know more. That's a great metrics outcome.

Next, let's see what "knowing more" looks like over time.

## Precision and Accuracy: Burndown and Updating over Time

**Note:** This is a more *advanced section*. It goes a bit deeper into R code and Bayesian data analysis concepts. I will still strive for concept over code.

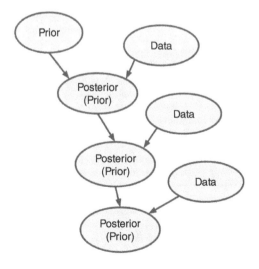

Baselining happens over time. The more data, the more certainty about our target rate. It is up to you to determine how much certainty is needed – how much precision and accuracy – to drive a decision. Bayesian approaches make this process easier.

Let's explore baselining over a whole year. In our first month, we mesh an SME's prior with data. Each subsequent month gets its prior from the previous month's posterior. Logically, it looks just like the previous image. Previous posteriors become the new prior. Sound complex? It's not. I'm going to show you how to do it step by step. You will be able to make your own compelling graphs in the process.

## Building a Bayesian Burndown Chart

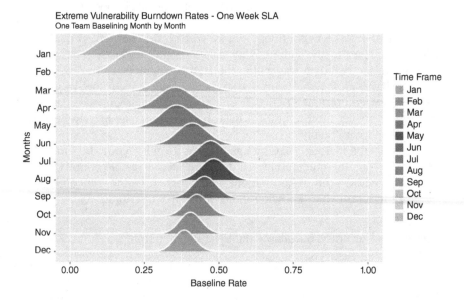

First step in graphing our data is creating a data frame. The tibble() function makes that easy. It is a special type of data frame brought to us via the tidyverse.[7] Think of data frames as spreadsheets. This one has three columns: y-axis, Hits, and Misses. Hits holds a count of vulnerabilities fixed within the one-week SLA. Misses are the ones opened but not fixed within SLA. The y-axis in this case holds 12 months. Months run along the y-axis.

After making our data frame we codify prior beliefs. Lastly, we make our graph.

```
# Jan includes Prior + first months data.
vulnData <- tibble(
  yaxis = c("Jan", "Feb", "Mar", "Apr", "May", "Jun", "Jul", "Aug", "Sep",
            "Oct", "Nov", "Dec"),
  hits   = c( 2, 4, 13, 4, 5, 12, 17, 7, 4, 3, 2, 4),
  misses = c(12, 11, 10, 9, 8, 7, 6, 5, 14, 13, 12, 16)
)

# Encode Prior Beliefs
eng_one_prior <- GetBeliefsHits(eng_one[1], eng_one[2],10)

# Build Tidy Data Frame for Visualization
eng_risk <- MakeVulnData(vulnData, eng_one_prior)
```

```
# Make Visualization
MakeRidgeChart(eng_risk,
               "Extreme Vulnerability Burndown Rates - One Week SLA",
               "One Team Baselining Month By Month",
               "Baseline Rate",
               "Months",
               "Time Frame")
```

That is all that is needed to make the chart above. Next, I unpack a couple of the function calls. I want to make the Bayesian updating portion explicit and expose you to more R.

We've covered the vulnData() data frame above. And we have also covered GetBeliefsHits() in some detail. Let's focus on the MakeVulnData() function call.

```
MakeVulnData <- function(vulnData, prior){

  # Vuln Data Can Have An Extra Group Column
  hasGroup <- length(vulnData)

  # Loop Through Data Frame
  for( i in 1:nrow(vulnData)){

    # If first row, add informative prior (beliefs)
    if( i == 1){

      # Update With Prior Beliefs
      hits <- vulnData$hits[i] + prior[1]
      misses <- vulnData$misses[i] + prior[2]
      yaxis <- vulnData$yaxis[i]

      # Used for multi-team chart
      if(hasGroup == 4){
        legend <- vulnData$legend[i]
      }else{
        legend <- yaxis
      }

      # Build Posterior Distribution
      res <- MakeBurnData(hits, misses, yaxis, legend)
      eng_risk <- res
    }else{

      # Update with previous posterior of hits and misses
      hits <- vulnData$hits[i] + hits
      misses <- vulnData$misses[i] + misses
      yaxis <- vulnData$yaxis[i]
```

```
    if(hasGroup == 4){
      legend <- vulnData$legend[i]
    }else{
      legend <- yaxis
    }
    res <- MakeBurnData(hits, misses, yaxis, legend)
    eng_risk <- bind_rows(res, eng_risk)
  }
}
return(eng_risk)
}
```

The meat of this function call is the Bayesian updating process. It occurs month over month. Of course, this can be applied to much smaller or larger time frames. As data rolls in, the model can learn and update.

The first month gets its prior from engineer 1. Do you see where the prior is added into the data? It's handled in the first if() statement. The rest of the months take the previous month's output as input, as a cumulative summary. Anywhere you see a "+" is where updating is occurring.

The updated data is passed into the MakeBurnData() function. It is responsible for making posterior distributions. Let's analyze the MakeBurnData() function:

```
MakeBurnData <- function(closed, misses, yaxis, legend){

  # An incremental list of x values
  x_vals = seq(from=0,to=1,length = 1000)

  # Return a score for each value of x_vals. It answers, "what is the
  # Likelihood of seeing each of these values given our shape data?"
  dens = dbeta(x_vals,closed, misses)

  # Normalize to sum to 1
  prob = dens / max(dens)

  # Create a new data frame to return
  res <- tibble(x_vals, yaxis , prob, legend, closed, misses, dens)

  # Get rid of "Inf" values
  return(res[res$dens != "Inf",])
}
```

The star in this function call is dbeta(). It creates the posterior. The prior is also a beta distribution. Thus, the prior and posterior are in the same family. This is a conjugate relationship. This makes updating our beliefs simplified. In this case, all we do is addition. We passed the new data plus previous priors in for closed and missed. They go into the dbeta() function. It returns the new posterior.

**Question:** Was there any improvement in burndown rate between January and December? A quick visual analysis shows that there is some overlap between their distributions. While Bernoulli's law of large numbers is at play – baselining data on the move – much of the data's wiggling overlaps. It makes it difficult to discern real differences visually.

Let's do some analysis to determine how much of January's plausible rates overlap with December's. I will explain all the code at the end.

> **Note:** There is data output in the code below. The main data points are the two HDIs and the ROPE value – which gets explained. HDIs measure the most plausible outcomes.

```
# Get beta shape parameters from eng_risk for january
jan <- eng_risk %>% filter(yaxis == "Jan") %>%
        select(closed, misses) %>% distinct()

# Generate 1,000 random probabilities constrained by shape params
jan_dist <- rbeta(10000, jan$closed, jan$misses)

# Get the 89% Highest Density Interval
jan_hdi <- ci(jan_dist, method = "HDI")
jan_hdi
# Highest Density Interval

89% HDI
------------
[0.07, 0.35]

# Get the shape parameters for Dec
dec <- eng_risk %>% filter(yaxis == "Dec") %>%
        select(closed, misses) %>% distinct()

# Generate 1000 probabilities constrained by shape parameters
dec_dist <- rbeta(1000, dec$closed, dec$misses)

# Get the HDI
dec_hdi <- ci(dec_dist, method = "HDI")
dec_hdi
# Highest Density Interval

89% HDI
------------
[0.33, 0.45]

# Get Diff Between Months
diff_dist <- dec_dist - jan_dist

# How much of Dec is credibly within Jan?
rope(diff_dist)

# Proportion of samples inside the ROPE [-0.10, 0.10]:

inside ROPE
-----------
17.85 %
```

FIGURE 4.3

## *Are We Improving?*

A lot just happened in the code above. Does it seem like overkill when all we want to know is, "Are we improving?" We get a hint at our answer at the end of the code. The final number is ~18%. It's our ROPE value. It's an indication of similarity. Dissimilar is 0%. Practically identical approaches 100%. Let's work our way to what our ROPE value means in context.

First, we can do a quick comparison between the average rate from December and January. We get the central tendency from each month's distribution. Let's also graph their distributions.

```
# Best central tendency point estimates
map_estimate(jan_dist)
MAP = 0.17

map_estimate(dec_dist)
MAP = 0.37

# Simple/Quick Plots
plot(density(jan_dist))

plot(density(dec_dist))
```

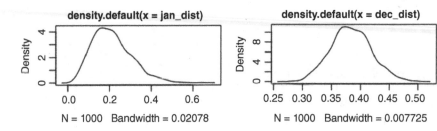

The map_estimation() function comes from the bayestestR library. You can think of it as a souped-up average. Technically, it is the most plausible central tendency based on the rate's density. MAP is short for "Maximum A Posteriori."

If you were to use only these two point estimates of 17% to 37% to draw conclusions, you might say, "Yes! We have a ~118% improvement!" (or, a difference of 20%). That may be very wrong. Why? Because you are ignoring a lot of plausible data. Look at the distributions above. There are a number (infinite in one sense) of rates that reach up toward the higher points in the distribution. A single point is a poor summary of all the data.

If you look at the HDI for each month, you can see a small amount of overlap: 7%–35% and 33%–45%, respectively. The graphs above also reflect some overlap. Intuitively, it seems that December is somewhat different from January.

Let's do one more check. We don't want to be fooled by our data. After all, we are going to make recommendations (or not) based on this analysis.

## Roping in Change

Turn your attention to the final couple of lines of code in Figure 4.3. We subtract the January distribution from December. This creates the diff_dist distribution. If these two distributions were mostly the same, the result would be centered around zero on the *x*-axis. In fact, if they were exactly the same, the results would be exactly zero. That is *not* what we see below. Things are shifted to the right. It's a complex graph. Let's unpack it.

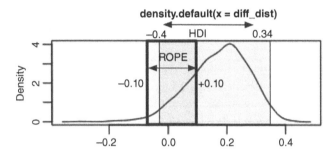

The first thing to note is the HDI of diff_dist. You can see that on top. It is −04% to +34%. It is a 95% HDI in this case. It's wide. The area it covers is shaded. That is where the most plausible values in diff_dist live. The next thing to notice is the shaded "ROPE" area from −10% to +10%. It has a bolded border.

ROPE stands for "Region of Practical Equivalence." That is a fancy term for a simple concept. If it could speak, it would say, *"Results inside my rope of −10% to +10% indicate no change. In this case, it means the more your process overlaps with me the more likely you have not improved."* We are using the rope to determine if the data-generating process itself is changing … improving. If the HDI were 100% inside the ROPE, we would say, *"There has been no demonstrable process improvement."*

The portion of the HDI and ROPE that overlap covers ~18%. If December was completely different from January, the HDI would be outside of the ROPE – off to the far right. Our ROPE score in that case would be 0%. That indicates change, ideally for the better.

But, the HDI does overlap with the ROPE region. It's only a partial, yet measurable, overlap. We could say that the results in terms of rate change (improvement in this case) are inconclusive.

**There are two challenges here.** First, January's data was sparse. It leads to a lot of uncertainty. Meaning, the graph was spread out. Imagine if it was so broad that almost any possibility was somewhat plausible? That's not quite the case here. December was far more certain with an HDI spanning a 10% range.

What if we started with June instead? The data seems to be baselining some. More data does that. Take a look at the colorful burndown graph. It's about a 20% spread if we just eyeballed the most plausible range. The difference between June and December doesn't seem like much. Let's see what our ROPE comparison says. Note, I wrote a function to make it easier to run.

```
GetRope(eng_risk, "Jun", "Dec")
# Proportion of samples inside the ROPE [-0.10, 0.10]:

inside ROPE
-----------
92.26 %
```

Based on our ROPE analysis, we would say that June and December are very similar. A ~92% ROPE is so close to be negligible in terms of differences. And let's be clear. We mean that June and December have similar data-generating processes in terms of rates.

## ROPE as a Decision-Making Tool

There can be some objections to the ROPE approach. First, the default rope range is arbitrary. I used the default range of –10% to +10%. That is not a hard-and-fast rule. The ROPE is a configurable decision-making tool. Its range can be changed to what makes sense given your context. And it is context that drives the amount of precision and accuracy needed.

In our case, we would conclude by saying that we are not 100% convinced that improvement has occurred. While there is evidence of progress, it is weak. This is partially a function of the small data size in January. While we need more data, it would be reasonable to say we need more progress! If progress were substantial, even with small data, the difference would indeed be measurable.

It is beyond the scope of this book to cover all aspects of the ROPE function. We largely stick to default ROPE ranges in conjunction with the HDI to better detect meaningful change. John K. Kruschke wrote one of the leading Bayesian books called *Doing Bayesian Data Analysis*. Chapter 12 covers ROPE in depth.[8]

## Wrapping Up Single Team Burndown

If I were wearing my CISO hat, I would be concerned after seeing the graph. Rates between January and December have a lot of overlap. The trend in the last few months *indicates* a worsening rate. Add our Bayesian change analysis (ROPE) to the mix and I would have a fairly grounded rationale for concern. There is some indication of *zero improvement*.

I would be motivated to find out if there is something systematically going on that is preventing betterment (particularly if I was expecting improvement due to security investments). And perhaps more importantly, is there something blocking (if not reversing) progress?

**This is how metrics work.** Confronting our capabilities with data and asking tough questions, and following the data. Notice that we did not rely on mere averages. That would have been a mistake leading to the "Flaw of Averages" – which is a great book by Sam Savage.[9]

# Final: Comparing Teams

I wanted to share one last example. It makes the Bayesian Updating concept crystal clear. It is a multiteam view.

First, we review a graph, then the code. There isn't really anything new in the code. It is just a different layout for pedagogical purposes.

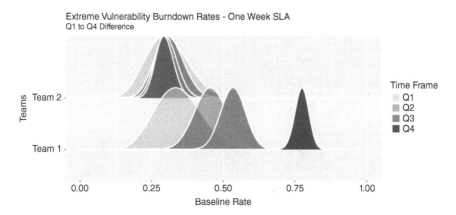

Imagine having all your product teams arranged this way. It's clear that Team 1 is absolutely progressing. Team 2 is not moving. They seem to be baselining around ~30%.

While there is some overlap in the data for team 1, the final quarter stands apart. This is a function of data volumes. The data learns from previous quarter's data, and that means every prior exerts some gravity on the new posterior. For Q4 to pull away as it has means an uptick in data.

You can see it clearly below. Q4 has 160 hits and 5 misses. I put that in there on purpose. I want you to see how much data it takes to make an obvious change when the data is cumulative for a long time frame.

Note how the data in Q4 is rather pointy for team one. Remember, with more data comes more certainty. Certainty (precision) expresses itself in less spread.

Below you can see the code for the team burndown chart. The functions are the same with one small change to the graphing function. It is Make-RidgeChart2().

```
# Build Team One Data Frame
teamOneData <- tibble(yaxis = "Team 1",
                      hits = c(10,24,46, 160),
                      misses = c(20,20,20,5),
                      legend = c("Q1", "Q2", "Q3", "Q4"))

# Codify Eng One Beliefs
prior <- GetBeliefsHits(eng_one[1], eng_one[2],10)

# Create Posterior Distribution
team1 <- MakeVulnData(teamOneData, prior)

# Build Team Two Data Frame
teamTwoData <- tibble(yaxis = "Team 2",
                      hits = c(10,15,20, 40),
                      misses = c(20,30,40,80),
                      legend = c("Q1", "Q2", "Q3", "Q4"))

# Codify Eng Two Beliefs
prior <- GetBeliefsHits(eng_two[1], eng_two[2],10)

# Create Posterior Distribution
team2 <- MakeVulnData(teamTwoData, prior)

# Combine Posteriors Into One Data Frame row by row
eng_risk <- rbind(team1, team2)

# Make Combined Chart
MakeRidgeChart2(eng_risk,
                "Extreme Vulnerability Burndown Rates - One Week SLA",
                "Q1 To Q4 Difference",
                "Baseline Rate", "Teams",
                "Time Frame")
```

## Wrapping Up

This chapter packed a lot of information. Here's what we learned:

- **Metrics data is simple.** Most metrics start with counting dates.
- **You can do a lot with a little code.** Everything in this chapter can be encapsulated in well under 30 lines of code. Thanks to an active community of R developers.

- **Burndown rates are useful for measuring remediation efficiency.** Burndown can be applied to numerous security processes.
- **Baselines are a function of the law of large numbers.** Rates stabilize as cumulative data increases. We baseline while rates are on the move.
- **Precision and accuracy requirements determine how much data is needed.** The HDI combined with the region of practical equivalence (ROPE) help navigate certainty requirements. The HDI reveals our most plausible rates. ROPEs provide a decision rule for detecting meaningful change.
- **Averages can be deceptive.** We need to measure using all plausible rates. A single rate can send us in the wrong direction. Earlier, we could have claimed a 118%+ improvement – the data in its entirety did not support that.

Let's take what we have learned on burndown rates and look at arrival rates. Arrival rates shift our attention left. We use arrival rates to better understand the data-generating process that allows risk to materialize. Burndowns were for better understanding and optimizing processes for eliminating risk.

## Notes

1. *Ars conjectandi.* (1713). Google Books. https://books.google.co.in/books?hl=en&lr=&id=XPOf7STJ3y4C&oi=fnd&pg=PA6&ots=LkXyfOVb7o&sig=pD7hNFo_EuAXm9V8UiXZIiRGnXE&redir_esc=y#v=onepage&q&f=false
2. Raper, S. (2018, August 1). Turning points: Bernoulli's golden theorem. Royal Statistical Society. https://rss.onlinelibrary.wiley.com/doi/full/10.1111/j.1740-9713.2018.01171.x
3. *Understand and Describe Bayesian Models and Posterior Distributions.* (2021). BayestestR. https://easystats.github.io/bayestestR/
4. Cook, J. D. (2020, April 21). Conjugate prior relationships. https://www.johndcook.com/blog/conjugate_prior_diagram/
5. Elsner, J. B., & Jagger, T. H. (2013). *Hurricane Climatology: A Modern Statistical Guide Using R* (1st ed.). Oxford University Press.
6. Albert, J. (2020). Intro to the ProbBayes Package. https://bayesball.github.io/Intro_ProbBayes.html
7. *Tidyverse.* (2021). R packages for data science. https://www.tidyverse.org/
8. Kruschke, J. (2014). *Doing Bayesian Data Analysis: A Tutorial with R, JAGS, and Stan* (2nd ed.). Academic Press.
9. Savage, S. (2019). *The Flaw of Averages: Why We Underestimate Risk in the Face of Uncertainty (Chinese Edition)* (1st ed.). CITIC Press Corporation.

# CHAPTER 5

# Risk Arrival Rates: Shift Left Security Metrics

*Probability is expectation founded upon partial knowledge.*

— George Boole[1]

## Introduction: Random Bombs and Horse Kicks

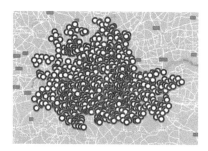

The image on the left is of the first ballistic missile. It's called the Vergeltungswaffe 1 (Vengeance Weapon 1, or V-1). During WWII, over 2,300 of them were dropped on London – the impact points are pictured on the right.

A young British actuary by the name of R. D. Clarke was deployed to help analyze hit rates and bombing locations of the V-1. His superiors wanted to know how much of a threat the V-1 posed.[2] Clarke was tasked with determining if the bombs were landing in random locations – or were they targeted?

Clarke focused on the likelihood of London munitions, rail, and other strategic sites being blown up. Was there anything in the data that revealed a nonrandom pattern? Hits to these sites would be devastating.

For a short and award-winning write-up on this story, read, "The Flying Bomb and the Actuary."[3]

Clarke made a grid over the bombed area. Imagine a grid of 576 boxes over the image on the right above.[4] Each box was a quarter kilometer squared. Some of the boxes would have had one or more dots (bombs) in them. Some would have had zero hits. He then counted up all the hits and misses to get a rate.

Here is what the real data looks like:

```
bombs <- tibble(hits = c(0,1,2,3,4,5),
                frequency = c(229, 211, 93, 35, 7, 1),
                ratio = frequency/sum(frequency))

> bombs
# A tibble: 6 x 3
   hits frequency    ratio
  <dbl>     <dbl>    <dbl>
1     0       229  0.398
2     1       211  0.366
3     2        93  0.161
4     3        35  0.0608
5     4         7  0.0122
6     5         1  0.00174
```

As you can see, there are many boxes with no hits, and one box with five hits. According to Clarke's analysis, the "bombs per square" average was 0.932.

**This chapter is about discovering rates like this.** In our case, it will be rates of vulnerabilities per week. So, if you get lost, remember that is all we are doing.

Clarke used his rate (.932) with the 576 squares to create a statistical model. That model had a near perfect fit to the original data. Meaning, meshing .932 with 576 simulated the real bomb drops quite well. Here is one run of Clarke's model. Note, each time you run it there will be slightly different, but generally correct, results:

```
> table(rpois(576,.932))

  0   1   2   3   4   6
229 216  85  35  10   1
```

**It gave the proof he needed. Bombs were indeed random and not targeted.** As a risk manager, this spelled some amount of relief. While bombs were devastating no matter where they hit, the enemy's capabilities were scattershot.

At the heart of Clarke's analysis is a statistical tool called the Poisson distribution. You can see it in the function call above "rpois()." It's used for analyzing and forecasting counts of relatively infrequent events. Events can be modeled spatially as in the case of bombs. Or, they can be considered over time. Let's look deeper into the Poisson distribution with our next historic example.

NICK THING, THIS HAVING TO DODGE FOR YOUR LIFE, ISN'T IT? AFTER MY TREATMENT THE HORSE HAS NO LONGER ANY DESIRE TO KICK.

Fifty years prior to WWII, the Russian economist and statistician Ladislaus Josephovich Bortkiewicz was counting rare and deadly events. He even wrote a book on counting infrequent events titled *The Law of Small Numbers*. His research, and that book, popularized the use of the Poisson process.

His examples leaned toward the macabre – his most famous study is accidental termination by horse kicks within the Prussian cavalry.[5]

Bortkiewicz's kick data covered 20 years and 10 regiments within the Prussian cavalry. That equates to 200 cavalry-years of death-by-horse-kick data. (Can you see how this is starting to sound similar to our bombing example?)

The data looks like this:

```
kicks <- tibble(victims = c(0,1,2,3,4,5),
                frequency = c(109,65,22,3,1,0),
                ratio = frequency/sum(frequency))

kicks
# A tibble: 6 x 3
  victims frequency ratio
```

```
        <dbl>        <dbl> <dbl>
1          0          109 0.545
2          1           65 0.325
3          2           22 0.11
4          3            3 0.015
5          4            1 0.005
6          5            0 0
```

Here is that same data unbundled. Think of it as 200 years of hit-and-miss data. Each number is a year. (The data values would obviously be randomly ordered.)

```
kick_amount <- c(rep(0,109), rep(1,65), rep(2,22), rep(3,3), rep(4,1))
length(kick_amount)
[1] 200
kick_amount
0 0 0 0 0 0 0 0 0 0 0 0 0 0 0 0 0 0 0 0 0 0 0 0 0 0 0 0 0 0 0 0 0 0 0 0 0 0 0 0 0 0 0 0 0
0 0 0 0 0 0 0 0 0 0 0 0 0 0 0 0 0 0 0 0 0 0 0 0 0 0 0 0 0 0 0 0 0 0 0 0 0 0 0 0 0 0 0 0 0
0 0 0 0 0 0 0 0 0 0 0 0 0 0 0 0 0 1 1 1 1 1 1 1 1 1 1 1 1 1 1 1 1 1 1 1 1 1 1 1 1 1 1 1 1
1 1 1 1 1 1 1 1 1 1 1 1 1 1 1 1 1 1 1 1 1 1 1 1 1 1 1 1 1 1 1 1 1 1 1 1 2 2 2 2 2 2 2 2 2
2 2 2 2 2 2 2 2 2 2 2 3 3 3 4
```

What is the average kick rate across the 200 cavalry-years? Here is the quick math:

```
sum(kick_amount) / length(kick_amount)
[1] 0.61
```

Practically speaking, we can't divide death up into portions. You die, or you don't. The .61 is similar to the .93 for bombs. It is an average rate spread across a type of unit. In the previous example, the units were square kilometers. In this example, the unit is cavalry-years.

We use these averages as inputs into a Poisson data model. Just like the V-1 bomb example, it models our horse kicking correctly – addressing the zeroes and fluctuations in the arrival of events.

This model works because of the relationship between the average horse-kick deaths and how much the total data varies. The vanilla Poisson distribution works well when the ratio of the data's variance over the mean is close to one.

```
var(kick_amount)/mean(kick_amount)
[1] 1.001565
```

Let's see how good of a job the Poisson distribution does in simulating 200 calvary-years of horse kicks. Here we add a new column of Poisson predicted results to the kicks data frame.

```
# Create 200 calvary-years of simulated data and add to kicks data frame

kicks$predicted <- round(200 * dpois(0:5,.61))
kicks
# A tibble: 6 x 4
  victims frequency ratio predicted
    <dbl>     <dbl> <dbl>     <dbl>
1       0       109 0.545       109
2       1        65 0.325        66
3       2        22 0.11         20
4       3         3 0.015         4
5       4         1 0.005         1
6       5         0 0             0
```

The model has a good fit to the data.

**This is the rough process we will use to baseline vulnerability arrival rates.** But, we are going to do it the Bayesian way. Meaning, we consider a distribution of plausible rates and update our beliefs as data rolls in. The flexibility of a Bayesian approach allows us to deal with complex data that may not be as tidy as bomb drops and horse kicks.

**Our ultimate goal** is baselining the rate at which extreme vulnerabilities arrive per week. But, we could model a variety of scenarios. Bombs, horse kicks, vulnerabilities, malware, logins, and phishing all have countable events that happen over time. Understanding the rate at which they materialize or are discovered is critically important. Once you understand your baseline arrival rates, you can take actions to better control those rates.

## From Burndown to Arrival

Last chapter's focus was extreme burndowns. These are risks that have already materialized. It's the first step toward identifying risk and optimizing for its elimination.

We learned that the law of large numbers drives baselining. At the same time, our rates are moving targets. Yet, with more data certainty emerges – but not perfect certainty. We often need to make decisions while data is small and rates are unstable. We may not have the time nor the money to eliminate our uncertainty before making a move.

Following Bernoulli's lead, can we make *satisfactory, safer, or more advantageous* choices while uncertain? Yes, with analytics tools like the HDI and ROPE. The highest density interval (HDI) and region of practical equivalence (ROPE) work together to support our decisions. They help us detect if change is occurring. They are only two of many analytics and decision tools you will be exposed to.

We also learned we can be tricked by focusing on specific numbers like the mean. That is opting for the veneer of *precision* while failing on *accuracy*. Instead, we confront our metric with all the plausible rates as they evolve. This gives us more truth – reducing the likelihood of being fooled by the flaw of averages.

In this chapter, we consider a new baseline. After all, burndown is just one tactic in an overarching metrics strategy. Now we shift our attention left to risk creation.[6] This is the other side of the metrics coin. Our intent is baselining the rate at which risks arrive.

In the BOOM framework this new metric is called the arrival rate. It is a count metric related to the Poisson distribution – the same one Clarke used for bombs and Bortkiewicz used for deadly horse kicks. Unlike them, our approach to arrival rates will be Bayesian.

## Simulating Arrivals

We are going to cover more code in this section. We start with a data-generating function called GetAdvSecResults(). Under the hood, GetAdvSecResults() uses a simulation tool for making scientific data. Chapter 11 covers simulation and this particular function in depth. I will touch on it lightly here.

We use GetAdvSecResults() to create three product teams' worth of vulnerability data. Product teams are composed of numerous squads. Each team has different rates at which they create risk, and they have different rates at which they remediate risk. Those rates change over time. Thus, our data reflects the random nature of security events.

Each function call has three inputs. The first asks for beliefs about event rates by risk tiers, of which there are three: extreme, critical, and high. You can alter this for your needs.

Each percentage in the first input is the probability of one or more events happening per day. The rate could be 0.005 or even less. If you believe you have on average five extreme "break-the-glass" events a year, then your rate is: 5/365 = 0.012. For a week, it would be 5/52 = 0.0961.

The second parameter in GetAdvSecResults() defines response efficiency. And the last number impacts risk creation rates. The two together represent a form of process maturity – or lack thereof. GetAdvSecResults(), in turn, uses various probabilistic functions to generate data from these inputs.

Please note that your results will likely differ from the data shown below and throughout the book. A lot of random noise gets injected into simulation results.

```
# See chp 5 scripts www.themetricsmanifesto.com

source("manifesto_functions.R")

# Make Vuln Data Table For Product Team 1
dtGroupOne <- GetAdvSecResults(c(.02,.03,.08),2,4)
dtGroupOne$group <- 1

#Make Vuln Data Table For Product Team 2
dtGroupTwo <- GetAdvSecResults(c(.03,.05,.10),1,2)
dtGroupTwo$group <- 2

#Make Vuln Data Table For Product Team 3
dtGroupThree <- GetAdvSecResults(c(.05,.07,.12),1,1)
dtGroupThree$group <- 3

# Merge Data Tables
dt <- bind_rows(dtGroupOne, dtGroupTwo, dtGroupThree)
```

The output is a 20-or-so-column-wide *data table* with several thousand records. Data tables are related to data frames. They are for larger data sets that need faster processing. You could create dozens of teams' worth of data quickly with these functions. Here is a snapshot of the data we are working with. Don't fret over the details – they are covered in Chapter 11.

```
> dt
    idTeam           team nDays  id dev_maturity audit exposure exposure_id
1:       1  external audit   106   1            4     0 external           1
2:       5  partner no audit   31   2            4     1  partner           2
3:       6 internal no audit   43   3            4     1 internal           3
4:       6 internal no audit   43   4            4     1 internal           3
5:       1  external audit    54   5            4     0 external           1

    severity hits severity_id    time_adj beta_prob fix_time fix_date status
1:   extreme    1           1  0.45327531 0.4501006       18      124      0
2:   extreme    1           1  0.37828240 0.3416041       22       53      0
3:   extreme    1           1  0.39376691 0.1394294       11       54      0
4:   extreme    1           1 -0.15441686 0.4796726       29       72      0
5:  critical    1           2  0.18977122 0.4615452       27       81      0

    first.seen  last.seen week.fseen week.lseen group
1: 2020-04-16 2020-05-04         16         18     1
2: 2020-02-01 2020-02-23          5          8     1
3: 2020-02-13 2020-02-24          7          8     1
4: 2020-02-13 2020-03-13          7         11     1
5: 2020-02-24 2020-03-22          8         12     1
```

We feed these results into an aggregating function that will make our arrival analysis easier. It groups data together like you saw in our bombing and kicking introduction.

```
vuln_wks <- GetVulnsOpenedByWks(dt)
vuln_wks
# A tibble: 52 x 5
   week.fseen extreme critical  high   all
        <int>   <dbl>    <dbl> <dbl> <dbl>
 1          1       5        6    14    25
 2          2      11        4     9    24
 3          3       5       16    16    37
 4          4       3        7    11    21
 5          5       5        8    11    24
 6          6       9        6     7    22
 7          7       0        6    22    28
 8          8       3        8    19    30
 9          9       5        6    12    23
10         10       9        3    19    31
# ... with 42 more rows
```

## *Quick Exploration of Arrival Data*

Let's do some basic data exploration to see how extreme counts break out per week. The table() function buckets vulnerability counts by week.

```
table(vuln_wks$extreme)
 0  1  2  3  4  5  6  7  8  9 10 11 14   # vuln counts
 2  3  3 11  4  9  7  4  2  3  2  1  1   # week counts
```

There were two weeks in the year that had 0 extreme vulnerabilities, and 11 weeks that had three extreme vulnerabilities. Again, this is just like our historical examples.

Here is an alternative view of the same data format using a simple bar chart:

```
# Barplot
barplot(table(vuln_wks$extreme),
        ylab="Number of Weeks",xlab="Number of Vulnerabilities")
```

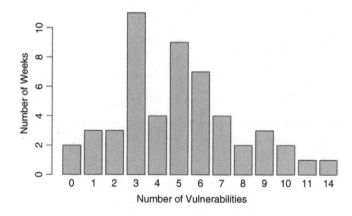

Let's consider how the data changes over time. Below is a very simple time series chart. It shows the change in counts per week for a whole year. As you glance at it, ask yourself, *"Are there any obvious trends?"* Or, *"Is the data relatively flat in the aggregate? Are arrivals particularly bursty in nature?"*

```
plot(vuln_wks$week.fseen, vuln_wks$extreme, ylab="Vulnerability Count",
    xlab="Weeks", type="l")
```

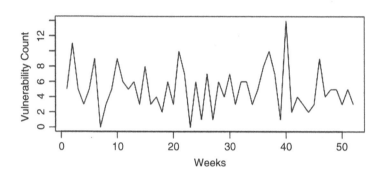

In terms of trend, I'm not seeing much. It might be moving slightly downward over time. It is moderately bursty. Do you see the two weeks with zero counts?

Let's add more vulnerability data and see if that provides any directional insights. Note the use of vuln_wks$all. It brings in extreme, critical, and high vulnerabilities.

```
plot(vuln_wks$week.fseen, vuln_wks$all, ylab="Vulnerability Count",
    xlab="Weeks", type="l")
```

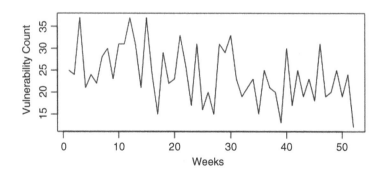

There does seem to be a light downward trend when we include all risks. Overlaying a trendline would be easy enough. If I saw this, I would be curious … and concerned. I would wonder, *"Are lower-risk vulnerabilities being remediated with higher priority than extreme risks?"* The data seems to indicate that may be occurring. After all, the downward trend didn't become obvious until the addition of lower-risk vulnerabilities.

## Simulating Rare Events

Let's run another simulation. I use 0.005, 0.01, and 0.02 as the event rate for extreme vulnerabilities for each product team. That is the probability of one or more extreme events happening per day.

> This is roughly the rate I saw as a cloud native CISO of a company with many hundreds of developers. We had a sign that counted the days between extreme events. I had a good feel for this, as did my team. It was similar to the "Days Without Accidents" sign you see in construction and manufacturing sites. It was very disruptive to development to push emergency fixes. **Reducing these events reduced breach and productivity risk.**

I pass the new simulation output to the GetVulnsOpenedByWks() function. I then ask GetVulnsOpenedByWks() for high-risk assets only. These are the assets (products) that are under audit and have external exposure. Setting audit_list to 0 and exposure_list to 1 queries the data for what we need. You can see how these fields are set in the data output above.

We will focus our energies on the "extreme" column in the vuln_wks data frame.

```
# Make Data For 3 Prod Teams Using Function
dtGroupOne <- GetAdvSecResults(c(.005,.03,.08),1,4)
dtGroupOne$group <- 1

dtGroupTwo <- GetAdvSecResults(c(.01,.06,.10),1,3)
dtGroupTwo$group <- 2

dtGroupThree <- GetAdvSecResults(c(.02,.08,.12),1,2)
dtGroupThree$group <- 3

# Load into one data frame.
dt <- bind_rows(dtGroupOne, dtGroupTwo, dtGroupThree)

# Get Aggregates for Critical Assets
vuln_wks <- GetVulnsOpenedByWks(dt,audit_list = c(0), exposure_list = c(1))
vuln_wks
```

```
# A tibble: 52 x 5
   week.fseen extreme critical  high   all
        <int>   <dbl>    <dbl> <dbl> <dbl>
 1          1       0        0     3     3
 2          2       0        0     4     4
 3          3       0        0     4     4
 4          4       0        2     1     3
 5          5       0        1     2     3
 6          6       1        1     3     5
 7          7       0        2     6     8
 8          8       0        0     2     2
 9          9       1        0     2     3
10         10       1        1     2     4
# ... with 42 more rows
```

Here is another view of the extreme count data. In this case, I print out the whole year. Note the output from the table() function. How would you characterize this data?

```
vuln_wks$extreme
0 0 0 0 0 1 0 0 1 1 0 0 0 0 0 0 0 0 1 0 0 0 0 2 0 0 0 0 0 0 1 0 0 0 0 0 2
0 0 0 0 0 0 0 0 0 2 0 0 0 0 0

table(vuln_wks$extreme)
 0  1  2  #Vuln Count
44  5  3  #Week Count
```

Consider that each time one of these vulnerabilities materializes, a portion of engineering comes to a full stop. A handful of team members would be focused on fixing the extreme vulnerability. It's also a race against the bad guys to get fixes in place.

## Arrival Prediction

Below we ask, *"What's the probability of more than zero, one, and two extremes arriving per week?"* This is the same question our actuary asked during WWII in the introduction.

```
hits <- 1 - ppois(0:2, lambda=mean(vuln_wks$extreme))
round(hits,3)
[1] 0.159 0.013 0.001
```

There is a 16% chance of one or more vulnerabilities per week. Two or more is rarer.

Do those probabilities seem right? Meaning, do they align with your subject matter expertise? Don't discount your expectations. You are the expert on security and your organization. Your expertise is what makes the data have meaning – particularly when it comes to making decisions.

**Let's generate some sample data.** We are going to use the Poisson distribution as a data-generating tool. We want to see how well the Poisson distribution mimics our real data to determine if the Poisson distribution is the right tool to use for this job. If not, it could lead to the wrong conclusions about the rate at which vulnerabilities tend to be created.

Let's start our validation of the Poisson distribution by passing in the mean rate for extreme vulnerabilities. It will spit out 52 weeks' worth of data given our mean rate. I will run it just a handful of times to see how it behaves. This is the exact same process we did in the intro.

First, we need to get the observed mean of our data:

```
mean(vuln_wks$extreme)
0.2115385
```

I run the rpois() function three times to get a feel for the data. This is for pedagogical purposes.

```
ext_wk <- rpois(52, lambda=mean(vuln_wks$extreme))
mean(ext_wk)
[1] 0.2307692
> ext_wk
 0 0 0 1 0 0 0 0 0 0 0 0 1 0 0 0 0 1 0 0 1 0 0 1 0 0 0 0 0 0 0 0 0 0 0 0 1 0 1 0 0
 1 1 0 0 0 1 0 0 0 0 0 2 0 1

ext_wk <- rpois(52, lambda=mean(vuln_wks$extreme))
mean(ext_wk)
[1] 0.1153846
> ext_wk
 0 1 1 0 0 0 0 0 0 0 0 0 0 0 0 0 1 0 0 1 0 0 0 0 0 0 0 0 0 0 1 0 0 0 0 0 0 0
 0 1 0 0 0 0 0 0 0 0 0 0 0 0

ext_wk <- rpois(52, lambda=mean(vuln_wks$extreme))
mean(ext_wk)
[1] 0.2692308
> ext_wk
 2 0 0 0 0 0 0 0 0 0 1 1 0 0 0 0 0 0 0 0 1 0 0 0 0 0 0 0 0 0 0 0 0 0 2 0 0 1
 1 0 0 0 0 0 0 0 0 0 0 0 0 0
```

There is quite a bit of variation in our mean vulnerability arrival rates. Yet, the distribution of the data looks *vaguely similar* to our real data in terms of the rate of arrivals. While eyeballing is fine, we need to be a little more thorough in testing the applicability of our data to the Poisson distribution.

As stated in the intro, our rule of thumb is that the ratio of the variance over the mean of the data should be close to one. If it is, it means that the data-generating process is *likely* Poisson based. **Warning:** Data rarely matches a distribution to a tee.

```
data_ratio <- var(vuln_wks$extreme)/mean(vuln_wks$extreme)
data_ratio
[1] 1.360071
```

> Our data *may be* a bit (if not a lot) wiggly for a standard Poisson distribution. Technically, it could be **overdispersed** or **underdispersed**. Underdispersion is rarer.
>
> There are alternative distributions that deal with seemingly over-dispersed data, all related in some way to the Poisson distribution. In this section, we address overdispersion using an approach called the **poisson-gamma mixture.** Another distribution to explore is the zero-inflated poisson distribution. While I don't cover it here, I will explore it at www.themetricsmanifesto.com.

## Bayes Meets Arrival Rates

To start this section, I am going to quickly simulate some new data using the GetAdvSecResults() function. Let's add two teams for a total of five. I will only print out what's new to save space.

```
# Create Two Additional Data Tables
dtGroupFour <- GetAdvSecResults(c(.03,.09,.15),1,3)
dtGroupFour$group <- 4

dtGroupFive <- GetAdvSecResults(c(.008,.04,.12),1,4)
dtGroupFive$group <- 5

# Load into one data table.
dt <- bind_rows(dtGroupOne, dtGroupTwo, dtGroupThree, dtGroupFour,
           dtGroupFive)

# Get Assets Under Audit With External Exposure
vuln_wks <- GetVulnsOpenedByWks(dt,audit_list = c(0), exposure_list = c(1),
           group_list = 1:10, week_list = 1:52)
```

There are 47 extreme vulns based on the most recent run. Again, each time I run this, the data-generating process spits out random results given the risk constraints I provided.

```
vuln_wks$extreme
0 4 6 1 0 1 1 3 0 1 3 0 0 1 0 0 0 1 3 0 0 0 2 0 1 0 4 0 0 3 0 0 0 0 0 0 0 0
0 0 3 1 2 1 0 2 1 0 1 0 1 0

table(vuln_wks$extreme)
 0  1  2  3  4  6
29 12  3  5  2  1
```

As you can see, I added a team above with a 3% chance of an extreme vulnerability – which kicked up our counts. I just added that for demonstration purposes. Our models should be able to accommodate both very sparse and more populated data.

Next, we are going to wind back the clock in our imagination. Imagine that only one quarter has passed. We want to start measuring, but the data is very sparse. Thus, we elicit subject matter expert beliefs about extreme arrival rates. This is the same process we did for burndown rates.

## Subject Matter Expert Interview

You turn to your team again and ask them, "*Knowing what you know about 'break the glass vulnerabilities,' what do you think the weekly arrival rate is?*"

Engineer 1 says, "*An exact average won't work. They can cluster together. It's bursty, random, and very chaotic.*"

You respond, "*Assume we can build a little machine that emulates random and bursty processes. If you think there are 10 a year, that's ~19% (10/52). If 30, then ~58% etc. (30/52).*"

Engineer 2 says, "*It feels like it's somewhere in the 20 to 40 per year vicinity. That jives with my experience. Let's call it 30.*"

To that, our first engineer says, "*That's totally off! It has to be closer to the 30 to 50 range. Call mine 40.*"

Before they get into a full-blown argument, you say, "*We can test your forecasts against a sample to see what's most consistent with the data. It's the same process that we did with burndowns.*"

```
# First quarter data
cnt <- vuln_wks$extreme[vuln_wks$week.fseen <= 13]
cnt
 [1]  0  4  6  1  0  1  1  3  0  1  3  0  0

# Get hits in 13 weeks for input below
sum(cnt)
[1] 20

# Add beliefs for each eng, and 20 hits sum(cnt) in 13 weeks
gscore <- ScoreGammaBeliefs(
              bias = c(0.5, 0.5),
              first_belief = c(40,52),
              second_belief = c(30,52),
              data = c(sum(cnt),13))

# Results will differ if sum(cnt) isn't 20…
gscore
first_belief
    10.61139
```

The score produced is an odds (Bayes factor). It says that engineer 1's forecast is nearly 11 times more consistent with the data than engineer

2's forecast. (*Note:* This function, like the previous belief scoring function, is a wrapper around ProbBayes.)

You may wonder, why don't we just use the average of the 13 weeks' worth of data as a prior? We can, and we do exercise this approach in the last section of this chapter. When we use previous data for priors, it's called *empirical Bayes*. We will be diving into empirical Bayes in Chapter 6. For now, we want to use reasonable beliefs to inform our tiny data.

## Building a Simple Bayesian Arrival Model

Let's model the team's beliefs about weekly vulnerability arrival rates. The belief that scored the best was 40 vulnerabilities in 52 weeks. As a ratio, that is very close to 3/4. Let's use that for our prior beliefs for the weekly vulnerability rate.

```
# Scaled Location of Rate
arrival_shape <- 3
arrival_rate <- 4

# Plausible Rates
plausible_arrivals = seq(0, 6, 0.001)

#Get Distribution of Beliefs
arrival_beliefs <- dgamma(plausible_arrivals, arrival_shape, arrival_rate)

# Plausible Rates Graphed
plotGammaAdv(plausible_arrivals,arrival_beliefs, ytop = 4,
            tlab = "Weekly Vuln Arrival Rate",
            slab = "Rates More Focused on .75")
```

Think of the arrival_shape and arrival_rate parameters as a numerator and a denominator. Here, it is 3/4. If we want our data to be tightly centered on a weekly rate of .75, we just make our values larger, like 6/8 or 9/12, etc. The larger the ratio in this case, the denser the distribution around .75.

Did you notice the dgamma() call above? It uses the gamma distribution. The gamma distribution has a conjugate relationship with the Poisson distribution. We covered conjugate priors in the last chapter. Again, *conjugate* is a fancy term for "easy math."

Think of the gamma distribution as a way to make flexible arrival rates. We use the gamma distribution when we have an average rate, but we know that average tends to move around – it's overdispersed. Formally, we would say that the rate is nonhomogeneous. Recall that we tested our data to see if it fit the Poisson model. The variance of the data was slightly larger than the mean. (Your simulations may have significantly more variation.) That is an indication of nonhomogeneity. Said plainly, there's more wiggle than expected. Thus, we use the gamma to model wiggle in our rates.

The following graph represents our spread-out weekly vulnerability beliefs. Most of the plausibility is far and to the left. Yet, our distribution stretches off and to the right. Its central tendency is vaguely around .75.

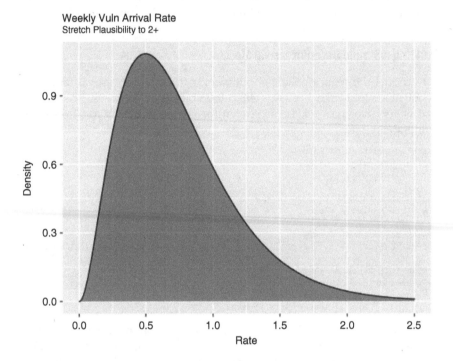

**Weekly Vuln Arrival Rate**
Stretch Plausibility to 2+

## Updating Our Beliefs about Extreme Arrival Rates

Imagine we start to progress through the year. Extreme vulnerabilities are arriving. Let's get two snapshots of data. We want to see how our model can learn about extreme arrival rates.

We start by pulling the first quarter's data below. It's small. Later, we will pull a whole year's data. The model will learn from the data and our beliefs, and then we will graph what that learning looks like.

Before we start, let's update our prior. I want to make the prior more focused. To do that, I set the prior to 9 and 12. It still represents

.75 per week extreme vulnerability rate. It is just scaled up and focused around .75.

```
# Scaled Location Of Rate
arrival_shape <- 9 #Updated
arrival_rate <- 12 #Updated

# Plausible Arrival Rates
plausible_arrivals = seq(0, 2.5, 0.001)

#Get Arrival Beliefs
arrival_beliefs <- dgamma(plausible_arrivals, arrival_shape, arrival_rate)

# Plausible Rates Scored
plotGammaAdv(plausible_arrivals,arrival_beliefs,ytop = 4,
             tlab = "Weekly Vuln Arrival Rate",
             slab = "Rates Closer To .75 Most Likely")
```

Now that we've codified our beliefs we mesh our new beliefs (prior) with the first quarter's data:

```
#Data
total_weeks <- 13   #Q1

# Subset vuln_wks to get the first 13 weeks of data
total_arrivals <- sum(vuln_wks$extreme[vuln_wks$week.fseen <= total_weeks])
mean_arrivals <- total_arrivals/total_weeks #optional

# likelihood of the data - FOR GRAPHING ONLY
arrival_likelihood = dpois(total_arrivals, total_weeks *
                           plausible_arrivals)

# posterior beliefs - mesh priors with data
posterior_beliefs = dgamma(plausible_arrivals,
                           arrival_shape + total_arrivals,
                           arrival_rate + total_weeks)
```

There is a lot going on above. I will explain each step as simply as possible.

Our first step is building our prior distribution, which we will build using the gamma() distribution. The dgamma() function takes in our plausible arrival rates and priors. The dgamma() function "scores" the plausible arrivals based on the prior. The most plausible rates get higher scores. Meaning, our graph will be higher where the score (density) is highest. That should vaguely be around .75.

I also call plotGammaAdv() to view the prior. Here is what the new prior looks like. You can see that things have shifted to the right, and are denser around .75.

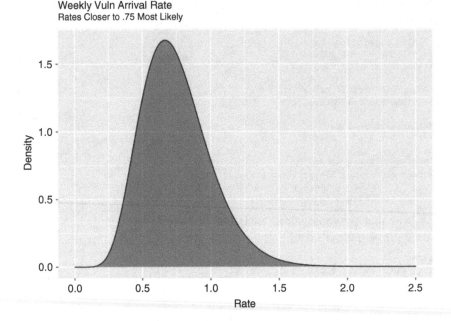

In the next section of code, we get the total_arrivals and mean_arrivals for the first quarter. We get the data by asking for the count of extreme vulnerabilities up to week 13.

Next, we determine the arrival_likelihood of the data against our plausible arrivals. The likelihood says, "*What is the likelihood of each plausible_ arrival rate, given our data.*

The posterior comes from the dgamma() function. It's a "likelihood-less" computation. Translation: It's mathematically and computationally easier due to the conjugate relationship with the prior. That is, it does not need the likelihood function – but our graph does.

The following chart helps visualize the updating process. It demonstrates how the posterior is a compromise between the prior and the likelihood of the data. Here is the code for making the graph.

```
# Mesh Prior Beliefs with New Data To Get Updated Beliefs
plot_posterior(plausible_arrivals, arrival_beliefs, arrival_likelihood,
               posterior_beliefs)

# Add a 95% Credible Interval To The Graph
abline(v = qgamma(c(0.025, 0.975), arrival_shape + total_weeks *
                  mean_arrivals, arrival_rate + total_weeks),
                  col = "seagreen", lty = 2)
```

Note how the posterior curve sits between the prior and the likelihood below. If your graph doesn't display this, it means we did something wrong and we need to check our work. Mathematically, it is a compromise between the two. The prior is pulling on the posterior. If the curve could talk, it would say, *"The data represented by the likelihood is biased. Move a little more this way."*

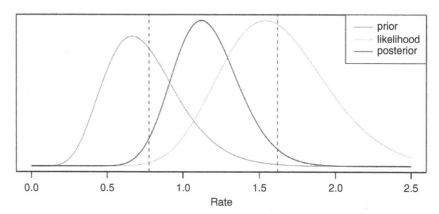

Here is the code for the plot_posterior() function. It uses standard (old school) graphing. It illustrates how the posterior is a compromise between the prior and the likelihood.

```
plot_posterior <- function(theta, prior, likelihood, posterior) {

    # Set Height of graph
    ymax = max(c(prior, posterior))

    # Normalize Likelihood - sums to 1 for graphing
    scaled_likelihood = likelihood * ymax / max(likelihood)

    # Plot Prior
    plot(theta, prior, type='l', col='orange', xlim= range(theta),
         ylim=c(0, ymax), ylab='',xlab='Rate', yaxt='n')

    # Plot Likelihood
    par(new=T)
    plot(theta, scaled_likelihood, type='l', col='skyblue',
         xlim=range(theta), ylim=c(0, ymax), ylab='' ,xlab='Rate', yaxt='n')

    # Plot Posterior
    par(new=T)
    plot(theta, posterior, type='l', col='seagreen', xlim=range(theta),
         ylim=c(0, ymax), ylab='',xlab='Rate', yaxt='n')
```

```
# Legend For Graph
legend("topright", c("prior", "likelihood", "posterior"), lty=1,
       col=c("orange", "skyblue", "seagreen"))
}
```

Let's run all the code from beginning to end. We are going to move forward in time to the end of the year. That means we have 52 weeks of data available for our analysis.

```
# Scaled Location Of The Prior Rate
arrival_shape <- 9
arrival_rate <- 12

# Plausible Rates
plausible_arrivals = seq(0, 2.5, 0.001)

#Get Prior Density
arrival_beliefs <- dgamma(plausible_arrivals, arrival_shape, arrival_rate)

# Plot Prior
plotGammaAdv(plausible_arrivals,arrival_beliefs,ytop = 4,
             tlab = "Weekly Vuln Arrival Rate",
             slab = "Rates More Focused on .75")

#Get One Year's Worth of Data
total_weeks <- 52
total_arrivals <- sum(vuln_wks$extreme[vuln_wks$week.fseen <= total_weeks])
mean_arrivals <- total_arrivals/total_weeks

# Get likelihood - for graphing
arrival_likelihood = dpois(total_arrivals, total_weeks *
                           plausible_arrivals)

# Get updated posterior
posterior_beliefs = dgamma(plausible_arrivals, arrival_shape +
                           total_arrivals, arrival_rate + total_weeks)

# Plot Posterior
plot_posterior(plausible_arrivals, arrival_beliefs, arrival_likelihood,
               posterior_beliefs)

# Add 95% Credible Interval
abline(v = qgamma(c(0.025, 0.975), arrival_shape + total_weeks *
                  mean_arrivals, arrival_rate + total_weeks),
                  col = "seagreen", lty = 2)

# Sample From Posterior
samples <- sample( plausible_arrivals , prob=posterior_beliefs,
                   size = 10000, replace = TRUE )

# Graph Posterior Alone
posteriorGraph(samples)
```

Here is the first of two graphs we will consider. This first one is the same format as the previous graph. What do you notice that is different?

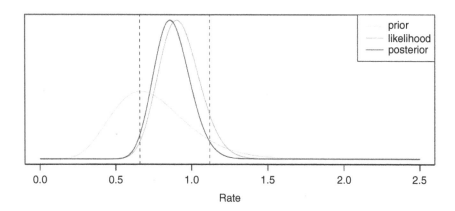

The likelihood and posterior distribution are significantly denser. The prior is still influencing the posterior – pulling it left. But, as we get more data, the prior has less effect. With enough data, the posterior and the likelihood (data) become nearly identical.

## Sampling Believable Reality

Notice the next-to-last function call above: sample(). We are using the posterior data as input to the sample() function. It creates yet another simulation. Sample() queries the posterior 10,000 times in a semi-random fashion. I say semi-random because the data that gets pulled has a higher likelihood of coming from the denser parts of the posterior. Those would be the portions between the two dotted vertical lines in the graph above – i.e., the HDI.

We take the results of the sampling process and pass it into the ci() function. It is used for getting credible intervals (CI). And the type of credible interval we are asking for is the HDI. Below is the 89% HDI and the 50% HDI.

```
ci_hdi <- ci(samples, method = "HDI", verbose = FALSE)
ci_hdi_small <- ci(samples, method = "HDI", ci = .50, verbose = FALSE)
ci_hdi
# Highest Density Interval

89% HDI
------------
[0.69, 1.06]

ci_hdi_small
# Highest Density Interval

50% HDI
------------
[0.79, 0.95]
```

Recall, our original mean value of the data was ~.22 vulns per week. By adding two more teams, and one with a high extreme vulnerability rate, our mean went to ~.90 for the organization.

Our model believes the rate now lives somewhere between .69 and 1.06 extreme vulnerabilities per week. Following is the graph created by calling posteriorGraph(samples) showing 89% and 50% HDIs. The latter HDI is more pedagogical than practical.

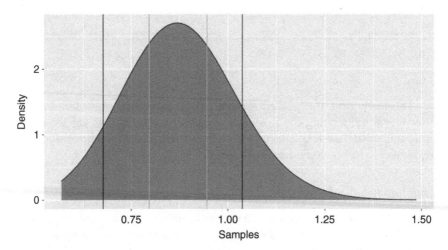

We can use the samples to simulate vulnerability values for a whole year. By themselves (like below), they are biased. That is why we simulate en masse from samples. Here are a few individual runs so you can get a feel for why we simulate en masse.

```
> rp <- rpois(total_weeks,samples)
mean(rp)
0.9615385
rp
 0 0 4 0 0 0 1 1 0 2 3 2 2 0 0 0 1 4 0 1 1 2 0 0 0 1 0 1 0 0 0 0
 1 3 2 3 1 0 0 1 1 0 2 2 0 4 1 1 1 0 1 0

> rp <- rpois(total_weeks,samples)
mean(rp)
0.8653846
rp
 1 0 1 0 1 0 2 2 0 0 2 0 2 1 0 1 2 0 1 0 1 3 1 0 0 2 1 0 2 3 0 1
 2 0 1 1 1 0 0 0 1 1 1 1 1 2 1 0 0 0 2 0

> rp <- rpois(total_weeks,samples)
mean(rp)
0.6730769
```

```
rp
0 0 2 0 1 1 0 1 1 1 0 2 2 3 0 1 0 1 3 0 0 0 1 1 0 0 0 1 1 0 0 0
1 0 0 1 1 2 0 0 0 0 1 0 0 0 0 0 2 1 1 2
```

There is quite a bit of variation in just three calls. We want the law of large numbers to kick in. Let's run rpois() 10,000 times. I then print out a simple graph of simulated extreme vulnerability arrival frequencies coming from those simulations.

```
reps = 10000
sims = rpois(reps, samples)

plot(table(sims) / reps, type = "h",
     xlab = "Number Of Extreme Vulnerabilities",
     ylab = "Simulated frequency",
     main = "Posterior predictive distribution",
     sub = paste0("Out of ",reps," simulations"))
```

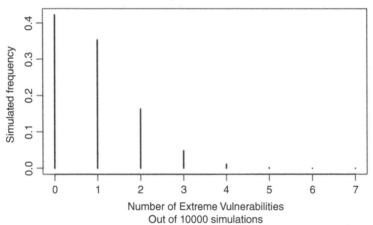

The new distribution, which is full of vulnerability counts by week, is called the **Posterior Predictive Distribution**. Using the posterior predictive distribution, we can ask for the frequency of extreme vulnerabilities per week. For starters, we can be 95% confident there will be 0–3 extreme vulnerabilities per week.

```
> quantile(sims, 0.95)
95%
  3
```

There is a ~58% chance of one or more extreme vulnerabilities per
week. And there is a ~6% of having three or more extreme vulnerabilities per week.

```
sum(sims >= 1)/reps
[1] 0.577

sum(sims >= 2)/reps
[1] 0.224

sum(sims >= 3)/reps
[1] 0.0612
....
```

## Advanced Prediction

We are going to take the ideas you just learned and expand on them. In this
case, we forecast vulnerabilities a year out.

My inspiration comes from code applied to hurricane predictions in a
wonderful book called *Hurricane Climatology*.[7] Hurricanes are relatively
rare catastrophic events. They are forecasted using years as opposed to
weeks. The same analytical principles apply just as well here. It's a count of
events happening within a flexible time frame.

The first portion of code develops our Bayesian prior. We optimize our
prior given a small sample of data. In this case, we have eight weeks of
data from the previous year. It's pulled from a ticketing system or perhaps a
spreadsheet. The following code develops the best gamma shape and rate
priors given a small sample of data.

```
source("manifesto_functions.R")

# Functions used to get optimized gamma values
boot_mean <- function(original_vector, resample_vector) {
  mean(original_vector[resample_vector])
}

obj = function(x){
  sum(abs(pgamma(q=qbs, shape=x[1], rate=x[2]) - c(.05, .95)))
}

# Get 8 weeks of data
prior_weeks <- 8
v_open <- c(0, 1, 0, 0, 3, 0, 1, 2)

# Simulate 2000 weekly vuln rates
```

```
mean_results <- boot(v_open, boot_mean, R = 2000)

# Print out a few weekly vulnerability rates
head(mean_results$t,10)
         [,1]
 [1,]  0.875
 [2,]  1.000
 [3,]  1.125
 [4,]  0.875
 [5,]  1.875
 [6,]  1.125
 [7,]  0.625
 [8,]  1.125
 [9,]  0.375
[10,]  1.500

# Get 95% interval from rates
qbs = quantile(mean_results$t, prob=c(.05, .95))

# Print Rates
qbs
  5%   95%
0.25 1.50

# Get best gamma() priors.
# Note obj takes in qbs values (95% CI) as a parameter
theta = optim(par = c(1, 1), obj)$par

# Print optimized shape and rate values for gamma function
theta
[1] 3.778991  4.958199
```

The gamma priors approximate a ~.76 weekly extreme vulnerability rate.

```
3.778991/4.958199
[1] 0.76217
```

We could have also just pulled the mean of v_open, but it is not as accurate in capturing the uncertainty in the data. And we wanted the two theta parameters. They control how much the mean varies.

```
mean(v_open)
[1] 0.875
```

Here is what the optimized prior looks like, given eight weeks of data. There is plenty of range for what the extreme vuln per week count may be:

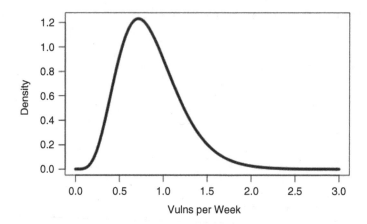

In this next section, we collect 26 weeks of data. This represents the first half of the year. And since we are using a conjugate prior, we simply update our priors with new data to make our posterior.

```
# Model the first two quarters of data
weeks <- 26

# Use clear names for priors
prior_shape <- theta[1]
prior_rate <- theta[2]

# Get count of extreme vulns for the first 26 weeks.
vulns <- sum(vuln_wks$extreme[vuln_wks$week.fseen <= weeks])

#BAYES CHART
# Posterior
curve(dgamma(x, shape=vulns + prior_shape, rate=weeks + prior_rate),
          from=0,to=2, xlab="Vulns Per Week",
          ylab="Density", col=1, lwd=4, las=1)

# Likelihood
curve(dgamma(x, shape=vulns, rate=weeks), add=TRUE, col=2, lwd=4)

# Prior
curve(dgamma(x, shape=prior_shape, rate=prior_rate), add=TRUE,
          col=3, lwd=4)

# Legend
legend("topright", c("Prior", "Likelihood",
      "Posterior"), col=c(3, 2, 1), lwd=c(3, 3, 3))
```

Following is the Bayesian update graph. I made it explicit in the code above so you can see the Bayesian updating in action. The prior here seems squished compared to the previous chart. It's the same as before. It's sharing space with the likelihood and the posterior.

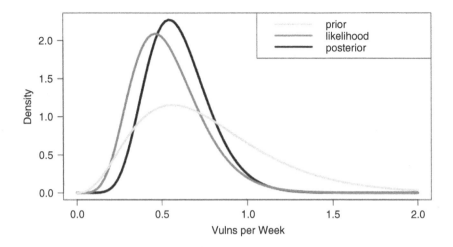

Lastly, we are going to make a forecast for 52 weeks. Note, there is a call to a new function called dnbinom(). This is called the negative binomial. Functionally, it is the same as the Poisson-gamma mixture model. In this case, it takes as its parameters the gamma mean and variance. It makes the prediction math simpler in code.

```
# PREDICTIVE CHART
new_weeks = 52   #weeks

# Mean
gamma_mean = new_weeks * (vulns + prior_shape)/(weeks + prior_rate)

# Variance
gamma_var = new_weeks * gamma_mean * (new_weeks + weeks +
            prior_rate)/(weeks + prior_rate)

# Rates along the x axis - the 4 and 1.8 help set the width
future_rates = round(gamma_mean/4):round(gamma_mean*1.8)

# Score (Density) for each of the future rates.
future_vulns = dnbinom(future_rates, mu=gamma_mean, size=gamma_var)

# Graph Histogram
par(las=1, mar=c(5, 4, 2, 4))
plot(future_rates, future_vulns, type="h",
     xlab="Number of Vulnerabilities",
     ylab="Probability", col="gray", lwd=4)

par(new=TRUE)

# Cumulative Probability Curve
p = pnbinom(future_rates, mu=gamma_mean, size=gamma_var)
```

```
plot(future_rates, p, type="l", col="red", xaxt="n",
    yaxt="n",xlab="", ylab="", lwd=2)

axis(4)
mtext("Probability of N% or less vulnerabilities",side=4,
      line=2.5, las=0)
par(new=TRUE)
```

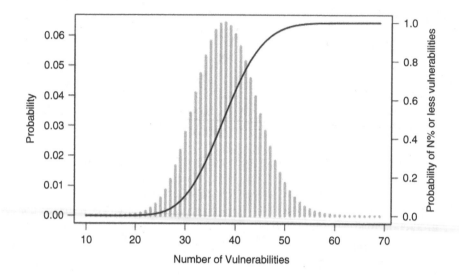

There is a 50% chance of ~40 vulnerabilities or less arriving in the next 52 weeks. That is based on the prior and 26 weeks of data. Also, the data was generated by five product teams.

We could have done the same forecast with only 13 weeks of data and with one team. The data would have been much smaller. There would have been far more uncertainty in the results. In fact, with one team over 13 weeks, the forecast would have been heavily reliant on subject matter expert–generated priors. Priors have more influence when data is very small.

**Prediction is not the goal. Baselining and making decisions is the goal.** Can you control the arrival rate? For example, how many arrivals could have been caught in development? How many of them could have been nullified through better configuration management or other mitigations? Or, is the arrival of extreme vulnerabilities completely random – like bombs dropping on London during WWII?

If the same product teams start producing a higher baseline rate, can you pinpoint why? What if the rate declines without apparent cause – can you discover the unapparent cause? This is the purpose (and joy) of measurement. Security gets their fingers on the pulse of risk creation and elimination.

The next baseline we explore is wait-times. It's very similar to arrival times. Instead of baselining the rate of new vulnerabilities arriving, we baseline the time between extreme vulnerabilities appearing. This metric has broad application in threat, vulnerability and other security domains.

## Wrapping Up Arrivals

Clarke forecasted bomb rates. Bortkiewicz forecasted death by horse kick. And we forecasted extreme vulnerability arrival rates. We only used a small (tiny) data set. It could have worked with larger data sizes. For example, if you wanted both extreme and severe vulnerabilities – this would have worked well enough. There are dozens of other security processes we can measure in terms of event arrivals.

Knowing the rates of risk removal and arrival is useful. What about wait-times between extreme events? While related to arrival rates, it is different. In the next chapter we focus on measuring wait-times between extreme vulnerabilities. It's the next step in filling out a complete metrics picture one baseline at a time.

## Notes

1. Boole, G. (2015). *An Investigation of the Laws of Thought, on Which Are Founded the Mathematical Theories of Logic and Probabilities.* Palala Press.
2. Clarke, R. D. (1946). An application of the Poisson distribution, *Journal of the Institute of Actuaries*. Cambridge Core. https://www.cambridge. org/core/journals/journal-of-the-institute-of-actuaries/article/abs/ an-application-of-the-poisson-distribution/F75111847FDA534103B D4941BD96A78E
3. Shaw, L. P. (2019, October 1). Royal Statistical Society Publications. Royal Statistical Society. https://rss.onlinelibrary.wiley.com/doi/10.1111/ j.1740-9713.2019.01315.x
4. R. D. Clarke, British statistician. (1946). *Encyclopedia Britannica.* https://www.britannica.com/biography/R-D-Clarke
5. Falk, M., Hüsler, J., & Reiss, R. (2010). *Laws of Small Numbers: Extremes and Rare Events* (3rd ed. 2010 ed.). Birkhäuser.
6. DevOps tech: Shifting left on security. (2021). Google Cloud. https:// cloud.google.com/architecture/devops/devops-tech-shifting-left-on-security
7. Elsner, J. B., & Jagger, T. H. (2013). *Hurricane Climatology: A Modern Statistical Guide Using R* (1st ed.). Oxford University Press.

CHAPTER 6

# Wait-Time Rates: Between Arrival and Departure Is...Waiting

*Chance favors the prepared mind.*

— Louis Pasteur

Survival and burndown rates measure your efficiency at removing risk. They are shift-right metrics: metrics that measure risk that's already deployed.

Arrival rates measure your efficiency at stopping risk from materializing in the first place. Arrival rates are a "shift-left" metric.[1] They turn your attention to the risk-creating process.

Escape rates are shift-left, too. We will cover escape rates in the next chapter.

In this chapter, we focus on a metric that is a sibling to arrival rates. I call this metric wait-times.

Wait-times measure the time between events – the interarrival time. I use both *wait-time* and *interarrival* interchangeably. This class of measurement is a big topic in reliability engineering, customer service, operations research,[2] queueing theory,[3] and much more.

The wait-times we focus on are for extreme events. That's because unplanned extreme events are disruptive – they cannot be ignored. They must be handled now. If they are not handled, they can quickly snowball into major incidents. That is the very definition of extreme.

> **Note:** If risk treatment can be scheduled for later, even a few days later, then it's not extreme by our definition. Not to say those risks aren't important. If they are going to require work and/or lead to compromise, then they too deserve measurement and optimization.

**I have some good news.** The measurement approach for wait-time analysis is nearly identical to arrival times. Meaning, the distributions and code are similar. This will give us an opportunity to expand on our methods of measurement.

## Non-Bayesian Wait-Times

Let's ease into the topic of measuring interarrivals (wait-times). To do that, we will first adopt a simple non-Bayesian approach. It will help you understand the goals of wait-time analysis. And, it will help you understand why we would want to take a Bayesian approach.

I start our analysis by creating 10 product teams. You may recall that a product team is composed of many scrum teams. The GetAdvSecResults() function doles them out across internal, partner, and external services. (Note, in the latter half of this chapter we will use historical security data.)

Unlike the previous chapter, where we created each group individually, I create them here in bulk by using a loop. It makes it easy to generate dozens (if not hundreds) of product teams. I encourage you to look through the code and its comments.

I added some randomness to the extreme, severe, and high-event inputs via the sample() function. Sample() randomly chooses values in a range. You can see those ranges in the "to" and "from" variables. The other inputs are also randomly selected. Probabilistic functions inside of GetAdvSecResults() then use those inputs to create our data frame.

```
# Code available on www.themetricsmanifesto.com

source("manifesto_functions.R")   #book functions

# Number of product teams
group_count = 10
```

```
# Empty Data Frame to hold results
dt <- tibble()

# Loop through count of groups
for(x in 1:group_count){

    # Get Ext,Sev,High random rates. See "from" and "to" ranges.
    extreme <- sample(seq(from = .005, to = .03, by= .001), size = 1)
    severe <- sample(seq(from = .031, to = .07, by= .001), size = 1)
    high <- sample(seq(from = .071, to = .15, by= .001), size = 1)

    # Set Random Maturity Values - get one value between 1-4 randomly
    patch_fail <- sample(1:4,size=1)
    dev_maturity <- sample(1:4,size=1)

    # Get Data Frame
    res <- GetAdvSecResults(c(extreme, severe, high),
                            patch_fail, dev_maturity)

    # Set Group Number
    res$group <- x

    # Append to master data frame - makes one large data frame
    dt <- bind_rows(dt,res)
}
```

Unlike the previous chapter, we won't be using the GetVulnsOpened-ByWks() function. Instead, we will manipulate the main **dt** data frame. As you may recall, the **dt** data frame is just over 20 columns wide. Several of its columns are for asset and vulnerability risk.

Below, I ask **dt** for all the rows with assets that are under audit, externally exposed, and with extreme vulnerabilities. I also ask for all weeks of the year. What I get back is a subset of the original data frame. I use that smaller data frame to get a list of wait-times (aka interarrivals), which I then graph as a histogram.

```
# Get Critical Rows And All Columns using subsetting
dte <- dt[(dt$audit == 0 & dt$exposure_id == 1 & dt$severity_id == 1 &
           dt$week.fseen <= 52), ]

# Get interarrivals. I.e. the difference between weeks numbers
interarrivals <- diff(sort(dte$week.fseen))

#make a histogram
hist(interarrivals, breaks=max(interarrivals))
```

The focus of this code is on retrieving interarrivals. I get those values by first asking for the number of the week. Each week in the year has a number from 1 to 52. Each of those weeks has zero or more extreme vulnerabilities.

Below, week "10" shows up six times. That means there were six extreme vulnerabilities in week 10. Here is the raw data:

```
dte$week.fseen
16 18 22 27 40 10 10 10 10 19 46  1  5 10 10 11 18 22 44 45 45 16 47 47 14  1 16 29
 3  3 19 31 31 36 2  9  49 9  17 41  7 7  8  12 15 16 16 16 19 19 26 28 30 31 34 36
37 37 37 52
```

There is one small problem. The data is not in the right order. To get interarrivals, we need to sequentially subtract weeks one from another. To get the data in the right order, we use the sort() function.

```
sort(dte$week.fseen)
 1  1  2  3  3  5  7  7  8  9  9 10 10 10 10 10 10 11 12 14 15 16 16 16 16 16 16 17
18 18 19 19 19 19 22 22 26 27 28 29 30 31 31 31 34 36 36 37 37 37 40 41 44 45 45 46
47 47 49 52
```

Now we are ready to find the differences between weeks, which we will do with a call to diff(). Below I run all the functions together:

```
diff(sort(dte$week.fseen))
0 1 1 0 2 2 0 1 1 0 1 0 0 0 0 0 1 1 2 1 1 0 0 0 0 0 1 1 0 1 0 0 0 3 0 4 1 1
1 1 1 0 0 3 2 0 1 0 0 3 1 3 1 0 1 1 0 2 3
```

```
hist(interarrivals, breaks=max(interarrivals))
```

Can you see what diff() does? Compare it to the output just above it. It is a simple sequential subtraction of weeks. Below, you can see the histogram of the diff() results.

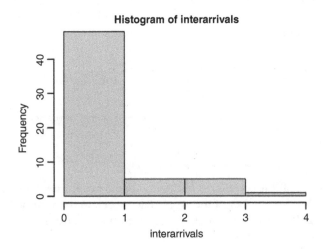

Histogram of interarrivals

## Wait-Time by Day

Many vulnerabilities arrive within one week of each other, or less. But, is a weekly analysis telling us everything we need to know to manage our queue of vulnerabilities? Let's break this down by day. The code is nearly identical.

```
# Same data frame for weeks
dte <- dt[(dt$audit == 0 & dt$exposure_id == 1 &
        dt$severity_id == 1 & dt$week.fseen <= 52),]

# Get interarrivals by asking for the day number
interarrivals <- diff(sort(yday(dte$first.seen)))

# Build a histogram of the arrivals.
hist(interarrivals,breaks=max(interarrivals))
```

The difference between the "by day" vs. week approach is the use of date stamps. It's that simple. The first.seen variable is the actual date the vulnerability was first seen. The yday() function returns the day number of the year. It is analogous to the week number. As before, we sort the dates by day number and apply the diff() function. The result can be seen in this histogram:

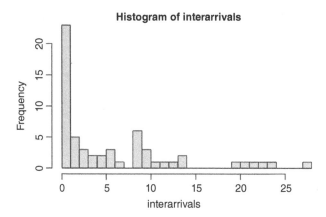

As you can see, the majority of interarrivals (wait-times) are less than a week. In fact, many are within one day. Yet, there is still some randomness to the data. It is spread out far and to the right.

The shape and spread of the data is modeled by an exponential distribution. The exponential distribution is related to the gamma and Poisson distributions. In fact, the exponential is a special case of the gamma distribution. You were introduced to both the gamma and Poisson distributions in the last chapter. Why do you care about the relationship among these distributions? You should care because using related distributions makes our job easier. You will see this as we move on into Bayesian data analysis.

From a metrics perspective, we can't do much with this data yet. We need to create a model – a wait-time model. We will need to make that model in order to make forecasts. We will base our model on the exponential distribution.

## Why Do We Need Models for Wait-Times?

Wait-times are used to measure queues of work. Think of a queue as things waiting in line – like the photo of cars at the beginning of this chapter. In our case, extreme vulnerabilities are in our queue. They arrive in the queue and get pushed through a work process.

The rate with which the queue gets filled is measured by interarrival rates. The smaller the interarrival rate, the faster the queue fills. And, the faster the work process connected to the queue needs to operate.

Interarrival models are like a speedometer for the queue. It lets you know how fast objects are approaching. Contrast that to arrival rates. Arrivals tell you the total events in a time frame. Arrivals and wait-times are tightly coupled and in fact inform one another.

We will pose questions to our interarrival model. For example, what is the probability of a critical vulnerability showing up within a week? If you find that the likelihood goes from 25% to 90% – you have learned something. You may need to take action, particularly if your burndown rates are starting to overflow.

### The Basic Wait-Time Model

The following code approximates our interarrival process. It picks up where our previous code left off. The comments will help you understand what is going on – even if you are new to R.

```
# Sum of individual interarrivals.
wait_time <- sum(interarrivals)

# Get count of vuln events. I.e ~60 vulns
n = nrow(dte)

# The ratio of vulnerabilities per day. I.e. 60/356 ~ .17
vulns_per_wait_time <- n/wait_time
```

```
# Average Time Between Event Days i.e. 356/60 ~6
avg_days = wait_time/n    #Avg wait time in days between extreme vulns

# Exponential Dist to Simulate data. It spits out 60 simulated results
# And each value will wiggle around 1/60 ~ .0167
simulated <- rexp(n, rate=n)

# Multiply simulated rates by 365 (in my case) to get 60 wait-times
sim_interarrivals <- simulated * wait_time

# Create a histogram (one of many since this is a random process)
hist(sim_interarrivals, breaks = max(interarrivals))
```

The results are shown in the following histogram. Note that each run would be slightly different. That's because the rexp() function generates random results within the constraints provided by the number and rate inputs.

The shape of the histogram looks a bit like the graph of the original data above. It is not an exact match – at least this run isn't. As you will see, the "average time" between the model and the data is close.

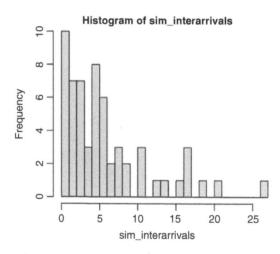

Below is the expected (average) next arrival from the vulnerability queue. It is one of several plausible expectations from the model.

```
avg <- mean(simulated) * wait_time
avg
> 5.895
```

If you look at the average time for the empirical data, we get the following:

```
avg_days
[1] 5.933
```

The average wait-time in days is pretty close between the model and the data. But don't get too excited. That is just one simulation of many thousand possibilities, and our data is still pretty small. When there is small data, there is high uncertainty. All that means is the model output will vary quite a bit on each run.

Let's use our interarrival data to ask questions about vulnerability arrivals. This was covered via a different angle in the last chapter. Here, I ask for the probability of a vulnerability arriving within a week:

```
# Chance of a vulnerability showing up in 0 to 7 days.
pexp(q = 7, rate = vulns_per_wait_time)
[1] 0.6926522
```

That's roughly 70%. It's based on the vulns_per_wait_time ratio, which was created by dividing the total vulnerabilities found by the total wait-times. In my particular example, that was 60/356, resulting in ~0.17.

That rate is then input into the pexp() exponential function. pexp() is a cumulative function that answers the question, "*What is the probability of a vuln materializing in 7 or less days?*" This means it adds up, or accumulates, all the probabilities from 0–7 days.

Here is another approach to that same question – with a much larger simulation:

```
# Simulated for 7 days
mean(rexp(n = 10000, rate = vulns_per_wait_time) <= 7)
[1] 0.6885
```

We just simulate 10,000 interarrival times. It is very close to our simpler result above. You need to see the inner logic to understand how we arrive at 69%. We are asking a true/false question. The logic looks like this:

```
# Simulate 10 boolean results, note how all are TRUE but one..its random
res <- rexp(10,.17) <= 7
> res
[1]  TRUE TRUE TRUE FALSE TRUE TRUE TRUE TRUE TRUE TRUE

# Get ratio of true to false results
mean(res)
[1] 0.9
```

Forecasting wait-times like this is easy. Let's use more of the data to create a cumulative graph. I will explain the details after we see the graph.

```
# Create Dataframe
tibble(x = 0:1000 / 100,
            prob = pexp(q = 0:1000 / 100,
            rate = vulns_per_wait_time,
            lower.tail = TRUE)) %>%
```

```
# Add a column to the data frame
mutate(Interval = ifelse(x >= 0 & x <= 7, "0 to 7", "other")) %>%

# Send the data frame to the graphing functions
ggplot(aes(x = x, y = prob, fill = Interval)) +
  geom_area(alpha = 0.3) +
  labs(title = "Probability Of Vulnerabilities Arriving",
       subtitle = "From 0 to 7 Days",
       x = "Days",
       y = "Cumulative Probability")
```

Probability of Vulnerabilities Arriving
From 0 to 7 Days

Let's decompose the code that produced this graph, starting with the data frame. The data frame was the input into the graphing functions. Here are the first five results of the data frame:

```
head(df, 5)
# A tibble: 10 x 3
        x    prob Interval
    <dbl>   <dbl> <chr>
1   0      0      0 to 7
2   0.01   0.00168 0 to 7
3   0.02   0.00337 0 to 7
4   0.03   0.00504 0 to 7
5   0.04   0.00672 0 to 7
```

The first column named *x* holds portions of days. It extends from 0 days to 10 by one-hundredth increments. The second column named "prob" holds the result of running each of the $x$ values (days) through the exponential function. For example, here is the result for the second value of $x$:

```
> pexp(.01,vulns_per_wait_time)
[1] 0.001683974
```

The data frame holds 1,000 values created in the same manner. The final column named "Interval" is used for the legend of the graph. It also tells the graph to fill areas based on the "Interval" values. We have two values so we get two fill colors.

Our original question was about the probability of an extreme vulnerability entering the queue within the next 7 days. It was just shy of 70%. You can also see that there is an 80% chance of a vulnerability entering in the next 10 days. It looks like there is about a 10% chance of vulnerabilities showing up in one day or less. A lot of information is conveyed in this simple metric and its graph.

I hope the concept of wait-times, or interarrival times, is getting clear. You will need it as we shift back to Bayesian data analysis. The good news is that the Bayesian models will look virtually identical to what you saw for arrivals in the last chapter.

## Bayesian Wait-Times

In the following sections, we do two things. First, we perform a quick Bayesian analysis on interarrivals (wait-times). We will use the same Bayesian approach from the last chapter – with some extra sauce.

Our second objective is an analysis of critical vulnerabilities from the National Vulnerability Database (NVD). I am going to analyze their release velocities from 2018 to 2021. As of this writing, the 2021 data is incomplete. But we won't let that stop us. I will use 2020 NVD data as a prior for 2021. This is an empirical Bayes approach.

Empirical Bayes will be covered in depth in the next chapter on escape rates, which is a topic that I want to ease into.

### More Code, More Functions, More Fun

There will be more code in this section. Part of the code is for making things simpler. We do that by making functions. Our first function will be for bulk data creation. We take the loop from earlier and wrap it in a function. This makes it easier to use. And like all our functions, they will be available on the book's site.

In the previous chapter, we called GetAdvSecResults() in a piecemeal manner. At the beginning of this chapter we put it into a loop. We did that so we could create any number of product teams. Now we wrap all of that code into a simple to call function.

We pass everything the function needs in as parameters. The first parameter specifies how many groups we want. It defaults to 10, but you can put any value in greater than 0.

The next three parameters specify the likelihood of extreme, severe, and high events. Each of those likelihoods is a vector of two values. Those values specify the lower and upper bounds of each likelihood. Values are selected randomly from those ranges.

```
# Function with default values that can be changed
GetVulnGroups <- function(group_count = 10,
                          ext = c(.005,.03),
                          sev = c(.031, .07),
                          hgh = c(.071, .15)){

  # data frame to hold results
  dt <- tibble()

  # loop through the group_count
  for(x in 1:group_count){

    # Get random likelihoods for each risk variable
    extreme <- sample(seq(from = ext[1], to = ext[2], by= .001), size = 1)
    severe <- sample(seq(from = sev[1], to = sev[2], by= .001), size = 1)
    high <- sample(seq(from = hgh[1], to = hgh[2], by= .001), size = 1)

    # Random maturity levels for key processes
    patch_fail <- sample(1:4,size=1)
    dev_maturity <- sample(1:4,size=1)

    # Create vuln data frame
    res <- GetAdvSecResults(c(extreme, severe, high),
                            patch_fail,
                            dev_maturity)

    # Add a group ID column
    res$group <- x

    # Append data frames
    dt <- bind_rows(dt,res)
  }

  # Return the complete data frame.
  return(dt)
}
```

Let's run our new function. And, let's query the results for the first half of the year's data. We do that by setting the total_weeks to 26. (Half of 52 weeks is 26.)

These are the key variables that are extracted below. The first two are the most important, as the latter two are generated directly from them.

- **n:** Count of Vulnerabilities
- **wait_time:** Sum of wait-times
- **avg_wait_time:** Average wait-time (wait_time / n)
- **vulns_per_wait_time:** Vulns per wait-time (n / wait_time)

```
# Get 10 product teams
dt <- GetVulnGroups()

# Retrieve first half years worth of data
total_weeks <- 26
dte <- dt[(dt$audit == 0 & dt$exposure_id == 1 & dt$severity_id == 1 &
          dt$week.fseen <= total_weeks),]

# Get a count of vulns - key variable
n = nrow(dte)

# Get Interarrivals
interarrivals <- diff(sort(yday(dte$first.seen)))

# Get Total Wait Time - key variable
wait_time <- sum(interarrivals)


# Get avg time per vuln
avg_wait_time = wait_time/n

# Get avg vulns per wait time
vulns_per_wait_time <- n/wait_time
```

## Empirical Bayes Prior

We want to get a stable baseline metric for the first two quarters (26 weeks) of the year. Unfortunately, the data is likely biased, due to its small size. It's small because extreme events are rare. What can we do to fix this?

This is where priors come in. Priors can update and regulate our data. We generate our *prior parameters* by using the previous year ... as a simulation.

Using previous data for our prior parameters is an alternative to subjective priors. Using historical data to create priors is called empirical Bayes. (*Reminder:* Empirical Bayes will be explored in depth in the next chapter.)

In the code block below, I introduce two new functions for generating our data-informed priors. The first is called GetFirstSeenHits(). It extracts a list of wait-times. Those wait-times are needed by a second function called GetGammaPriors().

GetGammaPriors() compresses our wait-times down to two optimized numbers. These two numbers summarize our prior data in terms of its central tendency and spread. The approach to making optimized inputs is formally called maximum likelihood estimation (MLE).

Think of our two prior parameters as the top and bottom of a ratio. That ratio is the average vulnerability arrival rate. For example, if one vulnerability materializes per week, then its average is 1 over 7 or 1/7. If that is a very certain ratio, then it would get scaled up perhaps to 7/49 or 10/70, etc. The larger the values, the more certainty there is in the result.

The GetGammaPriors() function will make the ratio "just right" in terms of numerator and denominator. That means it will not only get the average value right, but it will get the scale right, too.

```
# Get new data as if it came from the previous year
dtPrev <- GetVulnGroups()

# Pull only the last quarter's data. Week 40-52
dtePrev <- dtPrev[(dtPrev$audit == 0 & dtPrev$exposure_id == 1 &
                dtPrev$severity_id == 1 & (dtPrev$week.fseen > 39 &
                dtPrev$week.fseen <= 52)),]

# Get a list of all the day numbers with events..see example data
day_vals <- sort(yday(dtePrev$first.seen))
# [1] 281 281 285 295 311...  #example data

# Reformat the data for prior analysis
prior_int <- GetFirstSeenHits(day_vals, min = 275, max = 365)
# [1] 0 0 0 0 0 0 2 0 0 0 1 0 #example data

# Get optimal gamma priors - MLE
gvals <- GetGammaPriors(prior_int)
alpha = gvals[1]
lambda = gvals[2]

# Create a list of the possible rates (for graphing only)
theta = seq(0, .5, 0.001)

# Score possibilities using priors (for graphing only)
prior = dgamma(theta, shape = alpha, rate = lambda)
```

## Bayesian Updating

We are set to finish our analysis. We have our 26 weeks of data summarized in two key variables: $n$ and "wait_times." They are numbers. The first ($n$) is the total count of vulnerabilities. And "wait_times" is the summary of times between vulnerability arrivals. We also have our priors. These were generated from the previous year's fourth quarter. It's also summarized in two numbers:

```
gvals
[1] 7.013279 59.958270
```

Our priors say that a 12th of a vulnerability arrives per day: 7/ 60 ~ 0.12. It is what we think "prior" to seeing any new data – that is, before seeing data for the first 26 weeks of the current year.

We add the prior (gvals) to the data ("n" and "wait_times") to get the posterior. You see that occurring where the "+" signs are located below. This "easy math" comes from the conjugate relationship. We discussed this in some depth in the previous chapters.

This is all we need to perform our Bayesian data analysis. It's so simple it almost feels a bit like cheating.

```
# likelihood distribution - for graphing purposes only
likelihood = dgamma(wait_time, shape = n, rate = theta)

# Posterior - Conjugate prior update.
posterior = dgamma(theta, alpha + n, lambda + wait_time)

# Bayesian update graph
plot_posterior(theta, prior, likelihood, posterior)
abline(v = qgamma(c(0.025, 0.975), alpha + n, lambda + wait_time),
       col = "seagreen", lty = 2)
```

See the prior curve in the graph just below. It is the leftmost curve. Eyeballing it, it looks like plausible prior rates range from just above 0.05 to just over 0.23 with a central tendency around 0.12. The prior has some influence on the posterior. It pulls the posterior to the left.

The dotted lines are the 95% credible interval for the posterior. We generated the credible interval using this code:

```
qgamma(c(0.025, 0.975), alpha + n, lambda + wait_time)
[1] 0.1216472 0.2251792
```

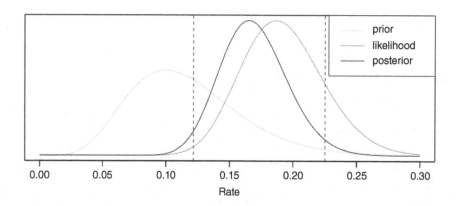

## Making Data and Forecasts from the Posterior

Given our data, and what we already know in terms of the prior, we would say that between a 12th and 23rd of a vulnerability will materialize per day. That, of course, does not make much sense. We don't experience partial vulnerabilities.

That is why we simulate data. We use what we have learned about wait-times to simulate vulnerability interarrivals.

In the following code we add our priors and data into two variables called **shape** and **rate**. It's for convenience. The rgamma() function takes in our new shape and rate parameters. It then returns 10,000 simulated rates. Most of the 10,000 rates will fall between the two dotted lines bracketing the posterior curve above.

We need to transform those 10,000 rates into actual days. To do that, we divide 1 by each rate. That provides the mean time between events. For example, 1/.17 is ~6 days. Now we are ready to graph interarrivals.

## The Grammar of Graphics

The histogram below is created using ggplot2(). The "gg" is short for "The Grammar of Graphics."[4] It's an open-source data visualization package. It is beyond the scope of this book to go into all its nooks and crannies. I will try to put informative (and non-distracting) comments in my ggplot code as I go along.

```
# Number Of Simulations
Nrep = 10000

# prior vuln count + num vulns from data
shape = alpha + n

# prior time + wait time from data
rate = lambda + wait_time

# Simulate 10K vuln day rates: .21, .17, .15, .22 etc
theta_sim = rgamma(Nrep, shape, rate)

# 1/theta_sim is the mean time between events 1/.21 = 4.76 days etc
scaled_sim <- 1/theta_sim

# Get 89% Highest Density Intervals for graph
ci <- ci(scaled_sim, method="HDI")

# Get Mean for graph
mean_sim <- round(mean(scaled_sim),2)
```

```
# Put scaled_sim into DF for graph
df <- tibble(sim=scaled_sim)

# Plot Mean interArrivals
ggplot(df, aes(x=sim)) +

  # Declare a histogram chart
  geom_histogram(aes(y=..density..), colour="black",
      fill="white",bins=100)+

  # Add a density curve
  geom_density(alpha=.2, fill="white")+

  # Add a vertical line for the lower CI value
  geom_vline(aes(xintercept=ci$CI_low),
             color="black", linetype="dashed", size=.5)+

  # Add a vertical line for the higher CI value
  geom_vline(aes(xintercept=ci$CI_high),
             color="black", linetype="dashed", size=.5)+

  # Add a mean line
  geom_vline(aes(xintercept=mean_sim),
             color="black", linetype="dashed", size=.5)+

  # Decorate the chart with labels
  labs(title = "Posterior Distribution of Mean interArrivals",
       subtitle = paste0("Mean Rate: ", mean_sim," | 89% HDI: ",
                  round(ci$CI_low,2), " To: ", round(ci$CI_high,2))) +
  xlab("Mean interArrival Rates") +
  ylab("Strength")
```

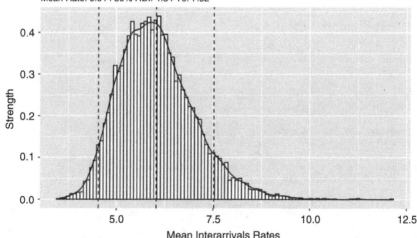

We have successfully created a Bayesian baseline for mean vulnerability interarrival times (wait-times). It is a key metric for understanding the velocity of risk creation. Now let's take a look at the same phenomena from a more "predictive" angle.

Should we expect a vulnerability every six days? No. That would be falling for the **flaw of averages**. If I can't be perfectly confident in six days – what can I be confident in? Let's try to answer that question.

The code for our confidence question is nearly the same as above. The big difference is the use of the exponential distribution. We do that by passing in the theta_sim vector created in the last example. I will skip the code used to develop the "theta_sim" results to save on space.

```
# Get interarrival values from the exponential distribution
y_sim = rexp(Nrep, rate = theta_sim)

# Get 95% and 50% quantiles - used for making vertical lines
val95 <- round(quantile(y_sim, 0.95),2)
val50 <- round(quantile(y_sim, 0.50),2)

# Pass interarrival data into DF
df <- tibble(sim=y_sim)

# Pass DF into ggplot
ggplot(df, aes(x=sim)) +

  # Declare histogram shape
  geom_histogram(aes(y=..density..), colour="black",
            fill="white",bins=100)+

  # Curve for chart
  geom_density(alpha=.2, fill="white")+

  # 95% or less vertical line
  geom_vline(aes(xintercept=mean(val95)),
            color="black", linetype="dashed", size=.5)+

  # 50% or less vertical line
  geom_vline(aes(xintercept=mean(val50)),
            color="black", linetype="dashed", size=.5)+

  # Labels for chart
  labs(title = "Posterior Predictive Distribution",
      subtitle = paste0("95% Chance of Vulnerability In: ",
              val95," Days Or Less | 50% In: ",
                    val50, " Or Less")) +
xlab("Days") + ylab("Strength") + xlim(c(0, 50))
```

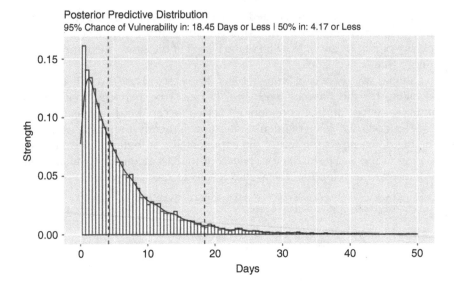

Posterior Predictive Distribution
95% Chance of Vulnerability in: 18.45 Days or Less I 50% in: 4.17 or Less

You can be fairly confident that vulnerabilities show up in 18 days or less. And it's a flip of a coin if an extreme vulnerability will show up in 4 days or less.

This result is based on 10 product groups with dozens of scrum teams. And it's based on critical vulnerabilities associated with externally accessible assets with regulated data. Meaning, it's not an infinite amount of teams, vulnerabilities, or asset combinations. It's a baseline for a specific use case.

You now have a baseline rate you can start tracking over time. And, you can set KPIs for improving it. Of course, this was a data simulation. What about applying it to real, seemingly chaotic, data?

That's what we are going to do next. **We are going to use everything we just learned for a large pedagogical case study.** It's a case study with lots of code. The good news is that you have already seen much of the code, in one form or another.

To make our lives simpler, we will create a series of small(ish) functions. These functions work like building blocks. They encapsulate complexity so you can focus on modeling.

My encouragement is to read through the text and the code comments. Get the concepts first. Then, if you feel inclined, run the code. And as always, the book's site has all the code ready for your use.

## Mitigatable Surprise

### *Bayesian Analysis Meet OSINT Using the National Vulnerability Database*

A large security research firm claimed that 2020 had a bumper crop of vulnerabilities. They believe it resulted in slower than usual patching. They further posited that this led to the ZeroLogon vulnerability getting lost in the shuffle.[5] Eventually, nation-state actors incorporated ZeroLogon in their playbooks. This got the attention of the Department of Homeland Security. Soon after, a patching frenzy ensued.

Was 2020 unusual? The data and analysis below says no. There must be some other cause for the ZeroLogon tardy patching.

How often do we assert "The sky is falling!" in our own environments? Momentary spikes in activity can lead to wrong conclusions. Alternatively, we may miss slow changes over time. Then, to our surprise, we are drowning in risk.

We shouldn't be surprised by trends we can observe. The good news is that vulnerability disclosure is public. Analyzing public data is a form of open source intelligence (OSINT).[6] This section is a simple case study that merges Bayesian data analysis with OSINT.

### *Start with the End in Mind*

Let's start with the final analysis. Then we can work backward into the details.

*Note:* Feel free to run this function after you have read the following section. You will want to download the required NVD zip files locally for years 2017 through 2021 first. They can be found here: https://nvd.nist.gov/vuln/data-feeds. If you set from_file to FALSE, it will attempt to download the zip files for you. You may get a cert-related error based on your system's configuration.

```
GetNVDAnalysis(2018:2021, new = TRUE, save = TRUE, from_file = TRUE)
```

GetNVDAnalysis() produces a series of graphs per year – in this case, covering 2018 to 2021. Each graph's data is informed by the previous year's data. For example, 2020 becomes the prior for 2021. Priors are important when data is small and biased. For example, in the first few months of 2022 our priors will matter. As more data is collected the priors have negligible influence.

In the following table, I share two of the three graph types GetNVDAnalysis() produces. All of these graphs should look very familiar – we just covered them in the section above.

The first row covers 2018. If we look at the chart on the left, we see there is a 95% chance that a vuln will arrive in ~2.4 days *or less*. The graph does extend out just beyond 8 days for edge cases. The mean wait-time on the right is less than a day. This process repeats itself through 2021.

The question to ask is, *"How much change is there year to year?"* The answer? Not much. At least, not as it relates to the subset of risks we are concerned with.

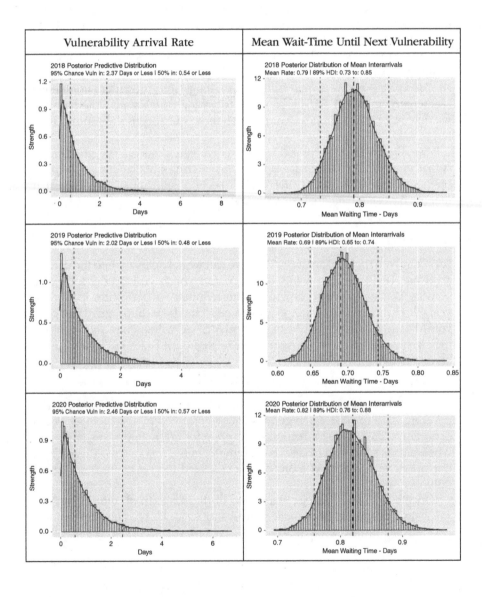

| Vulnerability Arrival Rate | Mean Wait-Time Until Next Vulnerability |
|---|---|

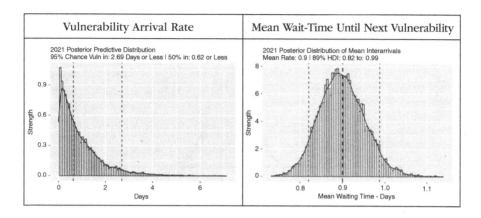

The final year is not complete – we are just over seven months into 2021. We used 2020 as a prior to support our forecast for 2021. The prior exerts minimal force. That's because the posterior has quite a bit of data – even seven months in.

Here is what the Bayesian update chart looks like for 2021. See how the posterior is infinitesimally shifted toward the prior. Note, this is a new version of the Bayesian Update chart – this one is implemented using more advanced ggplot capabilities.

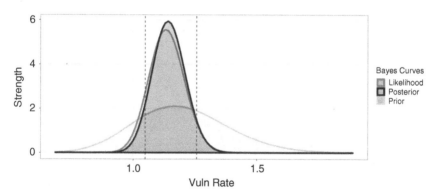

Priors matter most when data is small. Let's assume for the moment we are only 90 days into 2021. We can simulate that assumption by setting "end" to 90. GetNVDAnalysis() only analyzes the first 90 days of the year. The 2020 prior has much more influence now. Also, note how far to the right the data (likelihood) is. That's because the beginning of the year has a relatively slow rate for vulnerability arrivals.

```
GetNVDAnalysis(c(2021), end = 90, theta_range = c(.5,3.0))
```

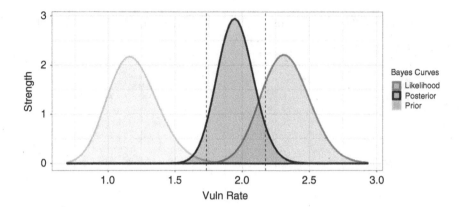

I do the same below with 140 days of data in 2021. The prior is exerting less force. Also, the posterior is baselining at a rate that is getting closer to the prior.

While 2021 is the slowest in velocity at the moment, I would be surprised if it ends up being significantly different than 2020. If it was indeed slower, I would be curious about causality.

```
GetNVDAnalysis(c(2021), end = 140, theta_range = c(.5,3.0))
```

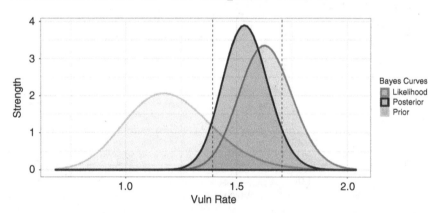

GetNVDAnalysis() can be run as frequently as you would like. The goal would be to observe any systematic changes that are out of the ordinary. If the arrival times are consistently getting shorter, then you can be alarmed – but not surprised! And you can take action to keep your head above water.

The rest of this section unpacks the code- and framework-based approach used to create our NVD analysis tool.

## NVD Analysis Decomposed

The NVD analysis follows these general steps.

The five steps are enabled by three layers of functions. The parent function is GetNVDAnalysis(). It's the first function pictured below. Its job is looping over its child functions – of which there are five. The first two children get the prior and likelihood (data), respectively. The last three functions are for simulation from the posterior and graphing. The functions, and the order they are called, mirror the process above.

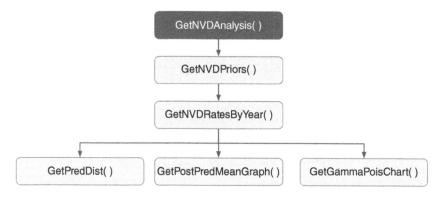

In addition to the child function, there are a handful of grandchild functions. To start, we will explore the five-step process and the five functions below. At the end of the section I will briefly cover some of the grandchild functions. All code is available on the book's site: www.themetricsmanifesto.com.

The five-step process is modeled inside of GetNVDAnalysis. You will see the child functions clearly, too.

```
GetNVDAnalysis <- function(years, sev_val = 9, prior_mult = 1,
                  end = 365, theta_range = c(.5,2.0),
                  new = FALSE, save = FALSE,
                  match_string = "default", from_file = FALSE){

  # Default text to search for in vuln description
  if( match_string == "default"){
      match_string="Windows|Microsoft|Office|Mac|Apple|Browser|cisco|java|Oracle|adobe"
  }

  # Reps for simulations
  Nrep = 10000
```

```
# Indicates if we are in the first loop
count = 1

# Loop through the years
for(year in years){

  # Get previous year
  prev_year <- year - 1

  # Prior Block
  if( count == 1){

    # Steps 1 & 2: Download prev year and Get Prior
    prior <- GetNVDPriors(prev_year,sev_val, new_file = new,
                          save_file = save, match_string,
                          from_file = from_file) * prior_mult

    # increment counter
    count = count + 1

  }else{

    # Step 2: Get Prior Only
    prior <- GetNVDPriors(prev_year,sev_val, match_string,
                          from_file = from_file) * prior_mult

  }


  # Step 1 & 3: Download current year and Get Rates
  data <- GetNVDRatesByYear(year, sev_val, day_start = start,
                            get_new = new, cache = save, match_string,
                            from_file = from_file)

  # Step 4 & 5: Simulate Data and Make Graphs
  ppd_graph <- GetPostPredDist(Nrep, prior, data, year)
  pm_graph <- GetPostPredMeanGraph(Nrep, prior, data, year)
  ggp_graph <- GetGammaPoisChart(prior, data)


  print(ppd_graph)
  print(pm_graph)
  print(ggp_graph)
  }
}
```

Were you able to see how the five-step process is modeled in the code? And did you notice all the child functions? The rest of the chapter unpacks the five-step process and supporting functions.

## Step 1: Download Data

GetNVDAnalysis() has three parameters that tell it how to get and save data: "new," "save," and "from_file." By default, they are set to FALSE. We set all to TRUE since it is our first run accept from_file per the note at the beginning of this section.

Downloads (or parsing from zip file) start with the first call to Get-NVDPriors(). It subtracts one from the current year to get 2017. It then queries the NVD site (or local zip file) and grabs the 2017 json and returns the priors.

The next download/parse is via GetNVDRatesByYear(). It fetches 2018 data and parses it. The 2018 data is then stored. In the next loop, Get-NVDPriors() subtracts one from 2019 and fetches the stored 2018 data. This process continues until all years are processed.

## Step 2: Get Priors

The values generated by GetNVDPriors() are called informed priors. Informed priors distinguish themselves from uninformed priors. The latter is also called a flat prior. As you may recall, a flat prior considers all possibilities as equally plausible.

An informed prior is not flat. It puts more plausibility on certain possibilities based on the data.

There are two ways an informed prior can be made. First, you can use subject matter expert beliefs. We did that many times in previous chapters. The other approach uses data. That is what we are going to do. As stated earlier, this particular approach to informed priors is called empirical Bayes.

Let's review GetNVDPriors. Be sure to read through the comments in the code. Some of it has already been covered.

```
GetNVDPriors <- function(year, sev_val = 9, optim_vals = c(1,1),
                  new_file = FALSE, save_file = FALSE,
                  match_string = "default", from_file = FALSE){


    # Pulls data from NVD site or from disc
    nvd_prev <- GetNVDData(year, new = new_file, save = save_file,
                  from_file = from_file)

    # Get critical findings
    prior_open <- GetCritDF(nvd_prev,sev_val, match_string)

    # Get publish day of year and sort
    prior_open <- sort(prior_open$pub_day)

    # Prepare data for prior optimization
    prior_open <- GetFirstSeenHits(prior_open, min = 1, max = 365)

    # Optimize Block - maximum likelihood estimation (MLE)
    g_priors <- GetGammaPriors(prior_open)

    # Create readable variable names for prior and return
    ptibble <- tibble(alpha = g_priors[1], lambda = g_priors[2])
    return(ptibble)
}
```

GetNVDPriors() returns our optimized priors. Do you see how it calls GetGammaPriors()? We covered that function in the last section. We name our prior values alpha and lambda in the code above.

## Step 3: Get Rates (from Data)

Priors come from the previous year. The function used to get current data is called: GetNVDRatesByYear(). Some of the code below should look very familiar. Indeed, it is building our two key data variables for the number of vulnerabilities and wait-times.

```
GetNVDRatesByYear <- function(year, sev_val = 9, day_end = 365,
                              get_new = FALSE, cache = FALSE,
                              Match_string, from_file = FALSE,
                              from_file = FALSE){

  # Download data and save if get_new and cache
  nvd_df <- GetNVDData(year, new = get_new, save = cache,
                       from_file = from_file)

  # Subset data based on day of the year. Default 365
  nvd_df <- nvd_df[yday(nvd_df$pub_date) <= day_end,]

  # Get Critical Findings
  crit_df <- GetCritDF(nvd_df, sev_val, match_string)

  # Get total wait time between vulnerabilities
  wait_time <- sum(diff(sort(crit_df$pub_day)))

  # Get count of vulnerabilities
  num_vulns = nrow(crit_df)

  # Get vulnerabilities per wait time
  vulns_per_wait_time <- num_vulns/wait_time

  # Get time between vulnerabilities
  avg_days = wait_time/num_vulns

  # Return what we learned as a data frame
  retTib <- tibble(wait_time, num_vulns, vulns_per_wait_time, avg_days)

  return(retTib)
}
```

The prior and rate data is passed into our three simulation and graphing functions.

## Steps 4 and 5: Simulate Data and Make Graphs

The following graphs were covered in part above. The difference being that we have turned the graph code into simplifying functions. I encourage you to walk through the code comments. It will reinforce the graphing approach and the simple five-step analytical approach.

The chart below asks, *"Given what we know about times between vulnerabilities, how soon will one arrive?"* It answers in terms of 95% and 50% confidence. If you give it one month of data, it will still answer, but that answer will be heavily influenced by the prior.

```
GetPostPredDist <- function(Nrep, prior, rates, year = "",
                            fill_curve = "white"){

  # Posterior shape and rate params using Bayes updating
  shape_val <- prior$alpha + rates$num_vulns
  rate_val <- prior$lambda + rates$wait_time


  # Simulate vuln arrivals the posterior
  theta_sim = rgamma(Nrep, shape_val, rate_val)

  # Simulate times to next arrival based on vuln arrivals
  y_sim = rexp(Nrep, rate = theta_sim)

  # Probability of event occurring or less
  val95 <- round(quantile(y_sim, 0.95),2)
  val50 <- round(quantile(y_sim, 0.50),2)


  # GGplot takes data as a data frame
  df <- tibble(sim=y_sim)

  # Format year with a trailing space for the graph title
  if( year != ""){
    year = paste0(year, " ")
  }

  # Return plot to "res" variable for printing later
  res <- ggplot(df, aes(x=sim)) +

    # Histogram chart type
    geom_histogram(aes(y=..density..), colour="black",
                   fill="white",bins=100)+

    # Add density curve overlay to histogram
    geom_density(alpha=.2, fill=fill_curve)+

    # Add 95% line to chart
    geom_vline(aes(xintercept=mean(val95)),
               color="black", linetype="dashed", size=.5)+
```

```
# Add 50% line to chart
geom_vline(aes(xintercept=mean(val50)),
          color="black", linetype="dashed", size=.5)+
labs(title = paste0(year, "Posterior Predictive Distribution"),
      subtitle = paste0("95% Chance Vuln In: ", val95,
                  " Days Or Less | 50% In: ", val50, " Or Less")) +
      xlab("Days") + ylab("Strength") + xlim(c(0, max(df$sim)))

  return(res)
}
```

The next graph measures the distribution of differences in mean arrival times. The smaller the time, the more frequently vulnerabilities arrive. Most of the codes should look very similar.

```
GetPostPredMeanGraph <- function(Nrep, prior, rates, year = "",
                                  fill_curve = "white"){

  # Update gamma parameters for posterior
  shape_val <- prior$alpha + rates$num_vulns
  rate_val <- prior$lambda + rates$num_vulns * rates$avg_days

  # Simulate vuln arrival rate
  theta_sim = rgamma(Nrep, shape_val, rate_val)

  # Get mean interarrival rates… day/simulated vuln arrival
  tratio <- 1 / theta_sim

  # Get HDI - for low/high line
  ci <- ci(tratio, method="HDI")

  # Get Mean - for middle line
  mean_sim <- round(mean(tratio),2)

  # Put space in front of year for print
  if( year != ""){
    year = paste0(year, " ")
  }

  # Data Frame for GGPLOT
  df <- tibble(sim=tratio)

  # Cache plot to var for print
  res <- ggplot(df, aes(x=sim)) +

    # Histogram chart
    geom_histogram(aes(y=..density..), colour="black",
                  fill="white",bins=100)+


    # Add curver over hist - with white fill
    geom_density(alpha=.2, fill= fill_curve)+
```

```
# Lower CI line
geom_vline(aes(xintercept=ci$CI_low),
           color="black", linetype="dashed", size=.5)+

# Higher CI Line
geom_vline(aes(xintercept=ci$CI_high),
           color="black", linetype="dashed", size=.5)+

# Mean Line
geom_vline(aes(xintercept=mean_sim),
           color="black", linetype="dashed", size=.75)+

# Labels for Graph
labs(title = paste0(year,
     "Posterior Distribution of Mean interArrivals"),
     subtitle = paste0("Mean Rate: ", mean_sim," | 89% HDI: ",
                       round(ci$CI_low,2), " To: ",
                       round(ci$CI_high,2))) +
xlab("Mean Waiting Time - Days") + ylab("Strength")

# Return Graph For Printing
return(res)
}
```

Lastly, we review the GetGammaPoisChart(). This is a standard Bayesian update chart. You saw this chart in action at the beginning of this section. The difference between this type of chart and the previous Bayesian update charts is the use of ggplot – it gives us an upgrade in power, flexibility, and aesthetics.

There is a lot of code below. It meshes together both simulation and graphing natively in ggplot.

```
GetGammaPoisChart <- function(prior,data){

# Posterior parameters
p_scale <- prior$alpha + data$num_vulns
p_rate <- prior$lambda + data$wait_time

# Generate best x-axis range by querying parameters for width
rng <- GetRanges(prior, data, p_scale, p_rate)

# Simulate posterior to get HDI Values for Graph.
sim_g <- rgamma(1000,p_scale,p_rate)
ci <- ci(sim_g,method = "HDI")

# Cache graph results for print
ggraph <- ggplot(data.frame(x = c(rng$min_r, rng$max_r)), aes(x = x)) +

          # Use ggplot dgamma stat function for prior
          stat_function(fun = dgamma,
            args = list(prior$alpha, prior$lambda),
            aes(colour = "Prior"), size = 1.5, geom = "area",
            fill="goldenrod", alpha=0.2) +
```

```
# Use ggplot dgamma stat function for likelihood
stat_function(fun = dgamma,
    args = list(data$num_vulns, data$wait_time),
    aes(colour = "Likelihood"), size = 1.5, geom = "area",
    fill="red", alpha=0.2) +

# Use ggplot dgamma stat function for posterior
stat_function(fun = dgamma, args = list(p_scale, p_rate),
    aes(colour = "Posterior"), size = 1.5, geom = "area",
    fill="blue", alpha=0.2) +

# Labels and Title
scale_x_continuous(name = "Vuln Rate")+
scale_y_continuous(name = "Strength") +
ggtitle("Normal function curves of probabilities") +

# Legend Configurations
scale_colour_manual("Bayes Curves",
    values = c("red", "blue", "goldenrod")) +

# Lower HDI for posterior
geom_vline(aes(xintercept=ci$CI_low),color="black",
    linetype="dashed", size=.5)+

# Upper HDI for posterior
geom_vline(aes(xintercept=ci$CI_high),color="black",
    linetype="dashed", size=.5)+

# White background
theme_bw()

    return(ggraph)
}
```

## Grandchild Function

There are two key grandchild functions that appear in both GetNVDPriors()
and GetNVDRatesByYear(). If you look at the code for each function, you
will see this code in each:

```
# Pull 2021 nvd data from site and saves it to disc
nvd_df <- GetNVDData(2021, new = TRUE, save = TRUE, from_file = TRUE)

# Get a critical subset of vuln based on vuln types and severity.
crit_df <- GetCritDF(nvd_df,sev_val = 9, match_string)
```

The first function is GetNVDData(). It downloads, parses, and stores
data. The second function is GetCritDF(). It queries the returned data set for
specific risk factors.

Let's unpack the GetNVDData() function first. Its core job is fetching
and parsing NVD json. The function takes three parameters to do this. The
first is the year. The second is the "new" parameter. If set to TRUE, it downloads the NVD data unless from_file is set to TRUE. If from_file is set to true,

local zip files are used. If new is set to FALSE, then cached data is used. The third parameter is "save." Save is set to FALSE by default. If set to TRUE, it will save the converted JSON to disc for future use.

## *Function: GetNVDData()*

```
# Years include digits like 2020, 2019 etc.  2002 is the earliest
GetNVDData <- function(year, new = FALSE, save = FALSE, from_file = FALSE){

  # This means you have a data frame on disc, and you want to use it
  if(new == FALSE){

    # Instantiate cached data frame from disk
    nvd_df <- readRDS(paste0("nvd_",year,".RDS"))

    # Return data frame and leave function
    return(nvd_df)
  }

  if( from_file == FALSE){

      # For caching json in memory - temp will hold our JSON
      temp <- tempfile()

      # Download json to temp. Note 'year' variable
      download.file(
         paste0("https://nvd.nist.gov/feeds/json/cve/1.1/nvdcve-1.1-",
                year,".json.zip"),temp)

      # Unzip and convert json into an R data frame
      nvd <- fromJSON((unz(temp, paste0("nvdcve-1.1-",year,".json"))))

      # Free up the memory that holds the large JSON file
      unlink(temp)
  }else{

    # Use nvd zip in current directory instead of auto download
    nvd <- fromJSON((unz(paste0("nvdcve-1.1-",
            year,".json.zip"),paste0("nvdcve-1.1-",year,".json"))))
  }

  # Extract CVE,Pub Date,Modify Date,Base Score,Severity and Description
  cves <- nvd$CVE_Items$cve$CVE_data_meta$ID
  pub_date <- nvd$CVE_Items$publishedDate
  mod_date <- nvd$CVE_Items$lastModifiedDate
  b_score <- nvd$CVE_Items$impact$baseMetricV2$cvssV2$baseScore
  sev <- nvd$CVE_Items$impact$baseMetricV2$severity
  desc <- nvd$CVE_Items$cve$description$description_data

  # Loop through descriptions to get exact text
  desc_vals = NULL
  for(x in 1:length(desc)){
```

```
  # append description values
  if( x == 0){
    desc_vals <- desc[[x]]$value
  }else{
    desc_vals <- c(desc_vals, desc[[x]]$value)
  }
}

# Create a tidy data frame
nvd_df <- tibble(cves,pub_date,mod_date,b_score,sev,desc_vals)

# Optionally save the data frame to disc
if( save == TRUE){
    saveRDS(nvd_df, file = paste0("nvd_",year,".RDS"))
}

# Return data frame for analysis
return(nvd_df)
}
```

The next function in our code-block queries for critical vulnerabilities. It does that by taking in the results of GetNVDData() as a parameter. You also specify a cvss score for the sev_val parameter. It will query for vulnerabilities that are that severity or greater. Lastly, you pass in a pipe "|" delimited list of strings. For example, if you wanted "Windows" or "Microsoft," your string would look like this: "windows|microsoft." The "|" means "or." It will match one or more of the pipe-delimited values.

## Function: GetCritDF()

```
# Create data frame of crit vulns
GetCritDF <- function(nvd_val, sev_val, match_string){

  # Filter data frame based on cvss score and string matches
  crit_df <- nvd_val %>% filter(b_score >= sev_val &
            grepl(match_string, desc_vals,ignore.case = TRUE))

  # Get vuln publish day of year
  crit_df$pub_day <- yday(crit_df$pub_date)

  # Get vuln modify day of year
  crit_df$mod_day <- yday(crit_df$mod_date)

  # Return crit data frame
  return(crit_df)
}
```

## Summary

This chapter presented a sister baseline to arrivals called wait-times. In this case, we measured the wait-time between extreme vulnerability arrivals. Think of it as a fine-grained approach to baselining the rate at which risk arrives.

Your operational goal would be to baseline this rate. Once you have a stable baseline, you can set goals for betterment. Betterment in this case would mean *expanding* (or *lengthening*) the rate at which vulnerabilities appear. In modern terms, this would require security to shift-left. That means security would influence how software and systems are built. And it would mean implementing policies that can block, and in some rare cases remediate, vulnerabilities pre-deploy.

You will know your shift-left capabilities are working because you will see an impact in wait-times. And you can optimize which policies seem to have the most impact.

The next chapter covers escape rates. If wait-times are a sibling to arrivals, then escape rates are like a cousin. They are the most shift-left metric of the bunch. Escape rates measure the rate at which risk moves across various boundaries. Boundaries include things like internal to external, or development to production, or in policy to out of policy.

I have some good news regarding escape rates. They use nearly the exact same statistical methods as burndowns. That will allow us to focus on empirical Bayes methods. We touched on empirical Bayes in this chapter. We go deep on empirical Bayes as it relates to escape rates.

## Notes

1. Seiersen, R. (2021, January 4). *A Modern Shift-Left Security Approach. Forbes.* https://www.forbes.com/sites/forbestechcouncil/2021/01/04/a-modern-shift-left-security-approach/?sh=764534857729
2. *What Is Operations Research?* (2021, March 6). Industrial Engineering and Operations Research. https://www.ieor.columbia.edu/about
3. Wikipedia contributors. (2021b, August 20). *Queueing theory.* Wikipedia. https://en.wikipedia.org/wiki/Queueing_theory
4. Wilkinson, L., Wills, D., Rope, D., Norton, A., & Dubbs, R. (2005). *The Grammar of Graphics (Statistics and Computing)* (2nd ed.). Springer.
5. Wikipedia contributors. (2021a, February 11). *Zerologon.* Wikipedia. https://en.wikipedia.org/wiki/Zerologon
6. Wikipedia contributors. (2021e, September 20). *Open-source intelligence.* Wikipedia. https://en.wikipedia.org/wiki/Open-source_intelligence

# CHAPTER 7

# Escape Rates

*Bayesian statistics is difficult in the sense that thinking is difficult.*

– Donald A. Barry

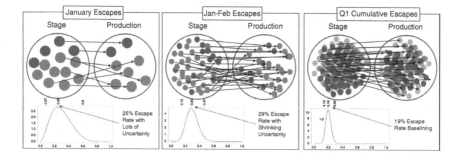

## What Is an Escape Rate?

If you google the words "escape rates," you will see articles on Brownian motion.[1] If you simply add one word – "defect escape rates" – you will see articles on measuring software quality. We will focus on the latter type of escapes – with a twist. First, our topic is security. Second, we will be doing things the Bayesian way.

Think of an escape rate as a measurement of risk movement. Or, with a mind toward process optimization, think of escape rates as measuring the *prevention* of risk movement. The lower the escape rate over time, the less risks are being exposed.

A canonical example is measuring the escape rate of software vulnerabilities. In the most general sense, a vulnerability found in production escaped from development.

The challenge is in knowing what could have been fixed in development. That is not an easy question to answer. It's a data, collaboration, and integration challenge. To be exacting, you would need to:

- Tag findings to releases.
- Correlate findings in build-time to findings found in run-time.
- Normalize (de-dupe) findings from different, possibly redundant, tools.
- Collect feedback from software and service owners regarding relevancy.

It is doable. There are solutions out there that can help. Unfortunately, the majority of teams likely don't have this level of maturity. Fortunately, there is an easier way to get started.

## Naive Escape Rates

The simplest escape rate is what I call a *naive escape rate*. It looks like this at a very high level:

**Production Vulnerabilities / (Stage + Production Vulnerabilities)**

I am using *stage* as a catch-all term. Whatever testing that is done *just prior* to deployment can be called stage or staging. You may have a number of pre-deploy environments like dev, test, uat, stage, pre-deploy, etc. Or, you may be working on a massive monorepo[2] doing trunk-based development.[3] I am lumping any testing done to code *just prior* to deployment as "stage."

If you're not doing security testing pre-deploy, or you don't have visibility into it, then your default escape rate is 100%. It is effectively an unmanaged process from a security point of view. Developers, DevOps, and Site Reliability Engineering (SRE) may say there are zero issues from software to infrastructure – they have it covered. And indeed, things may be humming along. But, you are the one accountable for security assurance. That means you can trust, but you still must verify.

### Why So Naive?

A naive approach will provide a useful, yet rough, measure of escape rates. After all, it's better to be approximately right than be exactly wrong.[4] *Exactly wrong* in this case means never getting started.

With a naive approach we don't have exact proof that a specific vulnerability has escaped – at least, not yet. But, we assume there is a relationship between vulnerabilities found in development to vulnerabilities found in production.

If you find there is no relationship (which is easy enough to measure), you have likely learned something ... there is a gap in your pre-deploy assessment process.

The good news is that the exact method you will learn here can apply to any type of escape rate measure, from naive to heavily integrated.

By way of example, let's assume the unadjusted, or raw count, of (high, severe, critical) vulnerabilities discovered in staging in January is 100. Unadjusted means vulnerabilities haven't been triaged to determine if they are false positives or simply irrelevant.

In January, you also find 10 *new* vulnerabilities in production. They may come from dynamic scans, bug bounty, customers, etc. Your naive escape rate ratio is: 10 / 110, or 9%. Let's graph this:

```
# Code available on www.themetricsmanifesto.com

source("manifesto_functions.R")   #book functions

MakeBetaGraph(10, 100, xlab = "Rate", ylab = "Strength",
              tlab = "January Escape Rates",
              slab = "Mean and Highest Density Interval", xadj = .001)
```

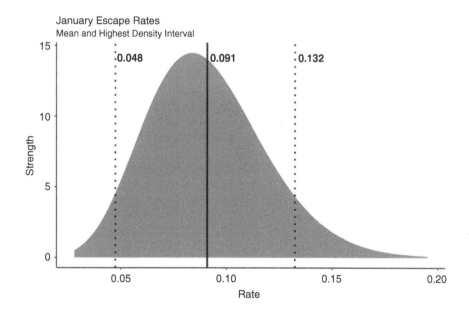

Congratulations, you just measured your first escape rate! You can be reasonably confident that given the data and this model, the true naive escape rate lives between 5% and 13%.

Each day there are new vulnerabilities added. As you get more data, your uncertainty about the baseline rate will reduce. Over time, you can groom your data and can eliminate vulnerabilities published after code was deployed – like zero-days. You can also remove false positives, irrelevant information, and other suppressed issues coming from development. We crawl, then walk, then run. With time, you can improve data quality without waiting to baseline escape rates.

## Baselined, Scaling, Accelerating

Is a 10% escape rate and a 90% burndown rate good? Before we go for qualitative assessments, let's state some useful distinctions. If rates over time don't fluctuate much, then you can characterize the process as **baselined.** If the volume of issues is increasing yet the rates are holding, then your process could be characterized as **scaling.** That means your capability is keeping up with risk volume. If escape rates and burndown rates are both improving over time, then your process could be characterized as **accelerating.**

*Good enough* is a function of **risk tolerance.** And risk tolerance is determined by the value at risk. Extreme risks (i.e., externally exposed, remotely exploitable, regulated data, etc.) will require rates that are scaling, if not accelerating. That is a policy statement. You will need to set those KRIs in relation to your business and the value at risk.

Hopefully, the full picture is emerging. Survival Analysis, Burndown, Arrivals, Wait-Times, and now Escapes work together. They collaborate to profile your security risk management capabilities. One baseline alone usually won't cut it. Focusing on reducing a shift-right metrics (like burndown) to the exclusion of a shift-left metrics (like escapes) won't cut it, either.

You will set objectives for managing cyber-risk. Then you invest in capabilities and measure their impact on your rates. That's the goal. Confront your security capabilities with data – and see if what you are doing is making a difference.

## Quick Bayesian Recap

**Subjective priors:** In the chapters on burndown and arrival rates we turned subject matter expert (SME) beliefs into data. Codified SME beliefs are called subjective priors. It's what we believe about a process prior to seeing any data.

**Empirical priors:** In the last chapter (on wait-times), we introduced priors based on previous data. Those priors are formally called empirical Bayesian priors. We used data from a previous year to get a count of risks (vulnerabilities), and we extracted the time between vulnerability arrivals. We called that data wait-times or interarrival times. We fed the vulnerability count and interarrivals into a function that gave us our optimized priors – gamma priors, to be exact. The method for getting optimized priors is called maximum likelihood estimation (MLE).

**Posterior simulation:** We mesh our optimal priors with current data. That "meshed" data is called our posterior. The posterior is what we believe based on prior and current data. We then use the posterior to create new data. The posterior simulation is formally called a *posterior predictive model*. We use simulated data to measure current processes and make forecasts about possible future rates.

We are going to follow this very same process for escape rates.

## Coding up Bayesian Escape Rates

Let's expand the empirical Bayes approach with escape rates. This section will first provide a code outline, consisting of four sections:

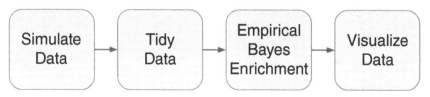

The code outline is followed by a narrative. The narrative explains what the code does and why, following the four-part outline. At the end of the code narrative, I then explain the main functions that support the outline. Like in the previous chapters, I try to emphasize concept over code.

> **Note:** At the end of the chapter, I do a complete analysis in 10 lines of longish code. I do that so you can see the forest from the trees. This type of analysis is easy. But, I want you to create as real of an experience as reasonably possible. That means we simulate lots of data.

## Code Outline

```
### Step 1: SIMULATE DATA ###
# First call takes ~ 4 mins and saves to disc
group_count <- 500
record_count <- 50000
dt <- GetLargeVulnGroups(TRUE,group_count)

# Extract samples as years
dt_year_one <- dt[sample(nrow(dt), record_count, replace = FALSE), ]
dt_year_two <- dt[sample(nrow(dt), record_count, replace = FALSE), ]
dt_year_three <- dt[sample(nrow(dt), record_count, replace = FALSE), ]

### Step 2: GET TIDY DATA ###
year_one_group <- GetEscapeGroups(dt_year_one, group_count)
year_two_group <- GetEscapeGroups(dt_year_two, group_count)
year_three_group <- GetEscapeGroups(dt_year_three, group_count)

# Put years into one data frame
group_vals <- AddEscapeDF(year_one_group, year_two_group)
group_vals <- AddEscapeDF(group_vals, year_three_group)

### Step 3: EMPIRICAL BAYES ENRICHMENT ###
# Get Basic Average
group_vals <- group_vals %>%
  mutate(escape_avg = prod_vuln / total_vulns)

# Get Long Run Groups That started in Q1
vgroups <- group_vals %>%
  filter(total_weeks >= 40)

# Get the Maximum Likelihood Estimation for Priors
mle_vals <- GetBurnMLE(vgroups$prod_vuln, vgroups$dev_vuln )

# Use MLE's to set alpha and beta prior vars
alpha <- mle_vals[[1]]
beta <- mle_vals[[2]]

# Beta average per group
group_vals <- group_vals %>%
  mutate(emp_bayes_avg =
    (prod_vuln + alpha) / (total_vulns + alpha + beta))

# Posterior update for each group
group_vals <- group_vals %>%
  mutate(alpha_update = alpha + prod_vuln,
         beta_update = beta + dev_vuln)

# Confidence intervals for each group
group_vals <- group_vals %>%
  mutate(low_ci  = qbeta(.025, alpha_update, beta_update),
         high_ci = qbeta(.975, alpha_update, beta_update))

### Step 4: VISUALIZE DATA ###
MakeBetaGraph(alpha, beta,"Empirical Bayes 'Prior' Escape Rate","Strength",
```

```
paste0("Escape Rates Derived From: ",sum(vgroups$total_vulns),
       " Vulnerabilities"),
paste0("Across ", nrow(vgroups),
       " groups supporting externally facing and audited services"),
xadj = .001)

# Get sample data for graph
short_year <- group_vals %>% filter(total_weeks <= 25) %>% head(25)
full_year <- group_vals %>% filter(total_weeks == max(total_weeks)) %>%
  head(20)

# Merge sample data into one df
example_df <- bind_rows(short_year, full_year)

# Make graph that makes empirical bayes impact apparent
MakeProportionChart(df_val = example_df, kpis=c(.05,.1,.2))
```

## *Step 1: Simulate Data*

The first code block simulates data. The GetLargeVulnGroups() function does this. It is an extension of GetVulnGroups() from the previous chapter. It saves simulated data to disk for later use. Just to refresh your memory, I have printed a subset of the dt data frame it creates below.

```
> dt %>% select(team, dev_maturity, audit, exposure, severity, beta_prob,

            week.fseen, week.lseen, group)
# A tibble: 222,935 x 9
   team          dev_maturity audit exposure severity beta_prob week.fseen week.lseen group
   <fct>                <int> <dbl> <chr>    <fct>        <dbl>      <int>      <int> <int>
1 external audit           4      0 external extreme     0.205           7          7     1
2 external audit           4      0 external extreme     0.407          12         15     1
3 external audit           4      0 external extreme     0.222          21         23     1
4 external audit           4      0 external extreme     0.0585         23         23     1
5 external audit           4      0 external extreme     0.115          27         28     1
# ... with 222,930 more rows
```

The simulation function takes two to three minutes to create 500 groups. In future calls, you would call the function as such: `dt <- GetLargeVulnGroups()` without any parameters. It will instantiate the data immediately – no waiting. This can be pumped up to a thousand or more groups. It just takes longer to produce.

The next step in the "simulate data" code block creates three years of data. It does that by sampling from the 200,000+ records associated with the 500 groups. Sampling from the pool of 200K vulnerabilities adds some additional randomness to our analysis.

Also, I wanted to increase the per-group data volume to cut across more than a year. You will have situations where you have both weeks and multi-years' worth of data. You shouldn't have to ignore small datasets – this is why we use an empirical Bayes approach. Our larger datasets can inform the smaller ones.

I want to display how we get random records for each year. We use some mildly fancy subsetting to do this:

```
dt[sample(nrow(dt), record_count, replace = FALSE), ]
```

Note how sample() below extracts indexes that are then passed to dt[...]. It returns 50,000 randomly selected vulnerability records.

```
> sample(nrow(dt), record_count, replace = FALSE)
64312  35859 191132  65074  99818   1348 179222 162523 111357 167788...
```

## Step 2: Tidy Data

The Tidy Data block of code does three things to prep our data for analysis. First, it aggregates vulnerabilities by group to make our escape rate analysis simpler. Here is what the output looks like for one year – note how simple the data actually is:

```
> year_one_group
# A tibble: 500 x 5
   group total_weeks prod_vuln dev_vuln total_vulns
   <int>       <dbl>     <int>    <int>       <int>
1      1          52        44      124         168
2      2          52        22      135         157
3      3          50        14      104         118
4      4          52        30      153         183
5      5          51        11       74          85
```

The second thing we do is stagger start times. Staggering is encapsulated in the GetEscapeGroups() function. A quarter of the groups start the last month of the year. Another quarter start the last quarter of the year. The remaining half operate for a full year or more.

This is how software development works – in fits and starts. Empirical Bayesian priors can help smooth some of the chaos created by small data and bumpy processes. You will see this clearly in the graphs.

The third and final thing the "tidy" code block does is indicate which vulnerabilities escaped. That is how you get the "prod_vuln" count in the data table above. Escapes are based on asset risk, vulnerability severity, and team maturity. I will unpack this in the functions section way below. In short, the higher the maturity and the higher the risk, the less likely escapes are to happen.

## Step 3: Empirical Bayes Enrichment

This code block creates our empirical Bayes priors. The first step is getting data. It needs to be long-run data. We use long-run data because the rate will be more stable and therefore more baselined. To get that, we pull records with 40 weeks or longer activity. We store that data in the vgroups data frame.

The vgroups data frame holds both development and production vulnerability counts. Those counts are imputed into the GetBurnMLE() function for creating optimized priors:

```
mle_vals <- GetBurnMLE(vgroups$prod_vuln, vgroups$dev_vuln )
> mle_vals
    alpha      beta
13.91220 64.43379
```

Those data-informed priors are then added back into the data. That means both long-run groups and groups with only weeks of data get updated. The mutate() function adds new columns to the group_vals data frame. It's simple Bayesian updating at work. Here is the code that does that:

```
# Posterior update for each group
group_vals <- group_vals %>%
  mutate(alpha_update = alpha + prod_vuln,
         beta_update = beta + dev_vuln)
```

We then use our new posterior data values to get credible intervals. That is the range of plausible values for the actual escape rate for each group. Here is how we get the lower and upper bounds of our 95% credible intervals:

```
# Credible intervals for each group
group_vals <- group_vals %>%
  mutate(low_ci  = qbeta(.025, alpha_update, beta_update),
         high_ci = qbeta(.975, alpha_update, beta_update))
```

Here is what our data is starting to look like. Can you see how it is all derived from simple counts of vulnerabilities?

```
group_vals %>% select(group, prod_vuln, dev_vuln, escape_avg, alpha_update,
beta_update, low_ci, high_ci)
# A tibble: 500 x 8
  group prod_vuln dev_vuln escape_avg alpha_update beta_update low_ci high_ci
  <int>     <int>    <int>      <dbl>        <dbl>       <dbl>  <dbl>   <dbl>
1     3        39      252      0.134         52.9        316. 0.109   0.181
2     6        21      186      0.101         34.9        250. 0.0870  0.163
3     9        28      170      0.141         41.9        234. 0.112   0.196
4    12        12      175     0.0642         25.9        239. 0.0650  0.136
5    15        39      239      0.140         52.9        303. 0.114   0.187
# ... with 495 more rows
```

## *Step 4: Visualize Data*

**The first visualization is of our empirical Bayes prior.** You have encountered the MakeBetaGraph() function before. It takes our optimized priors as inputs and returns a graph like this:

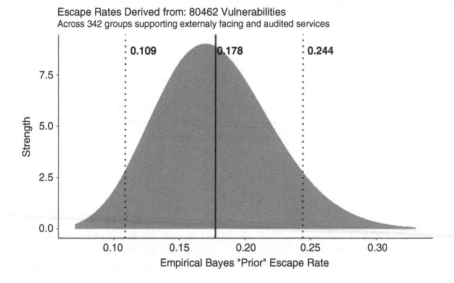

Note that the header has 80,462 vulnerabilities across 342 groups. The empirical Bayes prior is derived from that data set. Also, remember that this is three years of data. Some of the data has been removed to create a staggered effect in terms of group start. This leads to about 78 vulnerabilities a year on average per group. That is not the total vulnerability number, only those that would filter up to security's radar.

```
> 80462 / 342 / 3
[1] 78.423
```

**The second visualization is our empirical Bayes graph for 45 of the product groups.** It includes groups with a few weeks' worth of data as well as several years' worth. The shorter the width of the bar, the more certainty there is about the rate. The black dot is the Bayesian informed rate. The gray dot is the average for the specific group.

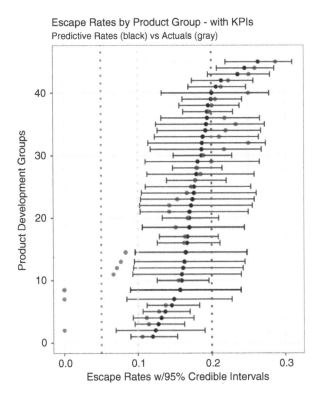

Escape Rates by Product Group - with KPIs
Predictive Rates (black) vs Actuals (gray)

Why, in some cases, are the gray dots so far away from the black dots? And why are some of the gray dots completely outside of the intervals? It's a function of data size. The wide bars have small data. The gray dots are averages. If the data is small, the average is not baselined and thus volatile. The black dots are informed by long-run trends. Specifically, from hundreds of groups that had 40 weeks of data or more – they are baselined.

For metrics purposes, we are mostly interested in the spread of the data. The spread of data retains both our certainty and our uncertainty about the underlying data generating process. We use the spread of data to measure our performance accurately. This is where KPIs come in.

I used three configurable KPIs above. Which teams "credibly" beat the 20% escape rate KPI? As you can see, it was the teams whose complete credible interval is to the left of the 20% KPI line. I count seven teams that beat the 20% KPI. This allows us to score teams reasonably well, even if their data is small and still baselining.

# Functional Decomposition

In this section I decompose each of the key functions used in our data analysis.

**The first function is GetLargeVulnGroups().** It should be familiar. It adds a small wrapper around the GetVulnGroups() function from the last chapter. GetLargeVulnGroups() can create hundreds of thousands (if not millions) of records. It takes time to generate that much data – there's a lot of math happening in the background.

Once you create *N* product teams' worth of data – GetLargeVulnGroups() saves the results to disk. On future runs, you just call it without any parameters. It will instantiate the data in minutes if not seconds.

```
GetLargeVulnGroups <- function(new = FALSE, group_count = 50,
    ext = c(.005,.03), sev = c(.031, .07), hgh = c(.071, .15)){

  # If new then build simulation
  if( new == TRUE){
    # Can take ~30 seconds to build
    dt <- GetVulnGroups(group_count, ext, sev, hgh)

    # Save for future use
    saveRDS(dt, file = "audit_df.RDS")
  }else{

    # Instantiated saved file
    dt <- readRDS("audit_df.RDS")
  }
  return(dt)
}
```

**Next comes GetEscapeGroups().** It returns a tidy aggregate dataset called group_vals. In the process, it determines which vulnerabilities escaped and which ones didn't. It also staggers our data. It does that by cutting records from certain groups, allowing us to more clearly see how empirical Bayes influences incomplete data. You saw this in the last graph. Be sure to read through the comments.

```
GetEscapeGroups <- function(dt, group_count){

  #Sets Boolean for escaped vulns
  dt$escaped <- GetEscapeVal(dt)

  # Final 25% of groups have one month of data (weeks 48-52)
  three_quarters <- group_count - round(group_count/4)
  dt_one_month <- dt %>%
    filter(group %in% three_quarters:group_count &
           (week.fseen >= 48 & week.fseen <= 52))
```

```
# Third quartile of groups has one quarter of data (weeks 39-52
half_count <- round(group_count/2)
dt_one_quarter <- dt %>%
  filter(group %in% half_count:(three_quarters-1) &
         (week.fseen >= 39 & week.fseen <= 52))

# The first half of the groups has a years worth of data
dt_full <- dt %>% filter(group < half_count & week.fseen <= 52)

# Integrate all of the data frames back into one
dt <- bind_rows(dt_one_month, dt_one_quarter, dt_full)

# Remove unwanted data frames - save on memory
dt_one_month <- dt_one_quarter <- dt_full <- NULL

# Create group aggregates
group_vals <- dt %>%
  group_by(group) %>%
  summarize(total_weeks = (max(week.fseen) - min(week.fseen)) + 1,
        prod_vuln = sum(escaped==1),
        dev_vuln = sum(escaped == 0),
        total_vulns = prod_vuln + dev_vuln,.groups = 'drop')

  return(group_vals)
}
```

**GetEscapeVal() is an important function embedded in GetEscape Groups().** Quickly read the comments prior to jumping into the narrative below.

```
GetEscapeVal <- function(dt){

  # Get random values the length of the dt dataframe
  rand_vals <- runif(nrow(dt))

  # Set the escape probability based on maturity level
  prob_escape <- dt$beta_prob/dt$dev_maturity

  # If the random val is less than the probability of escape set it to 1
  dt$escaped <- if_else(rand_vals < prob_escape,1,0)
  return(dt$escaped)
}
```

Escapes are not entirely random. They have a relationship to vulnerability severity, asset value, and dev team maturity. It's not a complete dependency. There are undoubtedly other influences on escapes that may not be observable. But, escape rates should be explainable in part by various risks as well as dev team maturity. In short, mature teams are less likely to let high-risk vulnerabilities escape – or so we hope.

The dt$beta_prob is a default variable, holding a probability that was generated based on the risk factors mentioned just above. We divide that value by the maturity level of the team. The result is the prob_escape variable. If the rand_vals is less than prob_escaped, then voilà! – the vulnerability escaped. The prob_escape variable ends up being slightly correlated to various risk factors and dev team maturity – as it should be.

In the analysis of your own data, if you were to discover that escapes have no relation to vulnerability severity, asset value, and team maturity – then you have likely discovered a problem. That problem may be in the model. Or, the process of controlling for vulnerabilities in development is not working as expected. Perhaps the problem is that teams think they are following a risk-based policy and the data shows that they aren't.

**The next critical function in our code is GetBurnMLE().** It has some advanced capabilities. I largely lifted it from David Robinson's great book, *Introduction to Empirical Bayes: Examples from Baseball Statistics*. Of course, he in turn "lifted" it from the amazing and supportive R community. I will only touch on this function in terms of *what* it does – less on the *how*.

```
GetBurnMLE <- function(hits,misses){
  ll <- function(alpha, beta) {
    x <- hits
    total <- hits + misses
    #print(total)
    -sum(VGAM::dbetabinom.ab(x, total, alpha, beta, log = TRUE))
  }

  m <- mle(ll, start = list(alpha = 1, beta = 10),
        method = "L-BFGS-B",lower = c(0.0001, .1))

  return(coef(m))
}
```

First, note the parameters for GetBurnMLE()? They are called *hits and misses*. A lot of security events can be understood as hits and misses. It's the discrete count of things that happened (hits) in relation to things that didn't (misses). It's formally called a *binomial relationship*. You can think of binomial from an etymological perspective as meaning "two names."

GetBurnMLE() searches through the mass of hit-and-miss data (binomial data) for the optimal summary of the data. It's looking for the right shape and central tendency of the data. Again, think dials on an Etch-A-Sketch. Central tendency is just a general term for the "average value" of the data. The shape can refer to the spread of data or direction of the spread – does it spread out further to the left or right, for example? The optimized summary is two numbers – our empirical Bayes priors.

**The last new function is MakeProportionChart().** It is the metrics chart I like for understanding escapes. It's easy to overlay KPIs on the data.

You are looking for teams to get their credible interval past the KPI. By past, I mean completely to the left of the KPI on the graph.

Of course, if the bar overlaps the KPI, one could claim partial KPI success. In fact, we could get very specific about how much KPI success there is. We touch on that in the dashboarding chapter.

There are several default parameters for this function. Most of them are labels. The last parameter is for setting three KPIs. You can obviously alter that to your needs.

```
MakeProportionChart <- function(df_val,
   xlab= "Escape Rates w/95% Credible Intervals",
   ylab="Product Development Groups",
   tval="Escape Rates By Product Group - With KPIs",
   sval="Predictive Rates (black) vs Actuals (red)",
   kpis = c(.05,.1,.2)){

   # The first parameter - a subset of the total data in this case
   df_val %>%

       # x-axis is bayes avg, y-axis ranked by avg.
       ggplot(aes(emp_bayes_avg, rank(emp_bayes_avg))) +

       # black dot for the emp_bayes_avg - i.e. prior
       geom_point() +

       # red dot for the data's average
       geom_point(aes(x = escape_avg), color = "red") +

       # horizontal bar for each group that is wide as the 95% ci
       geom_errorbarh(aes(xmin = low_ci, xmax = high_ci)) +

       # KP1 1 vertical line
       geom_vline(xintercept=kpis[1], color="maroon",
         size=1, linetype="dotted") +

       # KPI 2 vertical line
       geom_vline(xintercept=kpis[2], color="orangered2",
         size=1, linetype="dotted") +

       # KPI 3 vertical line
       geom_vline(xintercept=kpis[3], color="goldenrod",
         size=1, linetype="dotted") +

       # Chart Labels
       labs(x = xlab, y = ylab, title = tval, subtitle = sval) +
       theme_bw()
}
```

## Escape Rates in 10 Lines of Code

I get that some of the lines below are long. The point I am trying to make
is that you can do this sort of analysis easily – over lunch. You would need
data in the same format as I simulate it below.

I have 100 groups. I then sample 100 production vulnerabilities. I do the
same for development vulnerabilities. Your numbers do not need to fully
align with this. Your number of groups and vulnerabilities could vary widely
from what is listed here.

```
# Raw data
group_vals <- tibble(group = 1:100,
                prod_vuln = sample(10:70,100, replace = TRUE),
                dev_vuln = sample(70:300,100, replace = TRUE),
                total_vulns = prod_vuln + dev_vuln)

# Groups with over 300 vulns
vgroups <- group_vals %>% filter(total_vulns > 300)

# Get the Maximum Likelihood Estimation
mle_vals <- GetBurnMLE(vgroups$prod_vuln, vgroups$dev_vuln )

# Use MLE's to set alpha and beta vars
alpha <- mle_vals[[1]]
beta <- mle_vals[[2]]

# Bayesian Average Update All Groups
group_vals <- group_vals %>%
  mutate(emp_bayes_avg =
        (prod_vuln + alpha) / (total_vulns + alpha + beta))

# Posterior Update
group_vals <- group_vals %>%
  mutate(alpha_update = alpha + prod_vuln,
        beta_update = beta + dev_vuln)

# Credible Intervals
group_vals <- group_vals %>%
  mutate(low_ci  = qbeta(.025, alpha_update, beta_update),
        high_ci = qbeta(.975, alpha_update, beta_update))

# Basic Average
group_vals <- group_vals %>%
  mutate(escape_avg = prod_vuln / total_vulns)

# Final Chart
MakeProportionChart(df_val = group_vals)
```

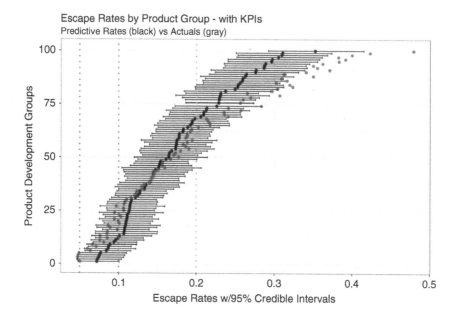

Escape Rates by Product Group - with KPIs
Predictive Rates (black) vs Actuals (gray)

## Chapter Summary

My goal with this chapter was twofold. First, to introduce escape rates. Second, to dive deeper into empirical Bayes. The good news is that the approach was not all that dissimilar to what we did for burndown rates. That was also true with arrival and wait-time rates.

The keen observer may have put this together already – we are using three algorithms for all of our baselines:

1. Survival Analysis: For measuring how long things live
2. Beta-Binomial: For measuring hit-and-miss events
3. Gamma-Poisson: For measuring the rate at which things materialize over time

The "beta" part provides our prior, informing our hits and misses. Hits and misses are a binomial process. The "gamma" portion provides our prior for the Poisson process.

Each of these prior distributions is closely related to its posteriors. Formally, they are called **conjugate priors**. Conjugate priors make moving from prior – to data – to posterior simple addition.

But alas, life is not always that easy. Data can be messy. That's because the processes that generate the data can be messy, too. We are going to upgrade our analysis. We are going to take what we learned from baselines into what I call **optimization analysis**.

Optimization analysis looks to understand what influences our rates. For example, how much does the severity of a vulnerability influence its time to live? How much does a team's assessed maturity level impact escape rates? These are just a few of the "optimization" questions we have. You will certainly have many more that are specific to your use cases.

The next part approaches these types of questions. Whole books and semester-long classes are dedicated to this topic. We are going to get as much done as we can in a quick chapter.

# Notes

1. Wikipedia contributors. (2021e, September 7). *Brownian motion.* Wikipedia. https://en.wikipedia.org/wiki/Brownian_motion
2. Atlassian. (2021a). *Monorepos in Git.* https://www.atlassian.com/git/tutorials/monorepos
3. Atlassian. (2021b). *Trunk-based Development.* https://www.atlassian.com/continuous-delivery/continuous-integration/trunk-based-development
4. Sauro, J. (2021). Better to Be Approximately Right than Exactly Wrong, *MeasuringU.* https://measuringu.com/approx-right/#:%7E:text=It's%20better%20to%20be%20approximately,famous%20economist%20and%20early%20statistician

# CHAPTER 8

# Optimization Basics with Bayesian Linear Regression

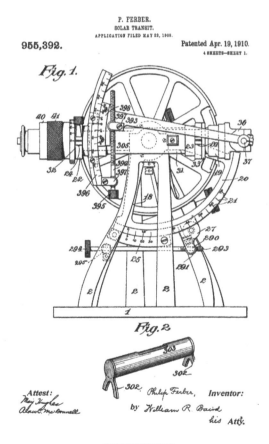

P. FERBER.
SOLAR TRANSIT.
APPLICATION FILED MAY 28, 1909.

955,392.

Patented Apr. 19, 1910.
4 SHEETS—SHEET 1.

*Fig. 1.*

*Fig. 2.*

Attest:

*Philip Ferber,* Inventor:

by *William R. Baird*
his Atty.

What do Pythagoras, Ptolemy, Pierre-Simon Laplace, Carl Friedrich Gauss, and Henri Poincaré have in common? Beyond being some of history's most elite mathematicians, they are all geodesists. Geodesists practice geodesy:

> Geodesy is the Earth science of accurately measuring and understanding Earth's geometric shape, orientation in space and gravitational field. The field also incorporates studies of how these properties change over time and equivalent measurements for other planets (known as planetary geodesy).[1]

Being a geodesist was all the rage back in the

day. One of its practical applications was shipping – and shipping was big money. Getting goods to their destination efficiently was key. Geodesy was like an early form of GPS – without the satellites.

Variables at play include the ship's position, various heavenly bodies, and other forces. The geodesist made models with these changing data points, analyzing their relationships one to another, to optimize the flow of goods.

Carl Friedrich Gauss must have been the Michael Jordan of geodesists. Although, his preoccupation was less nautical – he liked comets.[2] He thought geodesy was a bit pedestrian. He even quipped, *"All the measurements in the world are not worth one theorem by which the science of eternal truth is genuinely advanced."* His intellectual prejudices aside, he still published two volumes on geodesy.

Nestled in his measurement work was a simple method that interests us – a method so trivial that he originally ignored it. That is, until one of his peers published a paper on it. Only then did Gauss stand up and claim his invention.

Gauss's little "ignored" discovery is at the center of modern statistics and data science today.[3] What did he discover? A simple optimization tool based on a line. You have likely heard of it as the regression line – or regression analysis. I think that is an uninformative name for what is a simple concept. Gauss's discovery is simply about relationships – specifically, how data are related and influence one another.

We will work toward models that answer relational questions like, *"How much do risk scores influence remediation time? Do development team security capabilities make a measurable difference? Can we use these variables to better predict and plan for risk?"* We do all of this within a Bayesian framework.

It is in that spirit of squeezing relationship information out of data that we will ultimately explore optimization. Indeed, our main optimization tool is Bayesian regression analysis, but we need to crawl, walk, then run into that topic. In fact, there are whole semester-long graduate courses that focus on regression analysis. I can only dedicate a partial chapter to the topic. That means my goal for you is exposure to Bayesian regression analysis.

The good news is that there are ample APIs that take care of huge swaths of regression complexity on our behalf. We will get to those soon. First, let's add a new tool to our tool belt: grid approximation.

# Grid Approximation

Our metrics up to now have consisted of baselines. They are singular rate metrics. They are the workhorses of any metrics program.

Along the way, we upgraded our baselines with Bayesian data analysis. This enabled two things. First, the Bayesian approach keeps us honest. It forces us to retain our uncertainty – particularly when data is small. Second, it keeps us from obscuring what certainty we have.

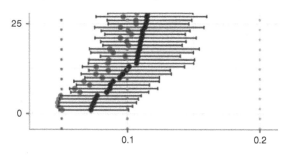

Look back to the last graph in the previous chapter. It is a perfect example of retaining our uncertainty without obscuring our certainty. The horizontal bands show our uncertainty about the true escape rate. The gray dot was a specific group average. The black dot is the empirical Bayes average – updated by all the data.

The bottom 25 groups clearly beat the 20% KPI. Do you see the vertical line to the far right? Also, it looks like only one team beat, or met, the 10% KPI. We would be skeptical of the 10% KPI. Depending on what is at risk, we may require more evidence that the KPI is thoroughly beaten.

Bayesian methods allow us to create metrics like this. Bayesian methods score what is plausible among the possible. For example, the last group in the image above scored the 5% to 10% range as most plausible. In fact, 5% to 10% is its 89% highest density interval (HDI). How did we score our data in this manner? We used grid approximation. We just didn't talk about it – until now.

## Introducing Grid Approximation

Hidden within our Bayesian baselines is a method we have used but skirted around. It's called grid approximation. It's a simple approach for exploring and scoring plausible rates. It's a conceptual steppingstone to a more advanced method called Markov Chain Monte Carlo, or MCMC for short.[4]

It will help to understand grid approximation prior to picking up MCMC. Unfortunately, we can only touch on the smallest portion of MCMC in this book. The good news is that our aforementioned APIs take care of all the MCMC complexity – so we can focus on analytic productivity. Nonetheless, a little bit of "point of view" work can go a long way toward making you productive.

## Beta-Binomial Grid Approximation

Our first example uses a simple beta-binomial model. Burndown and escape rates are in essence beta-binomial models. That means what I am about to share should be very familiar by now.

Our newest concept to introduce is grid approximation. It's a discreet method for exploring "probability space."[5] Probability space is the realm of possibilities that your algorithms will search through to uncover what is plausible – given your data and your model. It's a crude exploration tool, while MCMC is more expressive and powerful.

In the following code I call our grid the "possible_grid." It represents all possibilities in our search. In this case, it's a fine-grained grid of 10,000 possibilities ranging from zero to one.

**Here is the setup for our analysis:** It is the first quarter of the year. You have a one-week remediation policy for critical vulnerabilities. At the end of the quarter, you find that you have 9 critical (break-the-glass) vulnerabilities that were fixed within SLA and 21 that were not. That is a total of 30 critical vulnerabilities for the quarter. Your burndown average is 30%.

Of course, there is zero uncertainty in that number. We shouldn't trust it. In fact, you ask your team what they think. Let's assume they say they are ambivalent. To them, the true burndown rate is just as likely to be above 30% as it is to be below that number. In contrast, they are pretty darn sure the rate is almost always below 60%. We will use these values as our subjective priors.

Now let's run our model. The code should be familiar territory, so I won't go over many code details. As always, read the code comments.

## Beta-Binomial Example

```
# Code available on www.themetricsmanifesto.com

source("manifesto_functions.R")   #book functions

# Make grid of 10K sequential possibilities between 0 to 1
plausible_rates  <- data.frame(
     possible_grid = seq(from = 0, to = 1, length = 10000))

# Get Expert Beliefs (30% and 60%) About Burndown Rates
p_vals <- GetBeliefsEvents(.3,.6)

# Get Prior and Likelihood
plausible_rates <- plausible_rates %>%
  mutate(prior = dbeta(possible_grid, p_vals[1], p_vals[2]),
         likelihood = dbinom(9, 30, possible_grid))

# Get Posterior
plausible_rates <- plausible_rates %>%
  mutate(unnormalized = likelihood * prior,
         posterior = unnormalized / sum(unnormalized))
```

```
# Simulate 10K samples weighted on posterior
post_sample <- sample_n(plausible_rates, size = 10000,
                         weight = posterior, replace = TRUE)

# Get HDIs for graph
ci_hdi <- ci(post_sample$possible_grid, method = "HDI")
ci_low <- round(ci_hdi$CI_low,4) * 100
ci_high <- round(ci_hdi$CI_high,4) * 100

# Plot
ggplot(post_sample, aes(x = possible_grid)) +

  # Histogram and Curve (alter binwidth to the desired grain)
  geom_histogram(aes(y = ..density..), color = "white", binwidth = 0.01) +
  geom_density(alpha=.1, fill="white")+

  # HDI Low
  geom_vline(xintercept=ci_hdi$CI_low, color="black", size=1,
    linetype="dotted") +

  # HDI High
  geom_vline(xintercept=ci_hdi$CI_high, color="black", size=1,
    linetype="dotted") +

  # Make x-axis stretch full range
  lims(x = c(0, 1)) +

  # Labels for graph
  labs(x = "Plausible Rates",
       y = "Strength",
       title = "Beta-Binomial Example",
       subtitle = paste0("89% CI Low: ", ci_low , " CI High: ", ci_high)) +

  # Clean black and white theme
  theme_bw()
```

That code should seem very familiar. What is a little different is the method of simulation. The data we simulated populates our graph. Before we look at the graph, let's explore what our simulation actually did.

First, we created a data frame called post_sample. Here, *post* is short for "posterior." And sample referring to the fact that it is generated from sampling.

Sample() pulls records from the plausible_rate data frame and stuffs them into post_sample. It does this based on the posterior column values. The larger the posterior's value, the more records are sampled. You can see this below. I show the largest posterior probability value from post_sample:

```
> head(post_sample %>% select(possible_grid, posterior) %>%
arrange(desc(posterior)),5)
    possible_grid    posterior
1      0.2915292 0.0005140667
2      0.2915292 0.0005140667
3      0.2915292 0.0005140667
4      0.2915292 0.0005140667
5      0.2915292 0.0005140667
```

Based on the prior data, ~29% is the most plausible value. In fact, 10% of the post_sample records are in the 29% range. The associated posterior values look small. That's because they were transformed to sum to 1. You can see their pre-transformed value in the unnormalized column from post_sample here:

```
possible_grid    prior likelihood unnormalized     posterior
  0.2914291 1.868224  0.1564584    0.2922994 0.0005140663
```

The following graph shows the relative count of plausible grid elements after sampling. Where the bars are higher, there is more posterior probability.

We shouldn't fixate on any one rate. There is a band of credible values. The most credible values range between 18.55% and 42.89%. That's our 89% HDI. It is the smallest range of plausible values, with the densest (tallest) amount of probability. It helps us to be honest with what we do and don't know – given the data and our model. The grid approximation approach gave us these results.

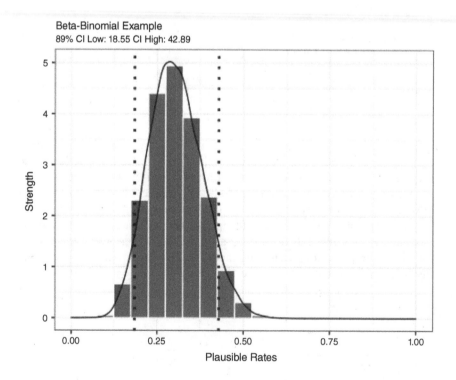

## *Gamma-Poisson Grid Approximation*

Let's do one more grid approximation. In this scenario, we will use the gamma-poisson model. Arrival and wait-time baselines use the gamma-poisson distribution. Much of the following code and concepts should be familiar. I will go through this example quickly.

> If you are looking for a very simple no-code and minimal-math explanation of both the gamma-poisson and beta-binomial models, I highly recommend the book *Bayesian Statistics for Beginners*.[6]

Imagine you are 10 weeks into the first quarter. During that time, 25 extreme vulnerabilities arrived. Your belief is that these vulnerabilities will arrive at a rate of three events every two weeks. Let's combine these four data values in a grid approximation to learn more about our vulnerability arrival rate.

```
# Subjective Priors, equals 1.5 per week i.e. 3/2
prior_events <- 3
prior_weeks <-2

# Data, which equals 2.5 per week 25/10
total_events <- 25
total_weeks <- 10

# Make grid of 10K sequential values between 0 to 5
plausible_rates    <- data.frame(possible_grid =
                        seq(from = 0, to = 5, length = 10000))

# Get Prior and Likelihood
plausible_rates <- plausible_rates %>%
  mutate(prior = dgamma(possible_grid, prior_events, prior_weeks),
        likelihood = dpois(total_events, possible_grid * total_weeks))

# Get Posterior
plausible_rates <- plausible_rates %>%
  mutate(unnormalized = likelihood * prior,
        posterior = unnormalized / sum(unnormalized))

# Simulate 10K samples weighted on posterior
post_sample <- sample_n(plausible_rates, size = 10000,
                        weight = posterior, replace = TRUE)

# 89% Highest Density Intervals
ci_hdi <- ci(post_sample$possible_grid,method = "HDI")
ci_low <- round(ci_hdi$CI_low,2)
ci_high <- round(ci_hdi$CI_high,2)

# Histogram of posterior sample
ggplot(post_sample, aes(x = possible_grid)) +
  geom_histogram(aes(y = ..density..), color = "white", bins = 100) +
  geom_density(alpha=.1, fill="white")+
```

```
# HDI Low
geom_vline(xintercept=ci_hdi$CI_low, color="black", size=1,
    linetype="dotted") +

# HDI High
geom_vline(xintercept=ci_hdi$CI_high, color="black", size=1,
    linetype="dotted") +

# Graph Labels
labs(x = "Plausible Rates",
     y = "Strength",
     title = "Gamma-Poisson Example",
     subtitle = paste0("89% CI Low: ", ci_low , " CI High: ", ci_high)) +
lims(x = c(0, 5))
```

Before we look at the graph, let's check in again on our sampled grid. The big difference between this grid and the last one is count data; yet the same sampling principles apply. Post_sample is filled with values in proportion to the posterior.

Querying post_samples reveals our most plausible arrival rates. We query for the highest posterior values to get the most plausible single rate. You see those rates in the possible_grid column below. Unsurprisingly, the top rate is very close to 2.5 events per week.

> **Note:** If you queried for the highest possible_grid value, you would NOT get the highest posterior value. Posterior is our index into our plausible rates.

Our data's empirical average was 2.5 events per week (25/10). The prior was at 1.5 (3/2). The prior has one week of data compared to the 10 weeks of data for the likelihood. So, the prior exerts some influence – but not overwhelming influence – on the likelihood. That influence produces our posterior values. And it is those values that point to our most plausible rates of 2.25 events per week, which is a compromise between the prior and the likelihood.

```
> head(post_sample %>% arrange(desc(posterior)),10)
    possible_grid      prior likelihood unnormalized      posterior
1       2.250225 0.2249009 0.06956647   0.01564556 0.0004592859
2       2.250225 0.2249009 0.06956647   0.01564556 0.0004592859
3       2.250225 0.2249009 0.06956647   0.01564556 0.0004592859
4       2.250225 0.2249009 0.06956647   0.01564556 0.0004592859
5       2.250225 0.2249009 0.06956647   0.01564556 0.0004592859
6       2.249725 0.2250259 0.06952782   0.01564556 0.0004592858
7       2.249725 0.2250259 0.06952782   0.01564556 0.0004592858
8       2.249725 0.2250259 0.06952782   0.01564556 0.0004592858
9       2.249725 0.2250259 0.06952782   0.01564556 0.0004592858
10      2.249725 0.2250259 0.06952782   0.01564556 0.0004592858
```

And here is our posterior predictive graph based on grid approximation:

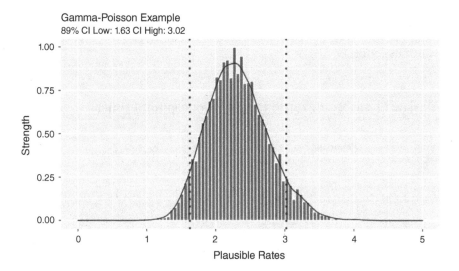

This wraps up grid approximation. You used it in previous chapters without even knowing what it was at the time. All we did here was get explicit about what a grid is and what it does. And the other difference was our extensive use of sampling across the Bayesian sets of priors, likelihood, posterior, and so on.

Now we drop grids and pick up chains. Specifically, we are going to start using MCMC.

Before we jump into MCMC modeling, let us explain what MCMC is and its purpose – as simply as possible. Statisticians and other scientists expect to see proofs and other maths. We, on the other hand, only need to know enough to use the tool...for now.

## Steps Toward Optimization: Using MCMC-Based Regression

This is the most technically challenging section of the book. What makes it challenging are the concepts of MCMC and regression modeling. As stated, multiple books have been written on these topics. The good news is that this chapter is relatively short. I can only hope to lightly introduce these new concepts to you in a friendly manner – and encourage you to go deeper.

The APIs we will use remove a lot of surface complexity. A small amount of conceptual understanding will help. I start by explaining MCMC. After that, we will jump right into regression modeling. My hope is that this section will set you up to explore the depths of Bayesian regression modeling on your own. It requires some amount of dedication, but it is well worth the effort.

## Markov Chain Monte Carlo (MCMC) Conceptual Primer

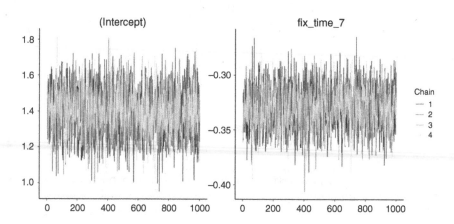

**Let's start by distinguishing MCMC from grid approximation.** Grid approximation relies on a discrete grid of possibilities. We had two types of possibilities in the previous section. The first grid held values between zero and one. These were probabilities. The second grid held values between zero and five. These were rates.

The values in the grid were sequentially compared to data. The values that were most compatible with the data scored higher. Meaning, they had more posterior probability and thus were the most plausible representatives of what we were measuring.

**Unlike grid approximation, MCMC doesn't have a tidy grid of sequential values to walk through.** Instead, MCMC randomly proposes values to explore. A proposal is like asking, "What do you think about .35?"

Proposals are either accepted or rejected. If they are accepted, then you move to that proposal. If they are rejected, then you stay put – for the moment. We accept or reject a proposal based on a set of rules. The "propose – move – stay" cycle repeats thousands of times. The result is the "chain" of MCMC simulation.

You can see a couple of chain examples in the images just above. They show how a range of possibilities are explored. The most plausible values are explored more frequently. Below, you see output of an MCMC as it runs, showing one of four chains. Each chain has many thousands of explorations across various proposals. The "warmup" phase is a learning phase where the MCMC warms itself to the data before jumping into the real "sampling" work.

```
SAMPLING FOR MODEL 'bernoulli' NOW (CHAIN 1).
Chain 1: Iteration:     1 / 10000 [  0%]  (Warmup)
Chain 1: Iteration: 1000 / 10000 [ 10%]  (Warmup)
Chain 1: Iteration: 2000 / 10000 [ 20%]  (Warmup)
Chain 1: Iteration: 3000 / 10000 [ 30%]  (Warmup)
Chain 1: Iteration: 4000 / 10000 [ 40%]  (Warmup)
Chain 1: Iteration: 5000 / 10000 [ 50%]  (Warmup)
Chain 1: Iteration: 5001 / 10000 [ 50%]  (Sampling)
Chain 1: Iteration: 6000 / 10000 [ 60%]  (Sampling)
Chain 1: Iteration: 7000 / 10000 [ 70%]  (Sampling)
Chain 1: Iteration: 8000 / 10000 [ 80%]  (Sampling)
Chain 1: Iteration: 9000 / 10000 [ 90%]  (Sampling)
Chain 1: Iteration: 10000 / 10000 [100%]  (Sampling)
```

MCMC succeeds when other methods (like grid approximation) fail. It is a much more efficient sampling algorithm for complex analysis. The good news is that the statistical APIs we use transparently run MCMCs. They take care of the details so you can focus on measurement.

## Steps Toward Bayesian Regression Modeling Using MCMC

We are going to create a predictive model. It is a Bayesian regression model that uses MCMC under the hood. **For now, think of regression as a tool for prediction and or analysis.** You are doing prediction if you want to know the likelihood of an event happening given a specific context. You are doing analysis if you want to know how much context matters in prediction – context being things like asset exposure, regulatory status, vulnerability, and/or threat severity, and so on.

The model we build analyzes remediation policy and predicts SLA achievement. Our first step is creating our data set and doing some quick analysis. After that, we will run our first MCMC simulation.

This section leverages work done by the authors of rstanarm, the API we will be using.[7] It is a probabilistic programming API. There is ample material online and several books on using rstanarm. A recent publication for beginners worthy of deep exploration is "Regression and Other Stories."[8]

We are reverting to piecemeal simulation by creating four specific product groups. Note how I incremented the event probabilities for each group. Group one has the lowest event likelihoods for each of the three severity levels, with the highest developer maturity level. We will see what (or if) our analysis can learn about these different groups.

```
# Build for product groups with vulns
dtGroupOne <- GetAdvSecResults(c(.03,.05,.15),1,4)
dtGroupOne$group <- 1

dtGroupTwo <- GetAdvSecResults(c(.05,.08,.18),1,3)
dtGroupTwo$group <- 2

dtGroupThree <- GetAdvSecResults(c(.07,.10,.20),1,2)
dtGroupThree$group <- 3

dtGroupFour <- GetAdvSecResults(c(.10,.15,.25),1,1)
dtGroupFour$group <- 4

dt <- bind_rows(dtGroupOne, dtGroupTwo, dtGroupThree, dtGroupFour)
```

We don't need all 20-plus fields from the dt data frame for our analysis. The following code creates a smaller eight-column data set. Note the addition of two new columns: fixed_in_sla and fix_time_7. The former variable is a Boolean flag. If the vulnerability was fixed within SLA, it gets a 1; otherwise it's a 0. The other column scales fix_time so that it is based on weeks. Lastly, we print out a graph that shows overall remediation policy compliance.

```
# Get basic subset of columns
basic <- dt %>%
    select(group, dev_maturity, audit, exposure, severity, fix_time) %>%

    # Check if SLAs were met based on risk
    mutate(fixed_in_sla = mapply(sla_check,fix_time,severity,exposure,audit))

    # Re-scale fix time from days to weeks
    basic$fix_time_7 <- basic$fix_time/7

# Plot policy histogram to compare fixed from not
ggplot(basic, aes(x = fix_time_7, y = ..density..,
    fill = fixed_in_sla == 1)) +
    geom_histogram() +
    scale_fill_manual(values = c("gray30", "skyblue"))
```

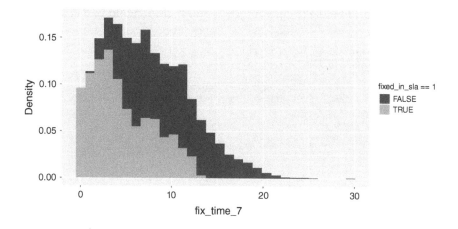

The gray and black chart above aggregates responses to a specific policy. The ideal chart is all gray. That means everything is within policy. Over time, it *may* be good to see the gray distribution shift left, indicating that policy requirements are getting shorter – and responses are happening quicker. That is a form of "acceleration."

If your business is creating more risk and your capabilities are keeping up (meaning no movement in the gray distribution), we would say you are scaling. Scaling may be adequate if risk is being managed to policy.

Lastly, it would be good to see a decrease in risk volume. That could be an indication of risk arrival and escape rate management effectiveness. Meaning, your shift-left capabilities are having a measurable impact on controlling for risk creation and policy achievement.

There is one new item in the code above. That is the call to mapply(). Think of it as a fast way of looping through data. As mapply() loops, it calls the sla_check() function.

The sla_check() function takes in the following data: fix_time, severity, exposure, and audit. It uses those values to determine if policy was met. If met, sla_check() returns a 1. If not, it returns a 0.

The code for sla_check() is just below. It represents a vulnerability management policy made from nine rules. It is more pedagogical than

practical. You should create your own rules given your particular data
and context:

```
# Returns boolean values based on policy check
sla_check <- function(fix_time,severity,exposure,audit){

  # Rule 1: Top Risk: Extreme, External, Audit
  if(severity == "extreme" & exposure == "external" & audit == 0){
    if( fix_time <= 7){
      return(1)
    }else{
      return(0)
    }
  }

  # Rule 2: External Risky Assets
  if((severity == "extreme" & exposure == "external") |
     (severity == "critical" & exposure == "external" & audit == 0)){
    if( fix_time <= 14){
      return(1)
    }else{
      return(0)
    }
  }

  # Rule 3: External Moderately Risk
  if((severity == "critical" & exposure == "external") |
     (severity == "high" & exposure == "external" & audit == 0)){
    if(fix_time <= 21){
      return(1)
    }else{
      return(0)
    }
  }

  # Rule 4: Introduce Extreme Partner Risk
  if((severity == "high" & exposure == "external") |
     (severity == "extreme" & exposure == "partner" & audit == 0)){
    if(fix_time <= 28){
      return(1)
    }else{
      return(0)
    }
  }

  # Rule 5: Partner Facing Risk
  if((severity == "extreme" & exposure == "partner") |
     (severity == "critical" & exposure == "partner" & audit == 0) ){
    if(fix_time <= 35){
      return(1)
    }else{
      return(0)
    }
  }
```

```
# Rule 6: Introduce Internally Facing Risk
if((severity == "critical" & exposure == "partner") |
   (severity == "extreme" & exposure == "internal" & audit == 0) ){
  if(fix_time <= 42){
    return(1)
  }else{
    return(0)
  }
}

# Rule 7: Internally Facing Risk
if((severity == "extreme" & exposure == "internal") |
   (severity == "critical" & exposure == "internal" & audit == 0) ){
  if(fix_time <= 60){
    return(1)
  }else{
    return(0)
  }
}

# Rule 8: Internal General Risk
if((severity == "critical" & exposure == "internal") |
   (severity == "high" & exposure == "internal" & audit == 0) ){
  if(fix_time <= 75){
    return(1)
  }else{
    return(0)
  }
}

# Rule 9: Longest Policy Timeframe
if(severity == "high" & exposure == "internal"){
  if(fix_time <= 90){
    return(1)
  }else{
    return(0)
  }
}
return(0)
}
```

Following you see what our basic data frame looks like. Our regression model will use this data for analysis and prediction:

| | group | dev_maturity | audit | exposure | severity | fix_time | fixed_in_sla | fix_time_7 |
|---|---|---|---|---|---|---|---|---|
| | <int> | <fct> | <dbl> | <chr> | <fct> | <dbl> | <dbl> | <dbl> |
| 1 | 31 | 4 | 1 | partner | high | 43 | 0 | 6.14 |
| 2 | 13 | 4 | 0 | external | critical | 35 | 0 | 5 |
| 3 | 61 | 4 | 0 | partner | high | 79 | 0 | 11.3 |
| 4 | 44 | 3 | 1 | external | high | 63 | 0 | 9 |
| 5 | 66 | 1 | 1 | external | high | 80 | 0 | 11.4 |
| 6 | 21 | 4 | 1 | external | high | 84 | 0 | 12 |
| 7 | 14 | 2 | 1 | internal | critical | 60 | 1 | 8.57 |
| 8 | 17 | 3 | 0 | internal | critical | 82 | 0 | 11.7 |
| 9 | 34 | 4 | 1 | external | high | 53 | 0 | 7.57 |
| 10 | 4 | 1 | 1 | internal | critical | 47 | 1 | 6.71 |

# A Brief Introduction to Regression Analysis

We are going to focus on two questions:

- What is the probability of meeting SLAs?
- What factors influence that probability?

In security, we have many time-bound activities. The time frame for action is based on risk. Risk considers threats, vulnerabilities, and value at risk. A response is considered out of policy if it doesn't happen in time based on risk. This is why policy analysis should be a core part of any security metrics program.

## *Regression Analysis Helps Us Understand Policy Achievement and Possible Outcomes*

Regression analysis helps us to understand what contributes to policy achievement and to forecast policy outcomes. An obvious contributing factor to policy compliance is time. As time increases, the likelihood of exceeding policy grows. Let's find out what the average SLA achievement rate is:

```
mean(basic$fixed_in_sla)
[1] 0.39
```

Across all nine rules that make up our SLA policy, we are achieving a ~39% SLA compliance rate. (That doesn't seem great.) Are high-risk vulnerabilities getting priority? Are teams with low capabilities responsible for the low compliance rate? Or, is there some other reason for poor rate?

---

**Note:** Some of the code for the following section is influenced by a free online book called *Bayes Rules! An Introduction to Bayesian Modeling with R*.[9] The chapters on logistic regression are useful.

While I am praising books, another that provides great coverage on Bayesian logistic regression is called *Reasoning with Data* by Jefferey M. Stanton.[10]

Almost any book on Bayesian data analysis will provide ample coverage for logistic regression. These two books are accessible to beginners – and the first is freely accessible.

## Logistic Regression for Policy Assessment and Management

When I want to analyze policy compliance, I turn to logistic regression. It analyzes yes/no, true/false, pass/fail, etc. outcomes. These are all binary responses. Logistic regression weighs the relationship between binary response rates and the data that influences them.

For example, do externally facing and regulated assets impact policy compliance? Are vulnerabilities that impact these assets more likely to meet policy than their internally facing counterparts? Should these vulnerabilities be fixed faster? And if so, by how much?

As a seasoned security expert, you know the squeaky wheel gets the grease. The most toxic vulnerabilities get the most attention. They are in the news and all eyes are on you to act. You likely see spikes in compliance for bad risks and a lull everywhere else.

Conversely, you may see less critical vulnerabilities with long lead times getting remediated within SLA. Worse, there may be exponentially more low-risk vulnerabilities getting fixed than their high-risk counterparts. There are many reasons for this. Often, it's a function of IT patch schedules. Or, it's a function of complexity. Easy-to-patch items on less critical assets go first. It's less disruptive.

I have worked with clients that thought they knew how their policies were being exercised. They were surprised to learn the truth – they had the wrong objects of measurement. (Think back to the WWII bomber story in Chapter 1.) What is your policy? Is it optimized for the right risks?

**Logistic regression excels at answering these sorts of questions.** It weighs how much something is likely to matter (or not), given your data. Does the fact that an asset is externally facing matter as much as you think it should? How much are other risk factors you care about having an influence on policy execution?

The weighing process in logistic regression is called an odds ratio. For now, you can think of it as the odds in gambling. The other tool logistic regression uses for measurement is the log scale. You can think of the log scale as a form of data compression. The larger the value, the more compression is applied. For example, $\log(10) \sim 2.3$ and $\log(100) \sim 4.6$ and $\log(1000) \sim 6.9$. Taken together, odds and the log scale are called **log odds**. **You don't need to think too hard about this.** You just need to be able to recognize it when you see it.

## Logistic Regression Priors

We know our vulnerability management SLA is met 39% of the time in the aggregate. As time passes, SLAs are put at risk. Likewise, with more time, more work gets done. It is a catch-22. Given this dilemma, where do we start measuring? Let's begin with the highest-risk items.

Of all the *extreme* risks you encounter, what percentage are closed within SLA? This is going to be the starting value for our regression models. Let's assume it's a value that only gets worse over time. That is because extremely exploitable risks (the ones in the news) get the lion's share of the attention. Lesser risk items get put on the back burner.

Extreme risks are the ones that are externally facing and remotely exploitable. In our use case, the most critical ones have a one-week SLA. Let's assume we *believe* those are closed within SLA 65% of the time – which is not great. We also believe it could be in the 80% to 50% range or more. We are highly uncertain.

The graph below represents our encoded prior beliefs about SLA compliance rates. It's called a prior predictive graph. Prior predictive graphs make our assumptions (beliefs) clear. As you can see, the graph expresses a lot of uncertainty. Yet, it also makes clear that as time progresses, policy achievement wanes. The code that created this graph is just below.

In this case, I consider our development of priors pedagogical. Our data set is large enough to overwhelm our priors. Also, the API we are using supplies weakly informative priors. We will be using those priors later in the chapter. Specifying your own priors matters most when data is small.

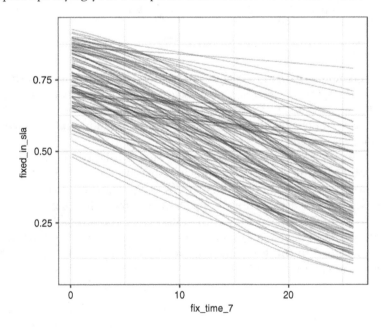

This is our first MCMC simulation. It creates the data for our graph. While we do pass a data frame in, it's only used to populate the axis of the graph. If prior_PD was set to FALSE, then the data values would matter. Since we are developing our priors, we set priore_PD to TRUE.

The portion we are going to focus on is the third and fourth lines of code with the two variables: prior_intercept and prior. They give the location and shape to the lines in our graph.

The values supplied for our variables are log odds. They help discover the probability of something being true or false, yes or no, on or off, etc., that would otherwise not be possible to find on a normal scale.

Read through the comments before moving on to the detailed narrative.

```
# Bayesian MCMC Logistic Regression Model
fit_prior_1 <- stan_glm(

    # How does meeting SLA relate to time?
    fixed_in_sla ~ fix_time_7,

    # What is the average prior probability of meeting SLA?
    prior_intercept = normal(0.62, .52),

    # How much influence does each week have on reducing SLA achievement
    prior = normal(-.08, .03),

    # We are using a binomial model with a log scale
    family=binomial(link="logit"),

    # Reference our data frame
    data=basic,

    # Return prior predictive results - as opposed to posterior
    prior_PD = TRUE)
```

Think of the prior_intercept as a *starter rate*. It is a rate that will have other values meshed with it to flesh out the policy.

The prior_intercept is modeled using the normal distribution. The normal distribution is frequently used for modeling continuous numbers that can be positive or negative. That is why we can use it to model log odds values. Log odds are continuous and either positive or negative. I am going to assume most readers have seen the bell curve associated with the normal distribution. Unlike some of the other distributions you have encountered to this point, this one is always symmetrical around its central tendency.

If log odds seem confusing, then rest assured you are not alone. Even experts have trouble translating between odds and probabilities – let alone log odds to probabilities. Don't overthink them ... yet.

In this particular use case, the normal distribution takes two log odds values as inputs. They define the central tendency and shape of our beliefs about the intercept. The first log odds value is 0.62. That translates to 65%. The second value tells us how spread out our uncertainty is around 65%. I wanted a value that was pretty wide ranging. Why? I am uncertain about the starting rate and where it really belongs. I use the second value to express that uncertainty.

Without getting too deep in the nitty-gritty of translating log odds to probabilities – we can use a function I wrote called getLogOddsInt(). It helps define the prior for our intercept. It's meant to jumpstart your prior exploration.

The getLogOddsInt() function takes a probability and scale value as an input. It returns two log odds values. The first value returned is the central tendency (0.62) and the other is the spread of that value. Both values are in log odds scale. You will want to adjust the second value to reflect your uncertainty – aka the spread of the lines.

```
getLogOddsInt(prob = .65, scale = 1.2)
[1] 0.62  0.60

getLogOddsInt <- function (prob, scale){

  # Turn probability into odds
  odds <- prob/(1-prob)

  # Turn odds into log odds
  logOdds <- log(odds)

  # Get spread around the central tendency
  sdev <- abs(round(logOdds/scale,2))

  # Return
  return(c(logOdds,sdev))
}
```

Back to our MCMC simulation, the second prior (called "prior") weighs time. It defines how much the SLA rate changes over time. It is commonly called the slope of the line. You can think of it as a value that changes the line's direction as time passes. We also use a normal() distribution to define this prior value.

Notice that the first parameter to the prior distribution is a relatively small negative value of –0.08. That is why the graph is gradually sloping downward from left to right. As each week passes, the line moves downward. If you wanted a steep slope, you would use a larger value. To slope a line in the opposite direction, you would add a positive value. The amount of movement (wiggle) on the slope is also relatively small. I set it for .03.

Now let's look at the code for the lined graph. It takes both the MCMC prior model output and portions of our data as input. It is quite short.

```
# Pipe in our data frame
basic %>% select(fix_time_7, fixed_in_sla) %>%

    # TidyBayes function for drawing values from prior (or posterior)
    add_epred_draws(fit_prior_1, ndraws = 100) %>%

    # Structure the x and y axis
    ggplot(aes(x = fix_time_7, y = fixed_in_sla)) +

    # Create lines based on prior definitions and data
    geom_line(aes(y = .epred, group = .draw), size = 0.1)+
    theme_bw()
```

What is not obvious is that we are simulating from the prior, creating about 400,000 records. The add_epred_draws() function does this. It's a function from the very useful tidybayes R package.[11] Let's look at the inner workings more closely.

Below, I extract the data from add_epred_draws(). First, I print out how many records were created using the nrow() function. It's a sizable sample. Next, I show a random sample of 10 records. The .epred values hop around, reflecting the uncertainty we encoded in our priors. I then get mean values for weeks 1, 5, and 10. I do that just to make the slope of the lines more apparent. Each week has over 3,000 records that we average over. (Note how weeks are fractional. My queries below consider those values using %in%. That just means I want to consider all the values within a range. For example, week five includes 5 to 5.99.)

```
# Pull data for graph into a data frame
res <- basic %>% select(fix_time_7, fixed_in_sla) %>%
    add_epred_draws(fit_prior_1, ndraws = 100)

# Show how much data add_epred_draws() simulates
nrow(res)
[1] 395700

# View values from res data frame
   fixed_in_sla fix_time_7 .epred
          <dbl>      <dbl>  <dbl>
1             1       2.57  0.781
2             1       1.71  0.547
3             1       6.57  0.673
4             1       8.29  0.762
5             1       5.14  0.450
6             1       3      0.933
7             1       8.29  0.659
8             1       0.143  0.577
9             1       5.29  0.491
10            1       7.71  0.576
```

```
# Get mean values based on fix_time_7 for weeks 1, 5, 10
> mean(res$.epred[(res$fix_time_7 <= 1 & res$fixed_in_sla == 1)])
[1] 0.77
> mean(res$.epred[(res$fix_time_7 %in% 5:5.99 & res$fixed_in_sla == 1)])
[1] 0.69
> mean(res$.epred[(res$fix_time_7 %in% 10:10.99 & res$fixed_in_sla == 1)])
[1] 0.60
```

Let's look at another view of our data, this time as a histogram. And this time we are going to mix our prior with real data to get our posterior model. The new model is called sla_model_1. We create sla_model_1 in the following section titled MCMC Posterior Quality. The histogram meshes our prior beliefs with the data. The prior only exerts minimal influence on the model due to the amount of data we have. We would say that the data overwhelms the prior's influence.

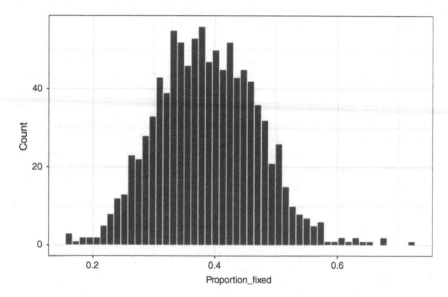

Here is the code that created this graph. It uses a somewhat similar function to our previous example for generating a massive amount of draws from the prior.

```
# Data frame as input
basic %>%

  # This first function creates millions of records.
  add_predicted_draws(sla_model_1, ndraws = 1000) %>%
  group_by(.draw) %>%
```

```
# Get proportion of fixed records
summarize(proportion_fixed = mean(.prediction == 1),.groups='drop') %>%

# Make a simple histogram
ggplot(aes(x = proportion_fixed)) +
geom_histogram(color = "white",bins=50)+
theme_bw()
```

## MCMC Posterior Quality

Next we are going to build the aforementioned posterior. That means mesh-ing our data with our prior. Before we get too far with our model, we also need to do some MCMC quality checks. We want to know if the model is reliable. To that end, I have added a few quality checks that we want to run after our model builds.

```
# Build Posterior Model
sla_model_1 <- update(fit_prior_1, prior_PD = FALSE)

# Inspect MCMC Chains - look for chain stability
mcmc_trace(sla_model_1)

# Inspect MCMC Posterior Distributions by Chain - look for overlap
mcmc_dens_overlay(sla_model_1)

# Auto-correlation check - look for quick drop to 0
mcmc_acf(sla_model_1)

# R-hat check - variance in chains over variance across - should be ~1
rhat(sla_model_1)

# Auto-correlation check - Above .1 desirable
neff_ratio(sla_model_1)

# Check posterior values for ROPE...should be 0% out of ROPE
describe_posterior(sla_model_1)
```

| Parameter | Median | 89% CI | pd | 89% ROPE | % in ROPE | Rhat | ESS |
|-----------|--------|--------|-----|----------|-----------|------|-----|
| (Intercept) | 1.550 | [ 1.426, 1.666] | 100.00% | [-0.181, 0.181] | 0 | 1.000 | 12354.545 |
| fix_time_7 | -0.289 | [-0.306, -0.273] | 100.00% | [-0.181, 0.181] | 0 | 1.000 | 11033.052 |

There are numerous tests you can run to ensure your model is stable.[12] The above code is just a start. The first function "**mcmc_trace**" created the two caterpillar graphs at the beginning of the section on MCMC. It shows that our MCMC chains stabilized. They effectively explored proba-bility space. That's why all four chains overlap well, making it look like a caterpillar.

The second function is called "**mcmc_dens_overlay.**" It profiles the distribution of each parameter for each chain. If the distributions for each chain look wildly different, you likely have a problem in your model. As you can see, these overlap fairly well:

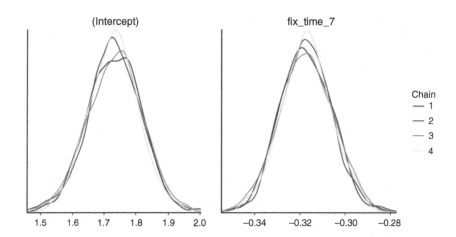

Next comes **mcmc_acf.** This is a check for autocorrelation. We want chains that are effective at discovering our parameters' values. If data is highly correlated, and hence not independent, then our MCMC simulations will get stuck. It won't efficiently discern which proposals matter. The following graph indicates that not much autocorrelation is occurring. On the far left, there is some autocorrelation between MCMC samples. But quickly, the model is able to learn from the data independently. Look for a quick drop to zero.

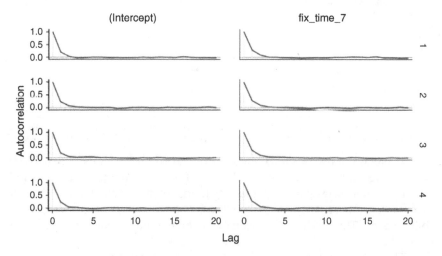

The calls to **rhat()** and **neff_ratio()** follow along these same lines. The rhat() function measures variance in chains and across chains as a ratio. We are looking for a value very close to one. neff_ratio() is used to measure the independence of draws. We are looking for a ratio over 0.1. In both cases, our model looks healthy with a 0.9999+ and ~0.60, respectively.

Last is our call to **describe_posterior().** The main value I look at here is the "% in ROPE." As you may recall, ROPE stands for "Region of Practical Equivalence." It is a range of values that are equivalent to zero. If the parameter of interest is inside that ROPE, you would say that the parameter is equivalent to zero and may have negligible influence on our model.

Good news for us. Our HDIs are completely outside the ROPE. It means that the time in weeks likely has a meaningful relationship to the probability of SLA achievement. This should come as no surprise.

## *MCMC Posterior Visualization and Prediction*

We have built a stable and simple model. Now it's time to do some simple visualizations and predictions. We will use tidybayse to help us simulate from the posterior.

First is the graph, and next comes the code. I will not spend as much time on the code. It should largely all be familiar by now.

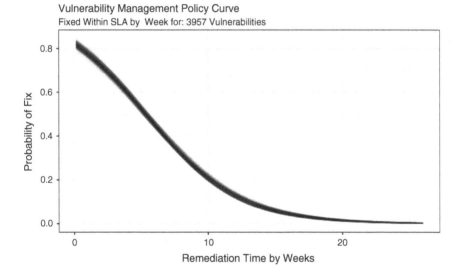

```
basic %>%
    # Simulates hundreds of thousands of draws
    add_epred_draws(sla_model_1, ndraws = 100) %>%

    # Graph Curve
    ggplot(aes(x = fix_time_7, y = fixed_in_sla)) +
    geom_line(aes(y = .epred, group = .draw), alpha = 0.15) +
    labs(x = "Remediation Time by Weeks",
        y = "Probability of Fix",
```

```
    title = "Vulnerability Management Policy Curve",
    subtitle = paste0("Fixed Within SLA By Week For: ",
                      nrow(basic), " Vulnerabilities"))+
theme_bw()
```

I thought I would add one more chart. It extends the basic curve above by incorporating evidence. This is a version of a chart found on the rstanarm documentation site.[13] Note how the evidence is incorporated on the top and the bottom of the graph. The gray bubbles on top are vulnerabilities fixed within policy. The black bubbles on the bottom are vulnerabilities that were not fixed within SLA.

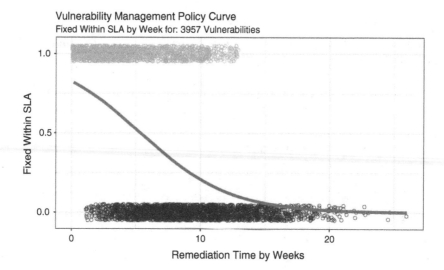

```
# Linear function - predicts sla rate based on week and MCMC params
pr_switch <- function(x, ests) plogis(ests[1] + ests[2] * x )

# Makes blue and black vulnerability points
jitt <- function(...) {
  geom_point(aes_string(...),
      position = position_jitter(height = 0.05, width = 0.1),
      size = 2, shape = 21, stroke = 0.4)
}

# Plot Curve
ggplot(basic, aes(x = fix_time_7, y = fixed_in_sla,
      color = fixed_in_sla)) +

  # Y axis
  scale_y_continuous(breaks = c(0, 0.5, 1)) +

  # Add colored vulns to chart
  jitt(x="fix_time_7") +
```

```
# Add curve to chart
stat_function(fun = pr_switch, args = list(ests = coef(sla_model_1)),
              size = 2, color = "maroon")+
labs(x = "Remediation Time by Weeks",
     y = "Fixed Within SLA",
     title = "Vulnerability Management Policy Curve",
     subtitle = paste0("Fixed Within SLA By Week For: ",
                       nrow(basic), " Vulnerabilities"))+
theme_bw()+
theme(legend.position = "none")
```

This is a useful approach for understanding the relationship between time and policy. Everything that is gray was remediated within policy. Everything in black failed.

Low-risk items have liberal policies. For example, the gray items to the right have longer SLAs. A perfectly executed policy would be all gray on top. The curve would be replaced by a straight line at the 1.0 mark on the *y*-axis. It would run left to right until the last gray value (vulnerability remediated within policy). The line would then drop straight down to day 90 – which is the maximum policy length.

## Forecasting Policy

How do vulnerability risk, asset value, and development team maturity play into policy achievement? And how can we use policy analytics to understand problem spots?

To answer that, I am going to create a number of quick models. For these models, we will use default priors within rstanarm. (If we had small data, we would want to consider creating informed priors.) Once we have a handful of models, we will compare them. Our goal will be to see which model predicts policy outcomes best. From there, we will use the best model to do prediction.

Let's create six models using various values within the "basic" data frame. Notice, I am not using fix_time_7 as a predictor. I used it to understand the relationship of time to policy. I am now focused on prediction. I want to see how vulnerability severity, asset exposure, audit, and development maturity can be used for prediction.

Let's create six models of varying complexity:

```
# vuln severity and asset exposure
policy_1 <- stan_glm(fixed_in_sla ~ severity + exposure,
            family=binomial(link="logit"),data=basic)

# vuln severity and audit
policy_2 <- stan_glm(fixed_in_sla ~ severity + audit,
            family=binomial(link="logit"),data=basic)
```

```
# asset exposure and audit
policy_3 <- stan_glm(fixed_in_sla ~ exposure + audit,
            family=binomial(link="logit"),data=basic)

# vuln severity, audit and exposure
policy_4 <- stan_glm(fixed_in_sla ~ severity + audit + exposure,
            family=binomial(link="logit"),data=basic)

# severity, dev maturity and exposure
policy_5 <- stan_glm(fixed_in_sla ~ severity + dev_maturity + exposure,
            family=binomial(link="logit"),data=basic)

# severity, dev maturity, exposure and audit
policy_6 <- stan_glm(fixed_in_sla ~ severity + dev_maturity + exposure +
            audit, family=binomial(link="logit"),data=basic)
```

Next we run each of the policies through describe_posterior(). As you may recall, it does a ROPE analysis. To save on space, I will tell you that the "audit" value consistently fell into the ROPE. This just means that "audit" has relatively low information value in this context – not zero value.

Next, I rank-order the models. The value used for ranking is called the **Expected Log-Predictive Density**, or ELPD. It is a score for determining posterior predictive accuracy. There is a lot of theory behind it, and apparently even interpreting the ELPD can vary quite a bit, given context. When comparing similar models, you want to consider the model with the highest ELPD score. Let's do that now using rstanarm's loo() function.[14] This function makes it easy to compare MCMC models.

```
# Use leave-one-out function to get elpd scores
(loo1 <- loo(policy_1))
(loo2 <- loo(policy_2))
(loo3 <- loo(policy_3))
(loo4 <- loo(policy_4))
(loo5 <- loo(policy_5))
(loo6 <- loo(policy_6))

# Compare and rank order scores
loo_compare(loo1, loo2, loo3, loo4, loo5, loo6)
          elpd_diff se_diff
policy_5     0.0       0.0
policy_6    -0.6       0.7
policy_1   -75.5      12.2
policy_4   -76.3      12.2
policy_2  -679.5      32.6
policy_3  -930.2      34.1
```

Based on this data, I am going to call a tie between policy_5 and 6. The standard error on policy_6 essentially negates any material differences.

Next, I ran the following checks. I won't print their output there. Everything turned out to be stable with the policy_6 MCMC:

```
# MCMC Model Checks

describe_posterior(policy_6)
mcmc_trace(policy_6)
mcmc_dens_overlay(policy_6)
mcmc_acf(policy_6)
rhat(policy_6)
neff_ratio(policy_6)
```

How well does our model predict our empirical data? Let's find out. Here is what the data says the mean value is across everything:

```
mean(basic$fixed_in_sla)
[1] 0.3903277
```

We simulate the average with a graph to express our uncertainty. It is a default graphing capability within rstanarm supported by the bayesplot package. The result is spot on:

```
# Function to get mean
proportion_fix <- function(x){mean(x == 1)}

# Run numerous simulations
pp_check(policy_6, nreps = 100,
        plotfun = "stat", stat = "proportion_fix") +
  xlab("probability of fix")
```

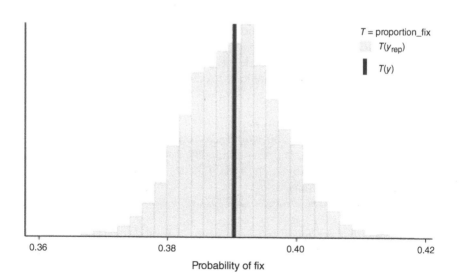

Probability of fix

## Posterior Policy Prediction

To close out this chapter, we are going to predict expected values given our parameters. We will use policy_6 because I like its rich context. And, since I know the domain and my data, I feel comfortable with the poor ROPE scores that showed up in two places.

This is the benefit of being the SME. It's a benefit you also share over an outside analyst. I can check my model's output against my background and work context. If the output seems correct, and the risk of being wrong is low, then I will carry on trusting in my experience.

After all, this is not brain surgery or rocket science. This is technology process optimization. The level of fidelity is simply different. Accuracy is critically important while perfect precision is likely a stumbling block. With that, let's produce some predictions and graphs.

I will show the raw prediction code first. Then, to save on space and typing, I will roll this as a function.

```
policy_prediction <-
  posterior_epred( policy_6, newdata = data.frame(
      severity = "extreme",
      exposure = "external",
      audit = 0,
      dev_maturity = 4),)

mean(policy_prediction)
[1] 0.85725
```

Look at the policy I specified. It's for extreme vulnerabilities impacting externally facing assets that are under regulatory audit. I then included the highest level of development team maturity. There are four levels of maturity. A rating of 1 means zero evidence of security capabilities in place. A rating of 4 means completely integrated security capabilities.

> The idea behind dev_maturity is that each of the maturity levels would be empirically auditable. You would have standards of implementation that can be validated with zero ambiguity in terms of what makes a level four maturity vs. three, etc. I liken this to the four tiers within the NIST Cybersecurity Framework.

The code that produced our 86% results is turned into a function and upgraded below. We are going to call it frequently.

```
policy_pred <- function(mcmc, sev, exp, dev_val, audit_val){

  # simulate from posterior
  res <- posterior_epred( mcmc, newdata = data.frame(
    severity = sev,
    exposure = exp,
    dev_maturity = dev_val,
    audit = audit_val))

  # Highest Density Interval
  ci_val <- ci(res, method = "HDI")
  ret_tib <- tibble(mean_est = mean(res),
                    ci_low = ci_val$CI_low,
                    ci_high = ci_val$CI_high)

  return(ret_tib)
}
```

Now I am going to run a series of predictions. Note, each time you run the function, the results could be slightly different. That is a function of the posterior_predict() function. It samples from the posterior. It's not a database of values – it's probabilistic reasoning over data.

Also, keep in mind that SLAs are based on risk. So, low-risk items have a longer time frame for remediation. That longer time frame may drive up remediation outcomes. That is because you have more time to fix things. Similarly, short time frames may drive SLA compliance down – despite the requirement for faster remediation.

```
# Extreme, External, Dev Mature: Excelling, Audited
policy_pred(policy_6, "extreme", "external", 4, 0)
# A tibble: 1 x 3
  mean_est ci_low ci_high
     <dbl>  <dbl>   <dbl>
1    0.858  0.820   0.895

# Extreme, External, Dev Mature: None, Audited
policy_pred(policy_6, "extreme", "external", 1, 0)
# A tibble: 1 x 3
  mean_est ci_low ci_high
     <dbl>  <dbl>   <dbl>
1    0.513  0.450   0.572

# Extreme, Partner, Dev Mature: None, Audited
policy_pred(policy_6, "extreme", "partner", 1, 0)
# A tibble: 1 x 3
  mean_est ci_low ci_high
     <dbl>  <dbl>   <dbl>
1    0.862  0.829   0.896
```

```
# Extreme, Partner, Dev Mature: Excelling, Audited
policy_pred(policy_6, "extreme", "partner", 4, 0)
# A tibble: 1 x 3
  mean_est ci_low ci_high
     <dbl>  <dbl>   <dbl>
1    0.973  0.964   0.983

# Critical, External, Dev Mature: Excelling, Audited
policy_pred(policy_6, "critical", "external", 4, 0)
# A tibble: 1 x 3
  mean_est ci_low ci_high
     <dbl>  <dbl>   <dbl>
1    0.306  0.241   0.366

# Critical, External, Dev Mature: None, Audited
policy_pred(policy_6, "critical", "external", 1, 0)
# A tibble: 1 x 3
  mean_est ci_low ci_high
     <dbl>  <dbl>   <dbl>
1    0.712 0.538   0.885

# High, Internal, Dev Mature: None, Not-Audited
policy_pred(policy_6, "high", "internal", 1, 1)
# A tibble: 1 x 3
  mean_est ci_low ci_high
     <dbl>  <dbl>   <dbl>
1    0.251  0.213   0.287

# High, External, Dev Mature: Excelling, Not-Audited
policy_pred(policy_6, "high", "internal", 4, 1)
# A tibble: 1 x 3
  mean_est ci_low ci_high
     <dbl>  <dbl>   <dbl>
1    0.658  0.605   0.709
```

We started at the aggregate policy level. Policy compliance, based on SLAs, was at 39%. We then created an MCMC model to measure the relationship between time in weeks and policy achievement. From there, we built a model to measure the relationship between risk ratings and policy outcomes. I call this policy rules analysis.

I also included a parameter for development team maturity. Dev maturity is not a policy component. It is an aggregation of capability maturity. Behind such a rating would be a set of empirically auditable capabilities.

As you review the policy analysis outcomes, keep two questions in mind. The first one is, "Are we underperforming based on risk?" The second question is, "Are we underperforming because we are overperforming on something less risky?" For example, it looks like externally facing extreme risk is not doing as well as partner-facing extreme risk. It may be a nonissue. But in theory, the attack surfaces are different. Everyone and their brother can see the external risks. It is a much larger attack surface. There may be an opportunity for optimization that transfers work effort from one class of risk to another.

The next step in examining metrics is setting KPIs for betterment. We touch on that in the dashboarding chapter.

## Final Chapter Thoughts

Logistic regression is one of many regression models to choose from. I favor it because of its obvious utility for measuring policy. A whole swath of security operations can be measured with this model alone.

Next steps for the adventurous are hierarchical (multilevel) models. These models allow you to take into consideration many confounding issues like different product teams, scrum teams, and the like. Many of the titles included in the Notes section below touch on this type of modeling. Probably the best book on this topic using Bayesian methods is *Statistical Rethinking*. Look to the book's site (www.themetricsmanifesto.com) for more advanced models including hierarchical models over time.

The next chapter takes a simplified approach to Bayesian A/B testing.

## Notes

1. https://en.wikipedia.org/wiki/Geodesy
2. Roeder. (1993). *Carl Friedrich Gauss*. Carl Friedrich Gauss. http://www.surveyhistory.org/carl_friedric.htm
3. *The Discovery of Statistical Regression*. (2015). Priceonomics. https://priceonomics.com/the-discovery-of-statistical-regression/
4. McElreath, R. (2020). *Statistical Rethinking: A Bayesian Course with Examples in R and STAN (Chapman & Hall/CRC Texts in Statistical Science)* (2nd ed.). Chapman and Hall/CRC.
5. Citizendium. (2011). Probability space. https://en.citizendium.org/wiki/Probability_space
6. Donovan, T. M., & Mickey, R. M. (2019). *Bayesian Statistics for Beginners: A Step-by-Step Approach* (Illustrated ed.). Oxford University Press.
7. Gabry, J., and Goodrich, B. (2020, July 19). *Estimating Generalized Linear Models for Binary and Binomial Data with rstanarm*. Rstanarm. https://cran.r-project.org/web/packages/rstanarm/vignettes/binomial.html

8. Gelman, A. (2020). *Regression and Other Stories (Analytical Methods for Social Research)* (1st ed.). Cambridge University Press.
9. Johnson, A. A., Ott, M. Q., & Dogucu, M. (2022). *Bayes Rules! An Introduction to Bayesian Modeling with R.* CRC Press.
10. Stanton, J. M. (2017). *Reasoning with Data: An Introduction to Traditional and Bayesian Statistics Using R* (Annotated ed.). The Guilford Press.
11. Gabry, J., & Modrák, M. (2021, June 13). Visual MCMC diagnostics using the bayesplot package. https://cran.r-project.org/web/packages/bayesplot/vignettes/visual-mcmc-diagnostics.html#general-mcmc-diagnostics
12. Gabry, J., & Goodrich, B. (2020, July 19). Estimating generalizing linear models for binary and binomial data with rstanarm. https://cran.r-project.org/web/packages/rstanarm/vignettes/binomial.html
13. Kay, M. (2021, August 22). CRAN – Package tidybayes. Tidybayes. https://cran.r-project.org/web/packages/tidybayes/index.html
14. Vehtari, A., and Gabry, J. (2020, December 3). Using the loo package. http://mc-stan.org/loo/articles/loo2-example.html

# CHAPTER 9

# ABC A/B Testing and Security ROI

## Get Better ROI for Security

This chapter exists because of a request from a fellow entrepreneur. He came to me, looking for a method for calculating ROI for his security product. His hope was to use something in the sales process that might motivate action.

What started out as a side project for a friend has evolved into a useful tool.[1] In the first half of this chapter we will focus on the higher-level concepts. The latter half will exclusively focus on the code.

> There were two resources that heavily influenced this chapter. The first and most influential is a video/article turned into a tutorial on DataCamp by Rasmus Bååth.[2] And of course, my first book that I co-authored with Doub Hubbard.[3] Both merge impact as dollars with Bayesian concepts and Monte Carlo–based simulations.

## Buying Security with Predictive Analytics

I'm proposing a simple approach for making faster and more informed security buying decisions. I call it ABC A/B testing, short for Approximate Bayesian Computation A/B testing[4] (heavy emphasis on the word *approximate*).[5] We have already covered ABC. Also, we are using ABC in conjunction with beta-binomial and gamma-poisson models. So, in one sense, much of this should be conceptually familiar territory.

ABC A/B testing uses subject matter expert (SME) beliefs and small sample data to compare product effectiveness. It specifically forecasts costs based on "proof of concept" (POC) outcomes, financial inputs, and plenty of uncertainty.


197

The model is largely based on my experience as a CISO and security buyer. I, like my CISO peers, ran countless POCs for new purchases. I felt we could do these faster and more "scientifically." This article and the associated code are for those of you who feel the same. The ideal user wants better products but has little time to test, never enough resources, and not enough data to make a truly informed decision.

Our first step is to turn your SME beliefs into data. If that sounds weird, don't worry. There's a lot of research on this topic. Our previous book goes over SME belief codification and the supporting research in detail. And we touched on this process in previous chapters.

## The Use Case: Web Application and API Scanning

**Note:** This method can work with just about any product you are evaluating. If the particular use case doesn't float your boat, substitute your own alternative.

Imagine you have a solution that scans web applications and APIs for vulnerabilities. These vulnerabilities are the kind that invariably escape out of development and get exposed to users and the bad guys. Let's explore some reasons why you are not happy with your current product's performance.

First, your product produces too many false positives (FPs). FPs create lots of wasted work for your team. The ones that get past your team to be later discovered by development are particularly annoying.

Then there's the false negatives (FNs). FNs create emergencies, particularly when a remotely exploitable vulnerability is discovered in production. Engineers have to stop what they are doing to remediate these – prior to the bad guys exploiting them. Additionally, security teams may have to resort to forensics just to be sure the bad guys didn't steal any treasure.

No matter the reason, you're in the market for a new product. Your goal should be to compare your existing solution to one or more alternatives, paying particular consideration to the financial impact of errors (FPs and FNs). Below, I will explore a three-step process for comparing your solutions.

## Step 1: Model Your Beliefs

Let's start with two reasonable assumptions. First, we should assume that you have the capability to measure the rate at which you find vulnerabilities. This includes true vulnerabilities, FPs, and FNs. The second assumption is that you already have some information about the underlying error rate even before you see the data. After all, you wouldn't be in the market for a solution if you didn't have at least a quasi-informed opinion about this.

To quantify your beliefs, you will require two numbers. (*I will define these technical terms via the example dialogue.*) The first is the *median error rate*. The second is the *90% boundary rate*. An informed practitioner might respond, "*Our median error rate is around 20%. That means I believe the true error rate is just as likely to be below 20% as it is to be above. I'm 90% confident the true rate is below 45%. After all, I have never in my life experienced a 50% error rate – but it might happen!*"

```
# Beliefs about error counts prior to testing
event_priors <- list()
event_priors["median_errors"] <- 0.20
event_priors["edge_errors"] <- 0.45
```

We use those numbers to create a graph of *all possible rates given those assumptions*. Check out the following graph (Figure 9.1). Any rate under the shaded curve is *possible* given your SME beliefs. But, the ones between the two lines are more *probable*. The ones near the apex are the most plausible, given your data, assumptions, and this basic model.

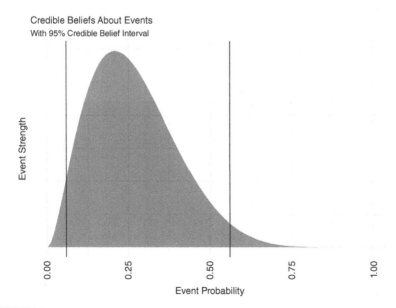

FIGURE 9.1

If this graph could speak, it would say, *"Given your beliefs about the rates and the particular model you are using, you should expect the true rate is likely between 6% and 56%."* This model allows for a lot of uncertainty about plausible error rates.

## Step 2: Mash up Data with Beliefs

Next, we are going to include real data. Real data is data that comes from the tools and processes you are running. We will literally combine the real data with the belief data (the shaded curve). *"Why on earth would you do that!?"* you say. We have *small* and *noisy* data – that's why.

> I use the words *tools* and *process* together to refer to *capability*. In this exercise, we are measuring a capability. It's pretty difficult to purely isolate a technology from its implementation, but we don't let that stop us! *We are interested in better outcomes over perfect measurement.*

Small data can refer to zero to hundreds of events. (In my previous book, we focused exclusively on zero events – all beliefs.) But your company may be a Netflix, Uber, AWS, etc., where you get many thousands of unique "vulnerability" events a day that interest you. Although I suspect most readers are dealing with much sparser data sets, this model would still apply.

When I say *noisy data,* I mean highly uncertain and incomplete data. Even 50 to 100 events will still leave you uncertain. You may wonder, *"Is this the real false positive rate? How can I be sure this is the false negative rate!? Was there a change in the environment we were scanning that I didn't know about?"* We call all that stuff noise and uncertainty. You use your SME beliefs to help control, and inform, the noise when data is small and incomplete.

Now let's capture your product data:

- The first configuration item below is the number of times you will run this analysis: 100,000. Running thousands of tests is another tactic for dealing with small and noisy data.
- The next two numbers are the distinct count of "critical vulnerabilities" found in a particular time period per product. Let's assume you ran two scanners against the same environment for 30 days. At the end of the period, you see that one product found 34 unique "critical vulnerabilities" and the other product found 37.
- Since you ran the test for a month, and we are looking to do a year-long cost forecast, you set the "time_multiple" variable to 12. If you ran your test for a day, then this number would be set for 365. If it ran for a week, then 52, etc.

```
# These parameters set the basis for the analysis in terms of simulations,
events and timeframe
base_configs <- list()
base_configs["n_draws"] <- 100000
base_configs["a_n_events"] <- 34
base_configs["b_n_events"] <- 37
base_configs["time_multiple"] <- 12
```

In the following code you input the errors of each product in relationship to their total events above. Errors are the sum of false positives and false negatives. Unfortunately, even the process of finding errors is ironically error prone. This is why your beliefs about events matter in this particular type of analysis. We are assuming small, messy, and noisy data. Again, *don't let the myth of perfect data halt measurement!*

```
event_counts <- list()
event_counts["product_a_errors"] <- 10
event_counts["product_b_errors"] <- 13
```

Using this data, we can now simulate 100,000 error rates. A sample of those rates for each product can be seen in the proportion_events table below. We get those rates from the "shaded beliefs" curve above. The curve "thinks" errors are most likely (but not exclusively) between 6% and 56%.

Using the total event counts of 34 and 37 for each product, we can generate error counts given the proportion_events. On the first row on the left, the model asks, "Given an error rate of ~2% and a total of 34 events, how many errors might I get?" This happens 100,000 times given the various proportion_events. The outcomes of each experiment are stored in the a_n_errors and b_n_errors columns, respectively.

```
  proportion_events a_n_errors
1 0.018300680       0
2 0.125779966       7
3 0.006415675       1
4 0.487886545       14
5 0.523474037       16

  proportion_events b_n_errors
1 0.4111845         13
2 0.1264897         2
3 0.0954012         5
4 0.1113773         4
5 0.2189808         9
```

Now this is where the ABC part comes in. From the above results, we filter anything that doesn't match real error counts of 10 and 13.

```
    proportion_events  a_n_errors
3           0.1749533          10
4           0.2456324          10
5           0.2598130          10
11          0.1888508          10
12          0.3207026          10
38          0.1997342          10

    proportion_events  b_n_errors
17          0.3407392          13
55          0.3759550          13
63          0.2985663          13
100         0.2950341          13
192         0.2728960          13
200         0.2291469          13
```

The point of view with Approximate Bayesian Computation is that there is an underlying random process that generates those specific error counts (10,13). That process has some constraints that will generate various "proportion_events." We are collecting all of those proportions that generate the exact error counts.

Next, we take these results and draw 10,000 random samples from each. I am going to assume that some of my readers might not be familiar with random sampling. In short, a sampler will randomly select rates from each of the tables above. The sampler is biased to select data in proportion to how frequently it occurs. Sampling also adjusts for noisy and incomplete data.

We can use the sampled data to answer some questions about the underlying data-generating process. For example, what is the most likely range of rates that produced the counts we are seeing? And if we had to choose one number to represent the rate, what might that number be? Below is a small posterior sample error rate for each product.

```
     prod_a      prod_b
1  0.3454845  0.4212118
2  0.3009141  0.3054843
3  0.3974528  0.3138465
4  0.3382859  0.4521465
5  0.2504374  0.2778871
6  0.1903597  0.4053522
```

Now that we have our posterior distribution, we can formally state what our new beliefs are in terms of error rates. For product A, we now believe the error rate is between 20% and 42% and centered near 30%. For product B, we believe the error rate is between 23% and 45% and centered near 34%.

Based on everything we have done to this point, our error rate model thinks there is a 33% chance that product B produces more errors than product A. Translated to English: You can bet on product B producing more errors in the long run. Either way, that is not a really big difference, and there is a lot of uncertainty here.

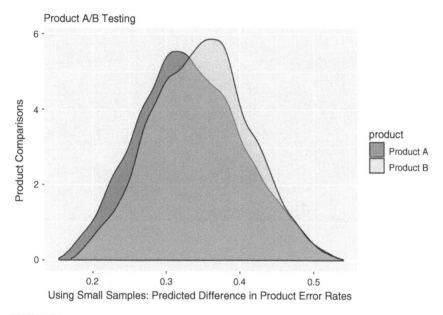

FIGURE 9.2

Figure 9.2 overlays product A and product B. Product B seems to make more errors. You can see this more clearly in the table below and the image that follows. The table shows the difference numerically. The more events that are in the negative shifts the graph further to the left. That's because product B has higher error rates. If, on the other hand, things are shifted to the right, it means that product A has higher rates (Figure 9.3).

```
       prod_a      prod_b prop_diff_events
1   0.3696819   0.4569722      -0.0872903018
2   0.2712881   0.2486014       0.0226867760
3   0.2125500   0.2794754      -0.0669254614
4   0.2512649   0.3242663      -0.0730013821
5   0.3109926   0.4130783      -0.1020857617
6   0.2513570   0.1555038       0.0958531637
7   0.2551497   0.4009451      -0.1457954142
8   0.3090410   0.3323398      -0.0232987345
9   0.2910907   0.3384736      -0.0473829085
10  0.3310631   0.3303720       0.0006910912
```

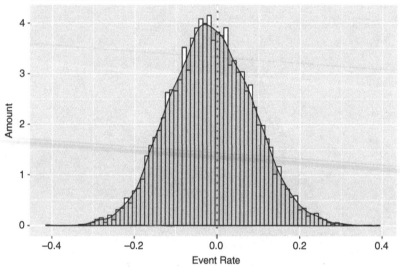

FIGURE 9.3

## Step 3: Forecast the Financial Impact of Errors

This particular part of the model is purposefully simple. The first thing I did was input a range of hours for addressing scan errors. The range of hours takes into consideration both security and developer time.

```
# Forecasted range of error response hours that can happen per event
eng_hour_range <- list()
eng_hour_range["mode"] <- 3   # Expect hours
eng_hour_range["low"]  <- 1   # Low hours
eng_hour_range["high"] <- 5   # Max hours
```

Next, I capture the engineering cost. This cost considers the possibility of multiple people being involved – typically, one security and one software engineer. You can adjust this to what you think is reasonable. Again, while this cost usually hovers around $600, it could range from $200 or well over $2,000.

```
# Forecasted cost of responding to an error event for ONE HOUR
eng_cost_range <- list()
eng_cost_range["mode"] <- 600    # Expected cost per event
eng_cost_range["low"]  <- 200    # Low end cost per event
eng_cost_range["high"] <- 2000   # High end cost per event
```

In the model, the hours are multiplied by the costs and the event probability. The final product of that calculation is the "expected value" of the impact. Expected value is a number frequently used for cost modeling. It is a single number that incorporates all the possibilities in a probability-weighted outcome.

I thought it might help to see what the underlying data frames look like. Just below you can see 10 lines of output from a much larger simulation. Note the two "diff" columns.

|    | prod_a    | prod_b    | prop_diff_events | prod_a_impact | prod_b_impact | prod_diff_impact |
|----|-----------|-----------|------------------|---------------|---------------|------------------|
| 1  | 0.1459609 | 0.4001620 | -0.25420109      | 312.4850      | 856.6994      | -544.21433       |
| 2  | 0.2085667 | 0.3861999 | -0.17763320      | 479.1112      | 887.1632      | -408.05192       |
| 3  | 0.2689256 | 0.4194196 | -0.15049400      | 555.1300      | 865.7875      | -310.65743       |
| 4  | 0.1887803 | 0.5001994 | -0.31141908      | 366.9279      | 972.2257      | -605.29784       |
| 5  | 0.3735295 | 0.3479386 | 0.02559085       | 592.6969      | 552.0907      | 40.60621         |
| 6  | 0.2432154 | 0.2614689 | -0.01825353      | 820.3245      | 881.8906      | -61.56610        |
| 7  | 0.2539515 | 0.3461273 | -0.09217576      | 1408.0478     | 1919.1213     | -511.07350       |
| 8  | 0.2691006 | 0.2915564 | -0.02245588      | 384.5159      | 416.6029      | -32.08704        |
| 9  | 0.2134581 | 0.2607941 | -0.04733601      | 654.6225      | 799.7902      | -145.16768       |
| 10 | 0.3185403 | 0.3612630 | -0.04272270      | 363.2587      | 411.9791      | -48.72034        |

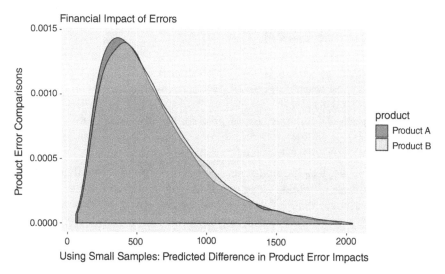

FIGURE 9.4

The difference visually looks pretty small (Figure 9.4). I would be ambivalent. What if we ratchet up the frequency of events? Now that we have a distribution of costs, we can do some simple aggregation to forecast the difference between product A and product B over time. We also need to add the licensing costs of each product and any available data on operational costs, though the latter is optional.

```
#Year 1 Deterministic Cost of Product A&B license or subscription etc
product_costs <- list()
product_costs["prod_a_cost"] <- 72000.00
product_costs["prod_b_cost"] <- 65000.00
product_costs["prod_a_run"] <- 10000
product_costs["prod_b_run"] <- 10000
```

In this code, you can see the program takes all of this information in and outputs the following:

- Product A is ~84% the total cost of product B.
- Product A (with base price of $72,000) is expected to cost to operate with errors: $159K a year.
- Product B (with base price of $65,000) is expected to cost to operate with errors: $191K a year.

This is not that motivating, right? I mean that cost difference is a rounding error for most large companies. But, what if we shifted this measurement to a weekly model? That would likely be more realistic for a Fortune 5000 company knee-deep in digital transformation. All you need to do is change the "time_multiple" variable to 52.

```
base_configs["time_multiple"] <- 52
```

Now we get the following:

- Product A is 73% the total cost of product B.
- The expected operation cost of product A with errors (with base price of $72,000) is $416K.
- The expected operation cost of product B with errors (with base price of $65,000) is $570K.

Just for kicks, let's assume your company is one of those that is doing tens of thousands of releases a year, just like my first cloud native CISO gig. Let's further assume that our sample was for one day only. In order to simulate a year's worth of data, all I need to do is change the "time_multiple" parameter to 365. I doubt anyone would do a one-day POC, but for illustration purposes:

- Product A is 68% the total cost of product B.
- The expected operation cost of product A with errors (with base price of $72,000) is $2.5M.
- The expected operation cost of product B with errors (with base price of $65,000) is $3.6M.

This is, of course, a "what-if" scenario based on a small scanning sample. It's only a model. That means "not real." I don't know that you would actually experience losses like this as if you were writing a check for millions of dollars. It's just a mechanism for comparing two things.

It's here that I remind you of George Box's famous phrase (with a little sauce from Doug Hubbard): "All models are wrong, but some are useful... *and some are measurably more useful than others.*"

Our goal was to create a mathematically unambiguous and consistent method of comparing products. We have also primed the model with our vague beliefs about actual error rates and costs. We munged all that together with actual error rates to help us make product comparisons over a one-year period.

Perfect? No. Useful? Yes. It is particularly useful when compared to the competition: your unaided intuition. That model usually goes by two names: "Wild Guesses" and "I'll Buy the Shiny One."

## What's Next!?

What we have demonstrated here is a simple scoring system for comparing products under POC. These analytics can be applied to any solution that has a binary outcome – that is, hit and miss, event and nonevent, exploit and nonexploit, escalate and nonescalate, etc. They can be used with events that occur in a bounded period of time: day, week, month, etc.

The goal is to compare capabilities using small data, and then forecasting costs. You can ultimately think of this model as a means for scoring how *capabilities may perform over time* – and then expand on it. For example, it can be a real-time learning system that alerts you to possible drift in your security services' performance.

That type of constant learning, informed by our uncertainty and incomplete data, is where the *Bayesian* in ABC comes in. Bayesian methods constantly update our beliefs about reality as data rolls in. Bayesian methods support including our prior beliefs (or prior data) about processes. The more data we have, the less reliance there is on subjective beliefs (aka SME forecasts).

# Code Details and Design

Note: All code is available on www.themetricsmanifesto.com. Go there for regular updates, error corrections, and new tools.

I suspect only a subset of readers will want to dig into the code. Although I make no claims to it being an example of R perfection, I do claim that this is a useful application of what you have learned up to this point. The following example also adds a new element of financial impact.

ABC, subjective priors, beta-binomial, and gamma-Poisson analysis also work together as a team. They provide a consistent tape measure for forecasting and evaluating competing security investments. And it is an example of *retaining our uncertainty without obscuring our certainty.*

As you read through, you can use the reference in the code blocks to see actual output. The references point to graphical elements already shown.

I have broken the code into blocks for ease of understanding. That means some things are explained out of order for better comprehension. To run this in its entirety, I encourage you to get the code from the book's site ... only.

Lastly, there are three things to note about how this code works. First, it is meant to run with minimal effort. It's one-click execution directly in RStudio. Second, it can also be run to produce a markdown page. That page functions as a self-contained tutorial. Third, I wrote it so that it could be easily integrated with Shiny – as a standalone web app. We will discuss Shiny in the next chapter. In short, it can be turned into a web application with ease.

## *Run Product Cost Comparison*

This is all you need to do to run the solution. You encountered all the configuration elements in the section above.

```
# Code available on www.themetricsmanifesto.com

source("manifesto_functions.R")   #book functions

# Declare list to hold configurations
base_configs <- list()

# Amount of simulation
base_configs["n_draws"] <- 100000

# Product A Events (bugs, phis, malware etc)
base_configs["a_n_events"] <- 34

# Product B Events (bugs, phis, malware etc)
base_configs["b_n_events"] <- 37
```

```
# Time Frame: Months(12), Weeks(52), Days(365)
base_configs["time_multiple"] <- 365.

### Slide #2
# Beliefs about error counts prior to testing
event_priors <- list()
event_priors["median_errors"] <- 0.20
event_priors["edge_errors"] <- 0.45

# True Error Counts
event_counts <- list()
event_counts["product_a_errors"] <- 10
event_counts["product_b_errors"] <- 13

### Slide #3
# Forecasted range of error response hours that can happen per event
eng_hour_range <- list()
eng_hour_range["mode"] <- 3 # Expect hours
eng_hour_range["low"] <- 1 # Low hours
eng_hour_range["high"] <- 5 # Max hours

# Forecasted cost of responding to an error event for ONE HOUR
eng_cost_range <- list()
eng_cost_range["mode"] <- 600 # Expected cost per event
eng_cost_range["low"] <- 200 # Low end cost per event
eng_cost_range["high"] <- 2000 # High end cost per event

### Slide #4
# Year 1 Deterministic Cost of Product A & B license or subscription etc
product_costs <- list()
product_costs["prod_a_cost"] <- 72000.00
product_costs["prod_b_cost"] <- 65000.00
product_costs["prod_a_run"] <- 10000 # Additional Operational Cost
product_costs["prod_b_run"] <- 10000 # Additional Operational Cost

# Command Line Option - run using "source" option or via CLI
runProductCostComparison(base_configs,event_priors, event_counts,
                    eng_hour_range, eng_cost_range, product_costs)
```

## *Wrapper Function*

I created a wrapper function to make the code easy to run. It's what you called above. This function calls a set of smaller functions. These functions fall into one of three classes:

- Functions that Get() data from calculations
- Functions that Cat() data to the screen and work with RMarkdown for HTML rendering
- Functions that Graph() data

Everything else is supporting computation for these function calls. Note, comments that looks like this "*#'*" are for RMarkdown. They get special HTML-based treatment when you execute the script to produce RMarkdown.

After I walk through this function, I will give a run-through of its child functions. I will finally enumerate a subset of the grandchild functions.

The wrapper function is a bit long, but most of the child functions it calls are relatively short.

```
#' ##Wrapper Function
#' Easy for users to call one function without much fuss.

runProductCostComparison <- function(
  base_configs, event_priors,event_counts, eng_hour_range,
  eng_cost_range, product_costs){

  # A Quick Check for missed false negatives etc
  update_count <- ErrorCheck(base_configs, event_counts)
  if( update_count[2] > 0){
      event_counts[update_count[[1]]] <- as.numeric(update_count[[2]])
  }

  #' ##Prior Beliefs About Error Rates
  #' In the *event_priors* config element above you specified what you
  #' think is the likely error rate given N events. This graph shows you"
  #' the spread of possible rates given our beliefs. It also gives some
  #' indication of where the most likely rates may cluster."
  CatPriorBeliefRates(event_priors)

  # Number of simulations, tests, and default array index sizes
  n_draws <- as.numeric(base_configs[["n_draws"]])
  a_n_events <- as.numeric(base_configs[["a_n_events"]])
  b_n_events <- as.numeric(base_configs[["b_n_events"]])
  size <- 10000

  # Create a list of simulated events and error RATES based on priors
  proportion_events <- GetProportionOfEvents(n_draws, event_priors)
  a_n_errors <- GetErrors(n_draws, a_n_events, proportion_events)
  b_n_errors <- GetErrors(n_draws, b_n_events, proportion_events)

  # Put simulations into dataframe
  a_prior <- data.frame(proportion_events, a_n_errors)
  b_prior <- data.frame(proportion_events, b_n_errors)

  # Select simulated prior data that correlates to product errors
  product_a <- a_prior[a_prior$a_n_errors ==
    event_counts[["product_a_errors"]], ]
  product_b <- b_prior[b_prior$b_n_errors ==
    event_counts[["product_b_errors"]], ]

  #Sample to create indices for posterior and load into data frame
  sample_a_indices <- sample( nrow(product_a), size = size, replace = TRUE,
    prob = product_a$proportion_events)

  sample_b_indices <- sample( nrow(product_b), size = size, replace = TRUE,
    prob = product_b$proportion_events)
```

```
posterior <- data.frame(
  prod_a = product_a$proportion_events[sample_a_indices],
  prod_b  = product_b$proportion_events[sample_b_indices])

#' Updated beliefs given real error rates
CatUpdatedBeliefRates(posterior, event_counts, base_configs)

#' Create and Print out Error Rate Graphs
GraphErrorRates(posterior)

#' Calculate the rate differences, graph and print out
posterior$prop_diff_events <- posterior$prod_a - posterior$prod_b
GraphErrorDiff(posterior)
CatErrorDiffProp(posterior)

#This gets our impact per event with lots of uncertainty packed in
eng_cost <- GetEngCost(size, eng_cost_range, eng_hour_range)

# Add expected cost to posterior for product a and b
posterior$prod_a_impact <- posterior$prod_a * eng_cost
posterior$prod_b_impact <- posterior$prod_b * eng_cost

#Load Median values into list of use later
impacts <- list()
impacts["prod_a_impact"] <- median(posterior$prod_a_impact)
impacts["prod_b_impact"] <- median(posterior$prod_b_impact)

# Add the column that holds the difference between the two costs
posterior$prod_diff_impact <- posterior$prod_a_impact -
    posterior$prod_b_impact

total_costs <- GetTotalCosts(impacts, product_costs,
    base_configs["time_multiple"], event_counts, event_priors,
    base_configs)

#' #Total Costs Differences
impact_res <- CatTotalCost(total_costs, product_costs)

#' Graph Impact Difference
GraphErrorImpact(posterior, impact_res)
}
```

## Calculate Subject Matter Expert Beliefs

This function takes in SME beliefs, simulates data, and creates a graph and prints results to screen. You have already encountered GetBeliefEvents().

```
CatPriorBeliefRates <- function(event_priors){

  # Labels For Graph
  xval = "Event Probability"
  yval = "Event Strength"
  tval = "Credible Beliefs About Events"
  sval = "With 95% Credible Belief Interval"
  beta_vals <- GetBeliefsEvents(event_priors[["median_errors"]],
    event_priors[["edge_errors"]] )
```

```
# Print graph to screen
print (ggplotBeta(beta_vals[1],  beta_vals[2],  xlab = xval, ylab = yval,
   tlab = tval, sval = sval))

#Get Beta Prior CIs
priorCI <- GetBetaCI(event_priors["median_errors"],
   event_priors["edge_errors"])

# Print text to screen
cat("------Prior Beliefs About Error Rates--------\n")

cat(paste(" You forecasted an ERROR RATE equally ABOVE/BELOW ",
   round(event_priors[["median_errors"]]*100), "%.\n", sep=""))

cat(paste(" You're also 90% sure the error rate is LESS THAN ",
   round(event_priors[["edge_errors"]]*100), "%.\n", sep=""))

cat(paste(" Given that forecast and the model we are using you you
   believe the true rate likely sits between ", priorCI[1],"% and ",
   priorCI[3], "%\n\n", sep=""))
}
```

## *Get Proportion of Events*

This function simulates events based on subject matter expert beliefs and
returns event probabilities. If you are paying close attention, this is the first
step for beta-binomial analysis.

```
GetProportionOfEvents <- function(n_draws,prior_events){
   error_beliefs <- GetBeliefsEvents(prior_events[["median_errors"]],
      prior_events[["edge_errors"]])

   #Make an n_draws length list of error beliefs
   proportion_events <- rbeta(as.numeric(n_draws),
      as.numeric(error_beliefs[[1]]) , as.numeric(error_beliefs[[2]]))

   # Return Simulated Events.
   return(proportion_events)
}
```

## *Get Error Rates*

We get errors using the proportion of events that were simulated in
GetProportionOfEvents(). This is the "binomial" portion of beta-binomial
analysis.

```
GetErrors <- function(n_draws, n_events, proportion_events){
   n_errors <- rbinom(n = n_draws, size = n_events, prob =
      proportion_events)
   return(n_errors)
}
```

## *Cat Update Belief Rates*

This function formats and presents forecasts "given small data, beliefs and lots of simulation."

```
CatUpdatedBeliefRates <- function(posterior, event_counts, base_configs){

  # Start of text output. This will be appended to.
  out <- "--------Updated Forecasts Given Small Data, Beliefs & Lots of
         Simulations--------------\n"

  # 89% Highest Density Intervals
  prod_a_points <- point_estimate(posterior$prod_a)
  ci_hdi_prod_a <- ci(posterior$prod_a, method = "HDI")
  out <- paste(out, " The previous product A forecast combined with ",
    base_configs["a_n_events"] ," events and ",
    event_counts["product_a_errors"] ," errors is between:",
    round(ci_hdi_prod_a$CI_low,2) * 100, "% and ",
    round(ci_hdi_prod_a$CI_high,2) * 100, "% \n    And centered near:",
    round(prod_a_points[[1]],2) * 100, "%\n\n", sep="")

  # 89% Highest Density Interval
  prod_b_points <- point_estimate(posterior$prod_b)
  ci_hdi_prod_b <- ci(posterior$prod_b, method = "HDI")
  out <- paste(out, " The previous product B forecast combined with ",
    base_configs["b_n_events"] ," events and ",
    event_counts["product_b_errors"]," errors is between:",
    round(ci_hdi_prod_b$CI_low,2) * 100, "% and ",
    round(ci_hdi_prod_b$CI_high,2) * 100, "% \n    And centered near:",
    round(prod_b_points[[1]],2) * 100, "%\n\n", sep="")

  # All text combined for singular output.
  out <- paste(out, "See the markdown report or plot tab graphs in rstudio
      to see forecasts combined with data.\n")
  cat(out)
}
```

## *Graph Error Rates*

The results of this function can be seen in the Figure 9.2 graph. It simply takes in data that has already been processed and produces an overlay of two beta-binomial related distributions.

```
GraphErrorRates <- function(posterior){
  # Create one tidy data frame as input into ggplot2
  newdf_a <- data.frame(posterior = posterior$prod_a,
    product = "Product A")
  newdf_b <- data.frame(posterior = posterior$prod_b,
   product = "Product B")

  # Merge two dataframes into one
  newdf_ab <- rbind(newdf_a, newdf_b)

  # Print out overlay graph
  print(ggplot(newdf_ab, aes(x = posterior, y = ..density..,
```

```
    fill = product)) +
    stat_density_ci(alpha = 0.5, n = 1024, geom = "density",
      position = "identity") +
    scale_fill_manual(values=c("#333399", "#CCCCFF"))  +
    labs(title = "Product A/B Testing",
      x="Using Small Samples: Predicted Difference In Product Error Rates",
      y = "Product Comparisons"))
}
```

## Graph Error Diff

You can see the result of this graph in Figure 9.3 – an alternative view of the difference between two products.

```
GraphErrorDiff <- function(posterior){

  xval <- posterior$prop_diff_events
  breaks <- pretty(range(xval), n = nclass.FD(xval), min.n = 1)
  bwidth <- breaks[2]-breaks[1]
  print(ggplot(posterior, aes(x=prop_diff_events)) +
    geom_histogram(aes(y=..density..), colour="black", fill="white",
      binwidth = bwidth)+
    geom_density(alpha=.2, fill="#333399") +
    labs(title="Event Amount Difference: Product A - Product B",
        x="Event Rate", y = "Amount")+
    geom_vline(xintercept=0, color="red", size=1, linetype = "dotted")
  )
}
```

## Cat Error Diff Prop

This function produces the following message when run: Probability that product A makes more errors than product B is 88%.

```
# Forecasted difference in error rates
CatErrorDiffProp <- function(posterior){
  error_rate_diff <- sum(posterior$prop_diff_events > 0) /
    length(posterior$prop_diff_events)

  cat(paste("--------Error Rate Difference For This Simulation--------\n
    Probability that product A makes more errors than Product B is",
    round(error_rate_diff * 100) ,"%\n\n", sep = ""))
}
```

## Get Engineering Cost

This function returns a distribution of costs.

```
GetEngCost <- function(size, eng_cost_pert, eng_hour_priors){

  mode <- as.numeric(eng_cost_pert[["mode"]])
  low  <- as.numeric(eng_cost_pert[["low"]])
  high <- as.numeric(eng_cost_pert[["high"]])
```

```
mode_hrs <- as.numeric(eng_hour_priors[["mode"]])
low_hrs <- as.numeric(eng_hour_priors[["low"]])
high_hrs <- as.numeric(eng_hour_priors[["high"]])

eng_rate <- rpert(size, min = low, mode = mode, max = high, shape = 4)
eng_hours <- rpert(size, min = low_hrs, mode = mode_hrs, max = high_hrs,
    shape = 4)
eng_cost <- eng_hours * eng_rate

return(eng_cost)
}
```

## *Get Total Cost*

This is where we see the use of gamma-Poisson. The process is largely encapsulated in functions. It is used to build an event rate forecast. That resulting event rate is used in an equation for total costs.

```
GetTotalCosts <- function(impacts, costs, time_multiple, event_counts,
                      prior_events, base_configs){

    product_a_counts <- event_counts[[1]]
    product_b_counts <- event_counts[[2]]

    # Gamma Prior for prod a feeds into poisson dist in GetEventFrequency()
    a_number_events <- as.numeric(base_configs$a_n_events)
    a_gamma_median_prior <- prior_events[[1]] * a_number_events
    a_gamma_sd <- prior_events[[2]] * a_number_events

    # Gamma Prior for prod b feeds into poisson dist in GetEventFrequency()
    b_number_events <- as.numeric(base_configs$b_n_events)
    b_gamma_median_prior <- prior_events[[1]] * b_number_events
    b_gamma_sd <- prior_events[[2]] * b_number_events

    prod_a_event_results <- GetEventFrequency(product_a_counts,
        a_gamma_median_prior, a_gamma_sd)
    prod_a_mean_events <- prod_a_event_results$mean
    prod_a_event_totals <- prod_a_mean_events * as.numeric(time_multiple)

    prod_b_event_results <- GetEventFrequency(product_b_counts,
        b_gamma_median_prior, b_gamma_sd)
    prod_b_mean_events <- prod_b_event_results$mean
    prod_b_event_totals <- prod_b_mean_events * as.numeric(time_multiple)

    prod_a_total_cost <- prod_a_event_totals * impacts$prod_a_impact +
        costs$prod_a_cost + costs$prod_a_run
    prod_b_total_cost <- prod_b_event_totals * impacts$prod_b_impact +
        costs$prod_b_cost + costs$prod_b_run

    return(c(prod_a_total_cost, prod_b_total_cost) )
}
```

## *Cat Total Cost*

In the script, this function will output text similar to this:

> Product A is 229.2% the total cost of product B.
> Product A (with base price of $72,000) is expected to cost to operate with errors: $555,991.
> Product B (with base price of $65,000) is expected to cost to operate with errors: $242,577.

```
CatTotalCost <- function(total_costs, product_costs){

  #Get Cost Ratios
  prod_a_total_costs <- total_costs[1]
  prod_b_total_costs <- total_costs[2]
  prod_ratio <- round( prod_a_total_costs / prod_b_total_costs, 3) * 100
  prod_ratio <- paste(prod_ratio, "%", sep = "")

  #Format as dollars
  prod_a_orginal_cost <-
      dollar_format()(as.numeric(product_costs["prod_a_cost"]))
  prod_a_total_final <-
      dollar_format()(round(as.numeric(prod_a_total_costs),2))
  prod_b_orginal_cost <-
      dollar_format()(as.numeric(product_costs["prod_b_cost"]))
  prod_b_total_final <-
      dollar_format()(round(as.numeric(prod_b_total_costs),2))

  #Print Message to stdout
  cat("--------Which Product Cost Most To Operate Given Forecasted
      Errors-------\n")
  cat(paste(" Product A is", prod_ratio , "the total cost of product B\n"))
  cat(paste(" Product A (with base price of ",
      prod_a_orginal_cost ,")
      is expected to cost to operate with errors: ",
      prod_a_total_final,"\n"))
  cat(paste(" Product B (with base price of ",
      prod_b_orginal_cost,")
      is expected to cost to operate with errors: ",
      prod_b_total_final,"\n"))
  cat("\n Still uncertain? Get more data by running more tests!")

  return(c(prod_ratio, prod_a_orginal_cost, prod_a_total_final,
        prod_b_orginal_cost, prod_b_total_final))
}
```

## Graph Error Impact

The graph in Figure 9.4 is created by this code. It will vary in how much differentiation it picks up. This graph in this example shows a negligible difference.

```
GraphErrorImpact <- function(posterior, impact){
  newdf_a_impact <- data.frame(posterior = posterior$prod_a_impact,
    product = "Product A")
  newdf_b_impact <- data.frame(posterior = posterior$prod_b_impact,
    product = "Product B")
  newdf_ab_impact <- rbind(newdf_a_impact, newdf_b_impact)
  impact_text <- paste(" Product A is", impact[1] ,
    "the total cost of product B\n Product A (with base price of ",
    impact[2] ,") is expected to cost to operate with errors: ",
    impact[3],"\n Product B (with base price of ",
    impact[4],") is expected to cost to operate with errors: ",
    impact[5],"\n")

  print(ggplot(newdf_ab_impact, aes(x = posterior,
    y = ..density.., fill = product)) +
    stat_density_ci(alpha = 0.5, n = 1024, geom = "density",
      position = "identity") +
    scale_fill_manual(values=c("#333399", "#CCCCFF"))  +
    labs(title = "FORECASTING APPSEC ERROR IMPACT\nUsing Bayesian A/B
      Testing\n",
        x="Using Small Samples: Predicted Difference In Product
          Error Impacts",
        subtitle = impact_text,
        y = "Product Error Comparisons")))
}
```

## Grand Child Functions

These are, for the most part, third-tier functions, with the important exception of the ErrorCheck() function. ErrorCheck() plays a key role fixing problems with key user inputs.

## Error Check

The ErrorCheck() function looks for logic errors in the configuration values you submitted. Specifically, it looks for implied false positives and false negatives. If FPs are found, the script stops and instructs you on how to update your config. If FNs are found, the script will take care of them.

Of course, later on through analysis you may find there are other issues missed. But, we are testing one product vs. another during a POC. If the math does not work, we can catch it and prompt you to make an update.

```r
ErrorCheck <- function(base_configs, event_counts){

  # Instantiate key variables
  a_total <- as.numeric(base_configs["a_n_events"])
  a_errors <- as.numeric(event_counts["product_a_errors"])
  b_total <- as.numeric(base_configs["b_n_events"])
  b_errors <- as.numeric(event_counts["product_b_errors"])

  #Remove errors to get on true events
  a_true <- a_total - a_errors
  b_true <- b_total - b_errors

  # Obvious misconfiguration
  if( a_total < a_errors){
    stop(paste("Exiting: Your errors for product A of: ", a_errors,
      " exceed your total events for product A of: ", a_total))
  }
  if( b_total < b_errors){
    stop(paste("Exiting: Your errors for product B of: ", b_errors,
      " exceed your total events for product B of: ", b_total))
  }

  # Catch False Positive Logic Errors
  if( b_total < a_true ){
    diff <- a_true - b_total
    cat(paste("Product B is missing", diff,
      " false positive error(s). Add ", diff ,
      " each to B's EVENTS and ERRORS\n"))
    stop("Exiting")
  }

  if( a_total < b_true ){
    diff <- b_true - a_total
    cat(paste("Product A is missing", diff,
      "false positive error(s). Add ", diff ,
      " each to A's EVENTS and ERRORS\n"))
    stop("Exiting")
  }

  # Update data due to false negatives
  if( a_true < b_true ){
    diff <- b_true - a_true
    cat(paste("Adding ", diff ,
      " FALSE NEGATIVE errors to product A for a new total of: ",
      diff + a_errors,"\n"))
    return(c("product_a_errors", diff))
  }

  if( b_true < a_true ){
    diff <- a_true - b_true
    cat(paste("Adding ", diff ,
      " FALSE NEGATIVE errors to product B for a new total of: ",
      diff + b_errors,"\n"))
```

```
    return(c("product_b_errors", diff))
  }

  return(c("No Change", 0))
}
```

## Get Event Frequency

This function is used in the GetTotalCost() function. See the code under "Get Total Cost." We use a gamma-Poisson wrapper function from the Bolstad library.[6]

```
GetEventFrequency <- function(event_counts, avg_event_count,
  event_variation, graph = FALSE){

  # Get priors for gamma poisson simulation
  event_count_priors <- GetRatePriors(avg_event_count, event_variation,
    graph)

  result <- poisgamp(event_counts, event_count_priors[1],
      event_count_priors[2], plot = FALSE, suppressOutput = TRUE)

  return(result)
}
```

## Get Rate Priors

This is the function featured in GetEventFrequncy() above. The rate and shape param algorithm is explained well by John Kruschke.[7] He is the author of the great book, *Doing Bayesian Data Analysis*.[8]

```
GetRatePriors <- function(mode, sd, graph = FALSE){
  # This function allows you to think in terms of mode and SD.
  # Note that everything is positive..
  #    so while the mode might be a small number that is close to 0
  # The SD can be large skewing far to the right,
  #    without going past zero on the left.

  # Here are the corresponding rate and shape parameter values:
  ra = ( mode + sqrt( mode^2 + 4*sd^2 ) ) / ( 2 * sd^2 )
  sh = 1 + mode * ra

  if(graph){
    x = seq(0,mode+5*sd,len=1001)
    plot( x , dgamma( x , shape=sh , rate=ra ) , type="l" ,
          main=paste("dgamma, mode=",mode,", sd=",sd,sep="") ,
          ylab=paste("dgamma( shape=",signif(sh,3),", ,
            rate=",signif(ra,3)," )",
                     sep="") )
    abline( v=mode , lty="dotted" )
  }

  return(c(sh, ra))
}
```

## Beta Simulation Functions

These last five functions are all related. They revolve around the beta distribution. Several of them you have seen in earlier chapters.

```
GetBeliefsHits <- function(hits, max_hits, events ){

  alpha_ratio <-  as.numeric(hits) / as.numeric(events)
  beta_ratio  <- as.numeric(max_hits) / as.numeric(events)
  q1 = list(p=.5, x= alpha_ratio)
  q2 = list(p=.9, x= beta_ratio)
  return( beta.select(q1, q2) )
}


GetBeliefsEvents <- function(belief, max_belief ){
  alpha_ratio <- as.numeric(belief)
  beta_ratio  <- as.numeric(max_belief)
  q1 = list(p=.5, x= alpha_ratio)
  q2 = list(p=.9, x= beta_ratio)
  return( beta.select(q1, q2) )
}

SimulateHits <- function(freq_hits, num_events){
  freq_miss <- 1 - freq_hits
  res <- sample(c("hit", "miss"), size=num_events, replace=TRUE,
                prob=c(freq_hits, freq_miss))
  hit <- sum(res == "hit")
  miss <- sum(res ==  "miss")
  return( c(hit,miss))
}

GetBetaCI <- function(hit,edge){
  betas <- GetBeliefsEvents(hit, edge)
  intervals <- qbeta(c(.025, .5, .975), betas[1], betas[2])
  intervals <- round(intervals * 100)
  return(intervals)
}

GetEngHours <- function(size, med = 10, ninety = 60, total_hours = 100){

  beta_vals <- GetBeliefsHits(med, ninety, total_hours)
  prop_hours <- rbeta(size, beta_vals[1], beta_vals[2])
  hours <- rbinom(size, total_hours, prop_hours)
  return(hours)
}
```

# Conclusion

This module can be easily expanded on, and there will likely be updates to this on the book's website. As stated, it could easily be translated into a Shiny-based application.

To that end, the next chapter explores dashboards with Shiny. After that, you will explore data simulation in depth, as the final chapter of this book.

# Notes

1. *Three Steps to Better Security ROI: When Fast Times Clash with Lean Reality* (2020, June 20). Getting Better ROI. https://get.soluble.cloud/posts/2020/06/three-steps-to-better-security-roi-when-fast-times-clash-with-lean-reality/
2. Bååth, R. (2017, February 13). *Video Introduction to Bayesian Data Analysis, Part 1: What Is Bayes? – Publishable Stuff.* Introduction to Bayesian Data Analysis. http://www.sumsar.net/blog/2017/02/introduction-to-bayesian-data-analysis-part-one/
3. Hubbard, D. W., Seiersen, R., McClure, S., & Jr., D. G. E. (2016). *How to Measure Anything in Cybersecurity Risk* (1st ed.). Wiley.
4. Hanington, J. (2021, March 12). *The ABCs of A/B Testing.* Salesforce Pardot. https://www.pardot.com/blog/abcs-ab-testing/
5. Hartig, F. (2014, June 3). *Explaining the ABC-Rejection Algorithm in R.* Theoretical Ecology. https://theoreticalecology.wordpress.com/2014/06/02/explaining-the-abc-rejection-algorithm-in-r/
6. Aut, J. C. C. (2021, January 8). *Poisson sampling with a gamma prior.* PoisGamp. https://rdrr.io/cran/Bolstad/man/poisgamp.html
7. Kruschke, J. K. (2021, September 29). *Parameterizing a gamma distribution by mode and sd.* Gamma Priors. http://doingbayesiandataanalysis.blogspot.com/2012/01/parameterizing-gamma-distribution-by.html
8. Kruschke, J. (2014). *Doing Bayesian Data Analysis: A Tutorial with R, JAGS, and Stan* (2nd ed.). Academic Press.

# CHAPTER 10

# Dashboarding with BOOM!

*You can see a lot, just by looking.*

— Yogi Berra

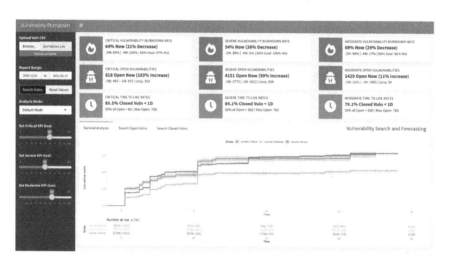

FIGURE 10.1

In this chapter, we will create a basic BOOM-based dashboard. This project is illustrative of what can be done using the BOOM point of view. It also provides exposure to the Shiny framework. The expectation is that you would use the fantastic set of open source solutions in R and Shiny to make dashboards for your bespoke needs. **Thus, this chapter is intended as a jumping-off point for learning – not a destination.** Note that with this

chapter's code, there is a .csv file for you to use as well. As always, look to
www.themetricsmanifesto.com for frequent updates as well as the specific
files for this chapter.

> As a reminder, BOOM stands for Baseline Objectives and Optimization
> Metrics. Burndown rates are a key BOOM metric. This particular dash-
> board has Vulnerability Burndown as the primary BOOM metric.

**A key feature of this dashboard is KPI measurement.** The method
of measuring KPIs may be new to most readers. It uses baseline rates over
time. That means KPI achievement is based on long-run data. Thus, when a
KPI is achieved, we can have more confidence in our capability. There will
be a whole section dedicated to the code behind this measurement.

Other metrics are included in this dashboard, including simple count
metrics, time to live, and survival analysis. The colored metrics objects (gray
scale here, colored when you run the code) at the top of Figure 10.1 merge
simple count and time to live metrics with burndown. Survival analysis is
seen in the bottom half of Figure 10.1. This provides a more holistic view
on burndown.

There is also a rudimentary application of security business intelligence.
This allows users to drill into specific metrics. BI functionality is accessed
through the additional tabs to the right of the survival analysis chart in
Figure 10.1.

The remainder of this chapter decomposes the dashboard piece by
piece. Each portion of the dashboard will be explored and supporting code
will also be reviewed. This application can be accessed via the site's website.

Lastly, this is meant to be run as a standalone browser app. I have also
built a containerized version of this that includes built-in authentication,
load balancing, and more. Look to the book's website for updates as the
BOOM metrics dashboard evolves.

## BOOM Metrics Objects

### Default Mode (Rate Mode)

CRITICAL VULNERABILITY BURNDOWN RATE
**95% Now (1% Decrease)**
-4W: 96% | -8W: 97% | 93% Goal: 100% Met

FIGURE 10.2

If I only have 5 seconds to stare at my dashboard, I will look at the top leftmost **metrics object** (seen in Figure 10.2). What do I see? I see a critical metric that is yellow. On this dashboard, yellow indicates that the rates are decreasing.

While my current burndown rate is 95%, there is a downward trend over the last eight weeks (–8W:97%). If my expected burndown rate is 95%, then it is fair to say that this metric is at risk.

> **Note:** The amount of weeks trended is based on the amount of data that is uploaded to the dashboard. As you will see in the objects below, which only trend four weeks of data.

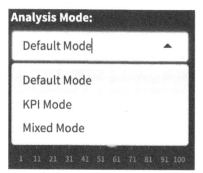

The dashboard is currently in "default mode" or "rate mode." That means its scoring algorithm is based on change. Colors change based on the rate of change. For example, yellow means a slight change for the worse. If the change over time was significant, the metric would be red.

Modes are set using the left-hand dropdown, as seen in Figure 10.1.

Notice the "93% Goal." That is saying that over the last several months, the highest rate that has been consistently beat was 93%. You can see that today you are at 95%, but your true burndown rate is likely at or below 93%. This protects us from overreporting on our capabilities' performance.

## KPI Mode

KPI mode allows you to explore different rate targets. The dropdown to the left in Figure 10.1 allows you to change the mode to KPI mode. And the sliders just below the dropdown are used for setting KPI targets. When you are in KPI mode, the metrics object algorithms change. Figure 10.3 is an example of a metrics object that is set to KPI mode.

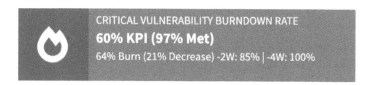

CRITICAL VULNERABILITY BURNDOWN RATE
**60% KPI (97% Met)**
64% Burn (21% Decrease) -2W: 85% | -4W: 100%

FIGURE 10.3

Note how the focus is now on KPI instead of rate change. (There is a whole section forthcoming that explains this algorithm – including code.) What does it mean for a 60% KPI to be only 97% met? Shouldn't it be 100%? After all, the burn rate is at 64%!

The 60% was a target set on the left-hand side via this slider. When you make a change to the slider, the metrics objects update. If I toggled the KPI goal down to 58%, we would indeed be at 100% met. If I slide the metric goal to 63%, the metric object turns yellow. And if I then slide it to 66%, the metrics object turns red. You can see what that looks like in the metrics object in Figure 10.4.

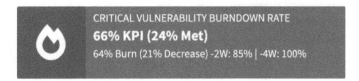

FIGURE 10.4

Note that the 66% KPI goal is 24% met. It is the 24% statistic that turned this metrics object red. There is a rule that looks at the data's long-run history. In light of that (and our uncertainty based on the amount of data), it was calculated that 66% is partially met. Thus, our confidence in that rate is low. Also, you can see that rates are slipping over the last four-week period.

As you can see, the burndown rate at the moment is at 64%. If that was our KPI, it would only be 56% met. That turns our metrics object yellow (see Figure 10.5).

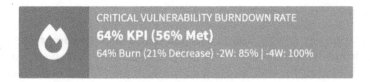

FIGURE 10.5

The KPI rule is simple:

- 75% to 100% is green.
- 25% to 74% is yellow.
- Less than 25% is red.

## Mixed Mode

If you need to be confident in your goal achievements, you can toggle the dashboard to run in mixed mode. Mixed mode is a conservative compromise between KPI and Rate mode. In short, if you have met a KPI and your rates are decreasing, you can't be "green" (Figure 10.6).

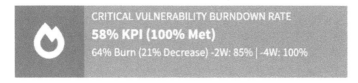

CRITICAL VULNERABILITY BURNDOWN RATE
**58% KPI (100% Met)**
64% Burn (21% Decrease) -2W: 85% | -4W: 100%

FIGURE 10.6

In mixed mode, the algorithm says, "*Great, you met your KPI. But, you are decreasing more than you should over time – I am going to say you are slightly at risk.*"

I personally prefer mixed mode. As a security leader, I tend to be conservative on metrics. Greenwashing our dashboards gets us into trouble. Also, as data accumulates, the fluctuation in rates tends to stabilize. So a move of 1–2% would take a considerable amount of data if you are looking at many thousands of results.

## Child Metrics Objects

Each of the metrics objects in the preceding section focused on burndown rates. They are arranged in columns by risk. There are three levels of risk. Nothing stops you from having more levels. My only encouragement is to include levels that have SLAs set to them. Think back to our chapter on regression modeling as a guide.

For each risk level of critical, severe, and moderate, I included supporting count and time to live–based metrics. These are purposefully rudimentary. They are meant to provide additional color to the main metrics, which are burndown rates.

## Count Metrics

This is the most basic of metrics objects. It is nothing more than a count of events over time. The reason you want counts is that a rate, which is a ratio over time, can hide the actual volume of events underneath it. This metric shows those details (Figure 10.7).

CRITICAL OPEN VULNERABILITIES
**818 Open Now (103% Increase)**
-1W: 403 | -1M: 872 | Uniq: 354

FIGURE 10.7

You can have a KPI that is being achieved, that is actually green, while this metric is red. The view is that you need just enough information to make a decision. For example, *"Yes we are at a 90% burndown rate, yet there are over 2000 critical open vulnerabilities!"*

### Time-to-Live Basic Metric

This is the other simple metrics that supports burndown. Time to live (TTL) is meant to give you a feel for open and closed rates (Figure 10.8).

CRITICAL TIME TO LIVE RATES
**85.5% Closed Vuln < 1D**
50% of Open < 6D | Max Open: 70D

FIGURE 10.8

### Scaling, Accelerating, Slowing

The TTL rate by itself may seem high performing. It needs to be considered in context. When I view the critical context for burndown, I would assess it as **slowing.** Critical vulnerabilities are coming and going. But the volume seems to be overwhelming the burndown rate. While the closed rate seems fast, those that remain open seem to linger.

CRITICAL VULNERABILITY BURNDOWN RATE
**64% Now (21% Decrease)**
-2W: 85% | -4W: 100% | 58% Goal: 100% Met

CRITICAL OPEN VULNERABILITIES
**818 Open Now (103% Increase)**
-1W: 403 | -1M: 872 | Uniq: 354

CRITICAL TIME TO LIVE RATES
**85.5% Closed Vuln < 1D**
50% of Open < 6D | Max Open: 70D

If the burndown rate was holding while critical open vulnerabilities are increasing, we could say that the burndown capability is **scaling.** Alternatively, if the burndown rate is improving while critical vulnerabilities are increasing, we would say that the burndown capability is **accelerating.**

Terms like *accelerating, scaling,* and *slowing,* when backed by real data, can be useful at the aggregate KPI level. You could report that "*Vulnerability remediation capabilities are scaling.*" And if appropriate, you could break out the underlying data that supports the assessment.

## Survival Analysis

You could consider survival analysis as time-to-live metrics' bigger and far more powerful brother. We had a whole chapter on it. It is included as a tab in the lower half of Figure 10.1. I have reproduced it in Figure 10.9.

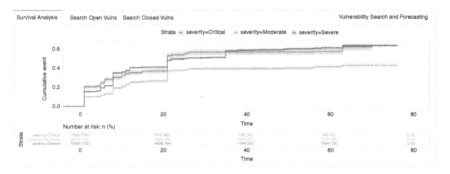

FIGURE 10.9

As you may recall, survival analysis both measures events that have happened as well as considers processes that have yet to experience an event. You can refer back to Chapter 2 for extensive details on this.

What we see above is fairly similar remediation across risk categories. In fact, the middle-tier risk seems to be slightly outperforming the highest-tier risk through the whole time period. This is a function of policy not being aligned with performance.

## *Assessment: Slowing and Unoptimized*

As an overarching characterization, I would say this is an example of "Slowing and Unoptimized" vulnerability burndown. I've grounded that assessment in data. While the data is empirical, and mathematically unambiguous, the distinctions I am using are indeed qualitative.

An optimized remediation policy would need to materialize in the data. In particular, the survival curves would look differentiated over time. In this case, they are somewhat undifferentiated.

What is making for the sluggish performance? Are there vulnerabilities or classes of vulnerabilities that are causing issues? Are there classes of vulnerabilities that may be drawing attention away from more pressing risks? Vulnerability Business Intelligence (BI) can help answer these questions.

## Vulnerability BI

This is a quick snapshot of the BI view. It allows you to search in the aggregate in the upper right, and it has search functionality in each column. The BI view allows for drill-in by risk and vulnerability. It is just a quick tool for understanding what is driving the metrics.

| Survival Analysis | Search Open Vulns | Search Closed Vulns | | | | | Vulnerability Search and Forecasting | | |
| --- | --- | --- | --- | --- | --- | --- | --- | --- | --- |
| | | | | | | | | Search | |
| severity | title | status | cvss | risk | ip | | time.open | first.seen | last.seen |
| | | | | | | | | | |
| ▶ Moderate (34) | | | | | | | | | |
| ▶ Severe (639) | | | | | | | | | |
| ▼ Critical (354) | | | | | | | | | |
| | ▼ Oracle WebLogic Obsolete (18) | | | | | | | | |
| | | NOT_REMEDIATED | 9.3 | 315 | 1.1.1.1 | | 70 | 12/7/20 | 2/14/21 |
| | | NOT_REMEDIATED | 9.3 | 315 | 1.1.1.1 | | 70 | 12/7/20 | 2/14/21 |

FIGURE 10.10

## Subsetting by Date

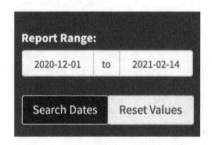

You will have questions about different time periods. For example, you may want to investigate the previous quarter vs. the current quarter vs. both together. This is possible through the report range search.

It informs the whole data set in memory. Not only are the metrics objects constrained by date, but the survival analysis view and vulnerability BI views are also.

## Data Upload

The last feature I want to discuss (which is the first one you would actually use) is data upload. I went old-school with this one because I can't predict what tools you may have in place from a vulnerability management perspective.

Perhaps you keep all your data in some form of log aggregation system or perhaps a GRC system? What I can be fairly confident in is that you can get your data out in a csv format. I am confident that you can manipulate your data to meet the simple format requirements for this tool.

The required fields are as you see them in Figure 10.10: Severity, Title, Status, CVSS, Risk, IP, Time Open, First Seen, Last Seen. These can be customized to your own needs.

Before we dive into Shiny in depth, I want to explain how KPI scoring works in more detail.

# KPI Analysis – Scoring the Scores

Think of a KPI as a rate you beat 100% of the time.

Imagine a two-month period where you have a burndown rate fluctuating from 61% to 93%. The average rate is 77%, but 60% is the highest rate you beat 100% of the time. It's just below 61%. If your goal (KPI) is a 60% burndown rate, then you met it. It's now your baseline. You set goals (KPIs) against your current baseline.

What if your goal was 75%? Using the KPI analysis mode, you find that you meet the 75% burndown rate only 45% of the time. Would you say you achieved your goal? Probably not. If you find that a 65% burndown rate was achieved by 90% – would you say you achieved your goal? Maybe. It depends on how strict you want to be.

Figure 10.11 shows our uncertainty about the current critical burndown rate. It's based on ~4,700 critical burndown events covering almost a quarter for a major enterprise.

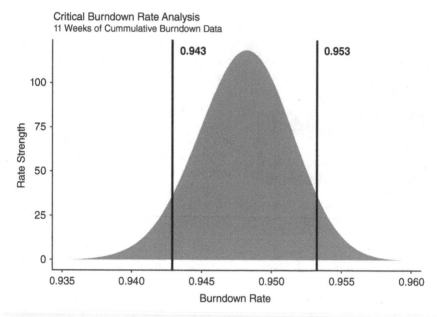

FIGURE 10.11

If you look to the far left on the *x*-axis of Figure 10.11, you will see a
0.935 (93.5% as a percentage). The distribution (purple bell-shaped curve)
actually stretches to just above 93%. If this graph could speak, it would
say, "*The highest-scoring KPI baseline is 93%. Anything above that has
some amount of uncertainty.*" How much uncertainty do we have with
rates above 93%? This is where we can flip the dashboard's analysis mode
to KPI mode.

In investigating a 94% KPI, we find that it is met 99% of the time in
Figure 10.12. The metric is green. It's a stable rate. Conversely, 95% is met
28% of the time. The metrics object is yellow. Given our uncertainty, I would
say 94% is passable.

FIGURE 10.12

The most plausible AVERAGE burndown rates (not the KPI baseline)
fluctuates between the ~94% and ~95% vertical bars in Figure 10.11. The
area between those two lines is the highest density interval, or HDI.[1] We
have encountered the HDI in earlier chapters. It's where the most plausible
rates live.

## KPI Sliders

The KPI slider in Figure 10.13 on the left is initially set to the baseline score – again, the highest rate you meet 100% of the time. In this case, that's 93%. Now we set the critical KPI slider on the right to 95%. It dynamically (reactively) updates the KPI goal with a new value. If you were using the dashboard, you would see that the metrics object moves from 93% to 95% with a new goal achievement of 28%, as seen in Figure 10.12.

That 28% rate has a technical name. It's called the **Posterior Inclusion Probability**, or PIP. And the opposite is the **Posterior Error Probability**, or PEP.[2] When using KPIs, I call it the **KPI Inclusion Probability**, or KIP.

Current Trend State: 93%

Current data at the bottom of the metrics object

-4Wk: 96%| -8Wk: 97%| 93% Goal: 100% Met

Future Trend State: 95%

After moving the slider, the data on the far right is dynamically updated

-4Wk: 96% |-8Wk: 97% | 95% Goal: 28% Met

FIGURE 10.13

Figure 10.14 repeats a graph you saw in Chapter 4 on burndown. Notice the dotted vertical lines. These are KPI lines for each quarter. Note that Q4 distribution for product team B. It's roughly 60% to the right of the Q4 KPI line. While Q4 rates seem to be trending in the right direction, the KPI goal hasn't been fully achieved. But, the Q3 goal was 100% achieved with zero uncertainty.

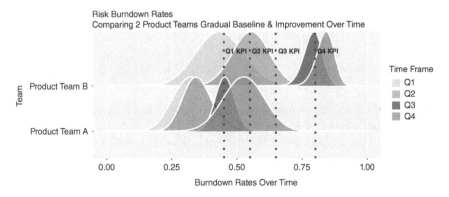

FIGURE 10.14

# KPI Scoring Using the HDI

Burndown metrics are a form of hit-and-miss measurement. And the statistical model behind that measurement is the beta distribution. Recall our hierarchy: Capability > Process > Metric > Measurement > Distribution(s). The beta distribution takes hit-and-miss *measurements* and returns a probability. Here are the cumulative hits and misses used for Figure 10.11:

```
> hit
[1] 4435
> miss
[1] 243
```

If the beta distribution could speak, it would say, *"Given these hits and misses, I'm pretty sure the rate (probability) is between 94% and 95%. It could be a little more, it could be a little less."* Here is the call to my souped-up beta distribution:

```
# Make Beta Graph
MakeBetaGraph(hit = hit,
              miss = miss,
              xlab = "Burndown Rate",
              ylab = "Rate Strength",
              tlab = "Critical Burndown Rate Analysis",
              slab = "11 Weeks of Cumulative Burndown Data"))
```

Under the covers, MakeBetaGraph() asks the beta distribution for 1,000 results and then asks for the HDI. Think of the HDI as the best-guess range for the burndown rate. Let's look at five samples from the 1,000 results from the beta distribution. Let's also look at the HDI. Don't worry about the code details – yet:

```
> posterior <- distribution_beta(1000, hit, miss)
> head(posterior,5)
[1] 0.9374848 0.9382534 0.9387232 0.9390667 0.9393394
>ci(posterior, method = "HDI")
# Highest Density Interval

89% HDI
------------
[0.94, 0.95]
```

This is important because it is what sits behind KPI scoring and the burndown metrics object at large.

## Making Shiny Dashboards

This will be a whirlwind tour of Shiny, R's web development framework.[3] Shiny is optimized for building analytics solutions quickly. It's also optimized for making single-page applications. Shiny excels at this in part because it uses a simple reactive programming framework.[4]

Reactive programming allows you to make web applications that behave just like desktop applications. If you update one field (think Excel formulas), other data fields can get updated dynamically, with no need for page refreshes.

Shiny allows you to code everything in R, which in turn creates javascript in the back end to support reactivity. If you need to make custom widgets, you can easily integrate javascript directly into Shiny.[5]

I am not a Shiny master – at least, not yet. But I am an API user. And I suppose you could say I am a domain expert. I suspect 99% of my readers are, too. Shiny is an easy-to-learn tool (API) that makes life much easier for the domain expert. But as easy as it is to learn, I will caution you that it is even easier to get lost in reactive programming.

I have spent a lot of time considering how data flows in and around our example Shiny app. I used various debugging and data flow tools to help. It took a lot of effort to make things simple. And you must make it simple. Because, there is complexity under the hood waiting to ooze out.

Figure 10.15 shows what our current app looks like in action on the back end. It is just one portion of the reactivity. For now, don't try to understand it. Just appreciate the fact that a lot is going on. If you ever intend to build anything "real" in Shiny, you will want to start simple.

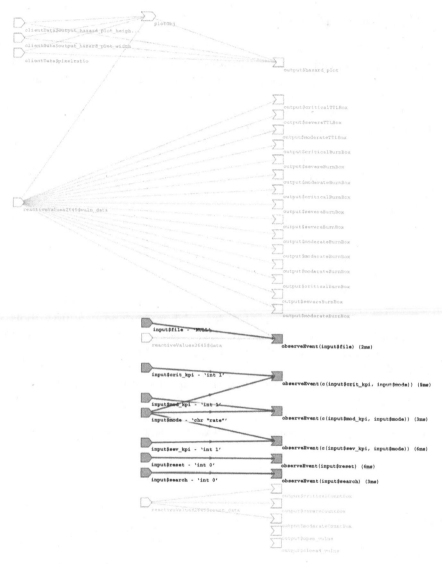

**FIGURE 10.15**

In the next section, I am going to cover the Shiny code used to make our application. There is some amount of abstraction to simplify things. I can't cover every piece of code like I did in the A/B testing example. Fortunately, for the curious you can explore the depth of the burndown dashboard code from the book's website: www.themetricsmanifesto.com.

# Shiny Code

When you execute the dashboard app, the following code will run in the back end. It is found in the helper_functions.R associated with this application. This executes transparently so as not to get in the way of Shiny starting up. My expectation is that you are using the code from the site. It will update frequently. The code is here mainly for concepts.

## *Dashboard Packages*

```
# Package names
packages <- c("readr", "tidyverse", "lubridate", "survival",
  "survminer", "shiny", "shinydashboard", "reactable",
  "shinyalert")

# Install packages not yet installed
installed_packages <- packages %in% rownames(installed.packages())
if (any(installed_packages == FALSE)) {
  install.packages(packages[!installed_packages])
}

# Packages loading
invisible(lapply(packages, library, character.only = TRUE))
```

## *Shiny UI Code*

Next comes the UI code. There is a direct correlation between this code and everything you can see in the ui() functions. I have added comments in the code. Take the time to skim through those. How this code relates to the UI should be easy to see.

```
# Allow large files to be uploaded
options(shiny.maxRequestSize = 30*1024^2)

ui <- dashboardPage(
  title="Vuln Burndown",

  dashboardHeader(title = "Vulnerability Burndown"),


  # Left hand sidebar elements of the dashboard
  dashboardSidebar(

    #CSS Settings For Scrolling and Button Colors
    tags$head(
      tags$style(
        HTML('#search{background-color:black;color:white}'))),
```

```r
tags$head(
  tags$style(
    HTML('#kpi_update{background-color:grey;color:white}'))),

#File Input
fileInput("file", "Upload Vuln CSV",accept = c(".csv")),
dateRangeInput("reportrange", "Report Range:"),

#Create Custom Buttons For Date Range
GetSearchButton(),
GetResetButton(),

# KPI Sidebar Elements
selectInput("mode", "Analysis Mode:",c("Default Mode" = "rate",
  "KPI Mode" = "kpi", "Mixed Mode" = "mixed"), selected = "rate"),
sliderInput("crit_kpi", "Set Critical KPI Goal:",1,100,.95),
sliderInput("sev_kpi", "Set Severe KPI Goal:", 1, 100, .95),
sliderInput("mod_kpi", "Set Moderate KPI Goal:", 1, 100, .95)
),

# Main Dashboard Body
dashboardBody(

  # Row of Burndown Metrics Objects
  fluidRow(
    verbatimTextOutput("text"),
    infoBoxOutput("criticalBurnBox"),
    infoBoxOutput("severeBurnBox"),
    infoBoxOutput("moderateBurnBox")
  ),

  # Row of Count Metrics Objects
  fluidRow(
    infoBoxOutput("criticalCountBox"),
    infoBoxOutput("severeCountBox"),
    infoBoxOutput("moderateCountBox")
  ),

  # Row of Time To Live Metrics Objects
  fluidRow(
    infoBoxOutput("criticalTTLBox"),
    infoBoxOutput("severeTTLBox"),
    infoBoxOutput("moderateTTLBox")
  ),

  # Survival Analysis and Vulnerability BI Tabs
  fluidRow(
    tabBox(
      title = "Vulnerability Search And Forecasting", width = 12,
      tabPanel("Survival Analysis", plotOutput("hazard_plot")),
      tabPanel("Search Open Vulns", reactableOutput("open_vulns")),
      tabPanel("Search Closed Vulns", reactableOutput("closed_vulns"))
    )
  )
)
)
```

Take a look back at Figure 10.1. Now, look at this code. Can you see the one-to-one correlation? This is the easiest part of working with Shiny – laying out the UI.

## Shiny Server Code

Now let's look at the server-side code. This all exists in the same file as the ui() code above.

You may have noticed that the above code is one function called ui(). The next function is called server(). You can separate the ui() and server() function into separate files. I kept them together. I abstracted much of the back end calculations into the helper file. This kept the code nice and tidy.

What you will see in the server() code is six calls to observeEvent(). These are six listeners. And they are waiting for things to happen in the UI. For example, the sixth call to observeEvent() listens to the file upload UI element. Notice the input$file variable?

If you look further into that specific function call, you will see that it instantiates the various UI objects. It does that after checking the file for correctness using helper functions. The objects the file function populates include: calendar, sliders, burn boxes (aka metrics objects), and tabs. I labeled everything very clearly so you should have no trouble following the first phase of dashboard instantiation.

Now the fun begins. This is where dealing efficiently with state change requires serious thought. Fortunately, this application is not that complex. Anything more would require more of a test-driven approach.[6] That's because small changes can set off reactive chains of events. Their source can be hard to trace.

The very first observeEvent() is listening for the "search dates" button to be pushed. As you may recall, the calendar allows you to subset your data. If you subset from six months of data to a quarter's worth, you want to be sure all the UI components update with the smaller data set.

For this project, you will likely want to go back to your original state – i.e., six months of data. You shouldn't have to upload a file again to do that. The second observeEvent() function below listens for the reset button. When pushed, the original dataset rehydrates the UI.

The next three observeEvent() functions are tied to the KPI sliders. The sliders only interact with the top row of metrics objects in the UI. In the back end, they run a series of calculations. I explained those in part in the "KPI Scoring Using the HDI" box above.

If you look closely at the slider code, you will see the use of the isolate() function.[7] This function puts a sandbox around that code, halting unwanted reactivity.

That's it in terms of the design of the application. I hope you can see how the back end and front end are stitched together. Most of the back end data wrangling and statistics complexity has been abstracted away into the helper_functions.R.

I did it this way both to keep things tidy and, possibly most important, to keep all the "reactivity" defined in the code below. It is the "reactive map" of the application. If the code was too cluttered, I would lose sight of which ui components were talking one to another.

```
server <- function(input, output, session) {

  #Empty data structure - waiting to be filled
  data_vals <- reactiveValues(data = NULL, vuln_data = NULL,
                              count_data = NULL)

  #If a date range is requested we need to update
  observeEvent(
    input$search, {

      #Fetch Data from global data() based on date inputs
      data_vals$vuln_data <- UpdateVulnData(data_vals$data,
        input$reportrange[1], input$reportrange[2])

      data_vals$count_data = GetVulnVariables(data_vals$vuln_data)

      crit_kpi <- reactive(GetBestKPI(data_vals$vuln_data, "Critical"))
      sev_kpi <- reactive(GetBestKPI(data_vals$vuln_data, "Severe"))
      mod_kpi <- reactive(GetBestKPI(data_vals$vuln_data, "Moderate"))

      #Update Sliders
      updateSliderInput(session, "crit_kpi", value = crit_kpi() * 100)
      updateSliderInput(session, "sev_kpi", value = sev_kpi() * 100)
      updateSliderInput(session, "mod_kpi", value = mod_kpi() * 100)

    }, ignoreInit = TRUE
  )

  observeEvent(
    input$reset, {

      #Reset Data To Original And Make Vars To Pass To Sliders
      data_vals$vuln_data <- GetUpdatedVulnData(data_vals$data)

      data_vals$count_data = GetVulnVariables(data_vals$vuln_data)

      crit_kpi <- reactive(GetBestKPI(data_vals$vuln_data, "Critical"))
      sev_kpi <-  reactive(GetBestKPI(data_vals$vuln_data, "Severe"))
      mod_kpi <-  reactive(GetBestKPI(data_vals$vuln_data, "Moderate"))

      #Update KPI Sliders
      updateSliderInput(session, "crit_kpi", value = crit_kpi() * 100)
```

```
    updateSliderInput(session, "sev_kpi", value = sev_kpi() * 100)
    updateSliderInput(session, "mod_kpi", value = mod_kpi() * 100)

    #Get Original Date Range and Update Calendar
    min_date <- min(mdy(data_vals$data$discovered_date))
    max_date <- max(mdy(data_vals$data$last_scan_date))
    updateDateRangeInput(session, "reportrange",start = min_date,
        end = max_date)

  }, ignoreInit = TRUE
)

observeEvent(c(input$crit_kpi,input$mode),{
  crit_kpi <- as.numeric(input$crit_kpi/100)
  mode <- input$mode
  output$criticalBurnBox <- renderInfoBox({ GetBurndownBox("Critical",
    isolate(data_vals$vuln_data), crit_kpi, mode)})
}, ignoreInit = TRUE)

observeEvent(c(input$sev_kpi,input$mode),{
  sev_kpi <- as.numeric(input$sev_kpi/100)
  mode <- input$mode
  output$severeBurnBox <- renderInfoBox({ GetBurndownBox("Severe",
    isolate(data_vals$vuln_data), sev_kpi, mode) })
}, ignoreInit = TRUE)

observeEvent(c(input$mod_kpi, input$mode),{
  mod_kpi <- as.numeric(input$mod_kpi/100)
  mode <- input$mode
  output$moderateBurnBox <- renderInfoBox({ GetBurndownBox("Moderate",
    isolate(data_vals$vuln_data), mod_kpi, mode) })
}, ignoreInit = TRUE)

observeEvent(input$file,{

  #Set Reactive Values - See Top Of Server Function.
  data_vals$data = GetFileData(input$file) # Cache for Reset
  if( is.data.frame(data_vals$data) == FALSE ){
    output$text <- renderText({data_vals$data})
    return()
  }
  data_vals$vuln_data = data_vals$data
  data_vals$count_data = GetVulnVariables(data_vals$vuln_data)

  #Get Slider Data
  crit_kpi_rate <- GetBestKPI(data_vals$vuln_data, "Critical") * 100
  sev_kpi_rate <- GetBestKPI(data_vals$vuln_data, "Severe") * 100
  mod_kpi_rate <- GetBestKPI(data_vals$vuln_data, "Moderate") * 100

  #Update Sliders W/Best KPI - These Create Burndown Boxes Above
  updateSliderInput(session, "crit_kpi", value = crit_kpi_rate)
  updateSliderInput(session, "sev_kpi", value = sev_kpi_rate)
  updateSliderInput(session, "mod_kpi", value = mod_kpi_rate)
```

```
#Get Calendar Data and Update Cal
cal_start <- min(mdy(data_vals$vuln_data$discovered_date))
cal_end <- max(mdy(data_vals$vuln_data$last_scan_date))
updateDateRangeInput(session, "reportrange",start = cal_start,
  end = cal_end)

#Count Boxes
output$criticalCountBox <- renderInfoBox({ GetCountBox("Critical",
  data_vals$count_data$critical) })
output$severeCountBox <- renderInfoBox({ GetCountBox("Severe",
  data_vals$count_data$severe)})
output$moderateCountBox <- renderInfoBox({
  GetCountBox("Moderate",data_vals$count_data$moderate) })

#TTL Boxes
output$criticalTTLBox <- renderInfoBox({ GetTTLBox("Critical",
  data_vals$vuln_data) })
output$severeTTLBox <- renderInfoBox({ GetTTLBox("Severe",
  data_vals$vuln_data) })
output$moderateTTLBox <- renderInfoBox({ GetTTLBox("Moderate",
  data_vals$vuln_data) })

#Survival Plot
output$hazard_plot <- renderPlot({GetSurvPlot(data_vals$vuln_data)})

#Not Remediated Search
output$open_vulns <- renderReactable({
  reactable(GetVulnTable(data_vals$vuln_data,"NOT_REMEDIATED"),
            groupBy = c("severity", "title"),
            filterable = TRUE,
            minRows = 10,
            searchable = TRUE,
            resizable = TRUE,
            striped = TRUE,
            highlight = TRUE)
})

#Remediated Search
output$closed_vulns <- renderReactable({
  reactable(GetVulnTable(data_vals$vuln_data,"REMEDIATED"),
            groupBy = c("severity", "title"),
            filterable = TRUE,
            minRows = 10,
            searchable = TRUE,
            resizable = TRUE,
            striped = TRUE,
            highlight = TRUE)
})

})# End observe event

}

shinyApp(ui, server)
```

## Conclusion

I hope this has piqued your interest in creating metrics dashboards. I think it is great fun, but it can also be full of frustration. Our approach was to use the core ui() and server() function as layouts and reactive maps, in which I extracted all the computation and dynamic ui creation out to another file. I think this is a fairly safe pattern, as anything more complex would need a test-driven approach.

## Notes

1. *Highest Density Interval (HDI) — hdi*. (2021). *HDI*. https://easystats. github.io/bayestestR/reference/hdi.html
2. *Understanding the Bayesian Approach to False Discovery Rates (Using Baseball Statistics)*. (2015, November 3). Variance Explained. http:// varianceexplained.org/r/bayesian_fdr_baseball/
3. *Shiny*. (2021). Shiny. https://shiny.rstudio.com/
4. *Shiny: Reactivity – an Overview*. (2017). Reactivity. https://shiny.rstudio. com/articles/reactivity-overview.html
5. *htmlwidgets for R*. (2015). HTMLWidgets. https://www.htmlwidgets.org/
6. Wickham, H. (2021). *Chapter 21 Testing | Mastering Shiny*. Scaling Testing. https://mastering-shiny.org/scaling-testing.html
7. *Shiny - Stop Reactions with isolate()*. (2017). Isolation. https://shiny. rstudio.com/articles/isolation.html

# CHAPTER 11

# Simulating Data Like a Pro

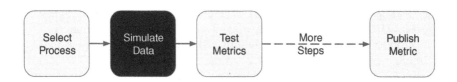

> **Note:** This is a *code heavy* chapter. That's why I pushed it to later in the book. Yet, you can read at least half of this chapter without having any desire to code. If you are one of those readers, I do think it is important for you to push ahead and read. Starting with simulation is an important metrics design concept, one that is novel to security – but old news to the sciences.

## Introduction

You can measure anything, but you can't measure everything. Why? Because measurement takes time. It takes skills. And, it takes money. If this wasn't true, more people would be doing it. That is why you need to prioritize what you are going to measure. Simulation can help.

Simulation forces you to think deeply about the object and methods of measurement. The object of measurement is the security process you want to improve. The methods are the metrics (algorithms) you will use.

Simulation helps you create rough but useful samples of the types of data you will ultimately consume. Those samples let you test out your algorithms (your metrics), removing a lot of the guesswork out of what might otherwise be an expensive and potentially fruitless effort.

**The good news is, with simulation you don't need to wait for data.**
Don't be fooled. Simulation is more than just spitting out data. It is modeling random data-generating processes. That means accounting for how events have a tendency to arrive, depart, and morph, and how their data is correlated.

In this chapter, we will focus on making data that grows and changes. We will then use this data in our chapters to see what we can learn about our data-generating processes.

The chapter has the following sections:

- **Warming Up to Simulation:** Background and motivation for simulation
- **Let's Make Some Data, Part 1:** Introduction do data-generating processes
- **Let's Make Some Data, Part 2:** Simulation deep dive using Simstudy
- **Enriching and Tidying:** Cleaning and readying data for analysis
- **Advanced Simulation:** Techniques for enriching and relating data

## Warming Up to Simulation

What do the following questions have in common?

1. What's the likelihood of having one or more emergency patches next quarter?
2. In the last year, how many times did phishing result in compromise?
3. How long does it take to respond to critical incidents?
4. How likely are you to experience a reportable data loss in the next year?
5. Are you accelerating, scaling, or decelerating toward your security KPIs?

These are all rate-based questions. Meaning, they measure events over time.

Let's look at the first bullet. Let's say you had 23 emergency patches in the last year, averaging out to 5.75 a quarter. Given this contrived scenario, what's the probability of having 0, 1, 2, or more emergency patches next quarter?

Following is a quick-and-dirty way to approximately answer that question.

```
patches <- 0:20
average <- 23/4
plot(p, dpois(patches, average), type="h", lwd=3,
     ylab="Probability Of Emergency Patch",
     xlab="Count Of Emergency Patches")
```

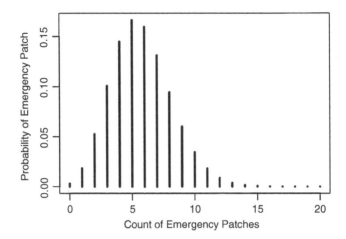

All we did here was simulate or, as measurement experts might say, we created a data-generating process. This one is simple. It's a standard approach for modeling and forecasting arrival rates. Arrival rates are one of the BOOM baselines.

The heart of this process is **dpois(patch, average).** Its job is to tell us the likelihood of seeing our data. The data is a list of critical patch counts like 1, 2, 3, etc. That data is then scored by comparing each count to our average belief – which was 5.75 per quarter.

The score returned from dpois() is a probability. You can see that clearly in the graph above, with the score being on the *y*-axis.

> Anytime you see a "pois" or "Poisson," you know we are dealing with counts – not French fish. And more specifically, we are looking to understand the rate at which things happen. It is one of many count functions you will encounter.

Our warmup was an example of a data-generating process. That is what this chapter is about – designing data-generating processes. Or, said more simply, simulating data. You will learn how to generate data like a pro – like a scientist. In fact, you will get exposed to an API used by scientists for generating data – even big data.

## Why Simulate First?

Why would I recommend simulating data first? As I alluded to in the intro, getting and tidying data is the most time-consuming and expensive effort in measurement. Indeed, you may have all the data you need in your log aggregation tool. But, getting that data out and formatted takes time – even if you are an expert data wrangler.

Before you go down the data-munging rabbit hole, it's best to have your metrics designs in order. It's a similar process to building a bridge or a skyscraper, or even a tiny house. Pros start with design, and that includes designing data prior to making metrics.

Understanding the primitive building blocks of the domain you are modeling is key to design. This is the topic of the next section – the very basic data types and dimensions of security metrics.

## Security Data Types and Dimensions

Security metrics consist of a standard set of data types and dimensions. Knowing these will help remove a lot of guesswork in modeling and measuring security processes. Let's start with data types:

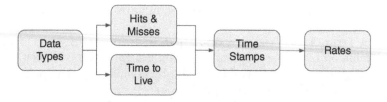

- **Security metrics are composed of two types of measures.** I call them hit-and-miss and time-to-live measures, or events and processes. Scientists might call them count and survival models.
- **Measures consist of one type of data – timestamps.** An event is a singular timestamp – something that happened at a specific time. An angry packet hitting a firewall, a beacon to a command-and-control server, and a vulnerability materializing are all examples of events. All events can be reduced to timestamps.
- **Time to live measures have two timestamps.** There is a first-seen timestamp and a last-seen timestamp. A vulnerability arriving and departing, an S3 bucket found open to the public and then closed, a user deprovisioning after a request – these are all time to live (process) measures.
- **Events are counted up over time to produce rates.** We just saw this in the introduction to this chapter. We want to see how rates change over time. Ultimately, we want to see how those rates respond to security activity. We want to know what sorts of activities or treatments matter

most in affecting those rates. (For example, is our new anti-malware solution making a difference?) This is how metrics lead to process optimization. Optimization is the third letter in the BOOM framework.

Now that we understand basic metrics data types, let's unpack their dimensions.

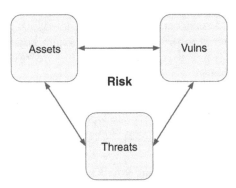

- **Security data has three *macro* dimensions:** threats, vulnerabilities, and assets. Taken together, they are commonly understood as risks.
- **Risks are ranked by their criticality.** Criticality tells us how quickly we respond to risks, and to what magnitude. *When the criticality of risks and their treatment get codified, we call it policy.* Metrics help validate that policy is being implemented as expected.
- **Lastly, most security tools provide data dimensions and types, as we just defined them.** You get data on threats, vulnerabilities, and assets with criticality directly from security tools, with timestamps provided by default.

In summary, the data we simulate revolves around these data types and dimensions.

- The fundamental data type is a **timestamp**.
- The fundamental dimensions are **assets**, **threats**, and **vulnerabilities**.
- The confluence of dimensions with **levels of criticality** can be characterized as **risks**.
- Treatment of risks codified is **policy**.

**That's it.** Our simulations will be a mashup of these elements.

## Let's Make Some Data: Part 1

In this section, we are going to model a hit-and-miss and time-to-live data-generating process. Most security phenomena you will measure are of these two types. The code is light here, so for concept-only readers – you should stick around.

In the second section of this chapter, I introduce a tool for scaling out the data-generation process. It supports very large and fast dataset generation. We use it to create the datasets we use throughout the majority of this book.

This is a long chapter, so strap in!

Lastly, these functions may get updates over time on the book's site, www.themetricsmanifesto.com. Refer to it as the authoritative source.

**Assume for a moment that you know absolutely nothing about security, computing, your company, etc.** You are maximally uncertain. Maximum uncertainty is our starting point for understanding data-generating processes. It's a clean slate on which to build.

I liken maximum uncertainty to a space alien attending their first baseball game. Assume this alien is from another dimension. They know nothing of our physics (gravity, wind resistance …) and nothing about baseball. If you asked the alien what the batting average is of a given batter, they would not know.

We can measure what knowing nothing (maximum uncertainty) actually looks like. As stated, it is an important backdrop for understanding what *knowing something* looks like when generating data.

When you know nothing about a process, you are in effect saying, *"All possible outcomes are equally plausible."* Why? Because you have no information. You have zero expertise, history, know-how, etc. So, for our alien, the batting average could be 1,000 or 0 or anything in between. Knowing nothing looks like this:

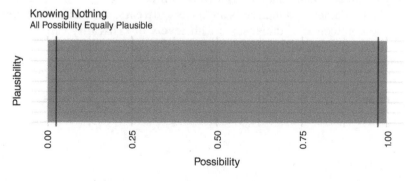

Knowing Nothing
All Possibility Equally Plausible

To make this more concrete, let's ask our resident alien about batting averages. (*Note:* The alien is good at math.)

"*In 1,000 at bats what number of hits would you expect from the average player? Make your most comfortable guess. Meaning, the true hit rate is just as likely to be above or below that comfortable number.*"

The alien responds, "*That's easy, 500! I am completely ambivalent about that number. The true rate is equally above or below that number from my highly uninformed point of view.*"

I then ask, "*What amount of hits is your likely maximum out of 1,000 tries? Meaning, the true rate has a 90% chance of being at or below this number?*"

The alien says, "*Another easy one, it must be 900.*"

## Let's Code It!

Let's feed those answers into R. To start, I am going to walk you through portions of code at a high level. **I'm shooting for concepts over code and you should, too.**

> These functions are all available on the book's site. *You are not required to understand all of this* – beyond knowing that this is a hit-and-miss model.

```
hits <- GetBeliefsHits(500, 900, 1000)
ggplotBeta(hits[1], hits[2], "Possibility", "Plausibility", "Knowing
Nothing","All Possibility Equally Plausible")
```

Our first function, which you have seen before, is a hit-and-miss data converter called GetBeliefsHits(). It converts hit-and-miss data into shape codes or shape parameters.

Shape codes control the shape of data. You can think of them as two dials on an Etch-A-Sketch. One dial moves things left to right and one dial moves things up and down (spread) – all on a graph. (Many statistical functions have shape parameters of one kind or another.) In our "no knowledge" case, our shape controls produce a straight line. You saw that in the graph above.

> You can look into the GetBeliefsHits() function in the GitHub repo for the book. It's something I created from work found here: https://bayesball.github.io/Intro_ProbBayes.html.[1] There's also a book that goes with the site called *Probability and Bayesian Modeling*. A free online version can be found here: https://bayesball.github.io/BOOK/probability-a-measurement-of-uncertainty.html.[2] It's one of many dozens of free resources on data analysis. I will reference resources like this throughout this book.

The two data-shaping values returned from GetBeliefsHits() are then fed into another helper function called ggplotBeta(). This function generates a small amount of data and graphs it using the shape codes. I cut some code out of the ggplotBeta() so we can focus on the data-generating portion.

```
x = seq(0, 1, 0.01)
y = dbeta(x, shape1=alpha, shape2=beta)
```

The portion of code above only does one thing: telling us how plausible our data ($x$ values) are given our shape values. It's very similar to the dpois() function we encountered at the beginning of this chapter. The difference here is that we are scoring probabilities. The $x$ value holds a set of 100 probabilities, aka possible batting averages:

```
> x = seq(0, 1, 0.01)
> x
  [1] 0.00 0.01 0.02 0.03 0.04 0.05 0.06 0.07 0.08 0.09 0.10 0.11 0.12 0.13 0.14 0.15 0.16 0.17 0.18 0.19 0.20
 [22] 0.21 0.22 0.23 0.24 0.25 0.26 0.27 0.28 0.29 0.30 0.31 0.32 0.33 0.34 0.35 0.36 0.37 0.38 0.39 0.40 0.41
 [43] 0.42 0.43 0.44 0.45 0.46 0.47 0.48 0.49 0.50 0.51 0.52 0.53 0.54 0.55 0.56 0.57 0.58 0.59 0.60 0.61 0.62
 [64] 0.63 0.64 0.65 0.66 0.67 0.68 0.69 0.70 0.71 0.72 0.73 0.74 0.75 0.76 0.77 0.78 0.79 0.80 0.81 0.82 0.83
 [85] 0.84 0.85 0.86 0.87 0.88 0.89 0.90 0.91 0.92 0.93 0.94 0.95 0.96 0.97 0.98 0.99 1.00
```

The dbeta() function scores each of those 100 values using our shape parameters. As you can see below, each $x$ value got an undifferentiated score of 1.

```
> y = dbeta(x, shape1=hits[1], shape2=hits[2])
> y
  [1] 1 1 1 1 1 1 1 1 1 1 1 1 1 1 1 1 1 1 1 1 1 1 1 1 1 1 1 1 1 1 1 1 1 1 1 1 1 1 1 1 1 1 1 1 1 1 1 1 1 1 1 1 1 1
 [55] 1 1 1 1 1 1 1 1 1 1 1 1 1 1 1 1 1 1 1 1 1 1 1 1 1 1 1 1 1 1 1 1 1 1 1 1 1 1 1 1 1 1 1 1 1 1
```

I call all those 1s *plausibility scores*. Plausibility scores also have a formal name – density. The higher the score, relative to other scores, the more plausible something is. There are 100 1s and they line up with each of the 100 probabilities.

Based on the data, is it possible to see a batting percentage that is most plausible – that stands out? The answer is no. Nothing stands out as everything is a 1. That's because our alien friend is maximally uncertain, meaning that 0.63 is just as plausible as 0.03.

## Ask the Expert

What if we were to ask an expert – aka a baseball fan? Let's say we have a true, deeply knowledgeable fan with us. Let's ask her the same set of questions we posed to our alien friend.

Her response is, "*I think the batting average is around .240 ... give or take. I am 90% confident that it's at or below .290.*" She is far more confident than our alien.

Let's put her data in our GetBeliefsHits() function, graph it, and see what sort of data was generated under the hood.

```
expert <- GetBeliefsHits(240,290,1000)
MakeBetaGraph(expert[1], expert[2],"Possibility","Plausibility","Knowing
Something","Not All Possibilities Equally Plausible")
```

> **Note:** I used a slightly different graphing function for this use case called MakeBetaGraph(). I did it simply because it adds some additional analytic sauce. It's what measurement experts call Bayesian data analysis. Bayesian analysis will show up frequently in this book, and I wanted to expose you to a tiny taste now.

Looking at the graph below, we can see that the scores are clustered around the pointy part of the gray curve. We would say that the probability is most dense where the graph is most pointy. It looks to be around the 24% mark. This is not surprising, given our expert's input of 24%.

The vertical black bars represent a thing called the "highest density interval," or HDI for short. You have encountered the HDI many times in this book in relation to Bayesian analysis. For now, consider the HDI the area most likely to hold the most plausible batting averages.

You're probably wondering, "*If we know the rate is 24%, then why all the fuss about an interval?!*"

If the graph below could answer you, it would say, "*Although 1,000 seems like a lot of swinging, we are still guessing here. Our expert said the rate is just as likely on one side or another of 24%. She also said she's 90% sure the true rate is at or below 29%. Given those assumptions and that amount of data – I'm still uncertain. If this sort of truthiness makes you uncomfortable, then go out and get more data. With more data, I get more certain – but never perfectly certain.*"

Apparently, our graph is Bayesian. Bayesians talk just like that. They leave plenty of room for uncertainty, which can be frustrating when all you want is a number. Yet, I find the Bayesian point of view aligns with security reality – which is fluid and chock full of uncertainty.

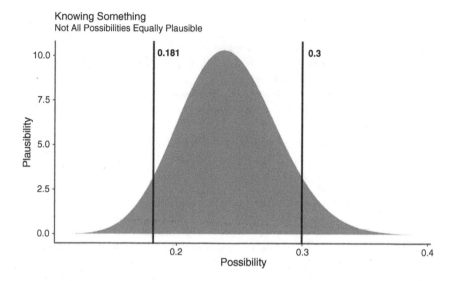

Here is the data-generating code used under the hood to make the graph above. Again, we focus on concepts over code.

```
posterior <- distribution_beta(1000, hit, miss)
ci_hdi <- ci(posterior, method = "HDI")
posterior %>% estimate_density(extend=TRUE)
```

I'm going to run each of these functions themselves and explain them. Again, this is all more for point of view.

```
posterior <- distribution_beta(1000, expert[1], expert[2])
head(posterior)
[1] 0.1385319 0.1445152 0.1482692 0.1510612 0.1533071 0.1551979
```

The three parameters for the first function are the total number of simulations (1,000) and the two expert shape parameters. The distribution_beta function fills a bucket up with 1,000 results.

We printed out the first five values from the bucket of results using the head() function. They are probabilities. The two expert shape parameters tell the function to fill the bucket with probabilities clustered approximately around the 24% mark.

The next thing you see is a call to get the HDI:

```
ci_hdi <- ci(posterior, method = "HDI")
ci_hdi
# Highest Density Interval

89% HDI
------------
[0.18, 0.30]
```

The ci() function looked at our pile of data and asked, *"What is the densest 89% portion of this data – where the probabilities are piled up the most?"* The answer is between 18% and 30%. It is not 19% and 31% or some other range; 18% to 30% is the thinnest range holding 89% of the probability.

> Why 89% and why not 90% or 95%? Some Bayesian experts say it's because 89 is a prime number. And primes have more fun. If you don't like 89%, you can change it.

The sample output below demonstrates plausibility scoring. I only listed four outputs out of a thousand due to space constraints. The *x* values are our hit probabilities and the *y* values are our plausibility scores (density). You can see how the probability rises up toward 24% while the plausibility increases. If you looked at all the data, you would see that 23.75% is paired with the highest density. That would be the tippy-top of our gray curve. If you get only one bet, 23.75% is it.

```
posterior %>% estimate_density(extend = TRUE)
            x          y
1   0.1157611   0.005106593
....
407 0.2242064   9.707605
....
457 0.2375617   10.31137
....
672 0.2949897   3.786227
....
```

**This is the basic concept of data generation.** We went from knowing nothing to knowing something. We learned that data tends to take on shapes, that summarizing the shape of data is key to measurement, and that we can score data to find out what's plausible among what's possible.

I hope you focused on the concepts without obsessing over the small amount of code and stats. As stated, it's about scores. The higher the score, the more plausible the data.

Now we are ready to generate some data at scale. I will unpack and expound on my points in this chapter and expose you to more!

# Let's Make Some Data: Part 2

We are going to create a data simulation piece by piece – function by function. Along the way you will get exposure to several data generating processes. A lot of code follows. For concept-only readers, you are welcome to stick around. But, this eventually gets into deeper waters.

In this section you will see fancy names like beta, binary, binomial, normal, and Poisson – all distributions. I will explain what they are good for in an intuitive and security-oriented manner. That means I will do my best to avoid getting mired in statistical jargon – a little bit is unavoidable.

To simplify and scale simulation, we will be using a library called simstudy: https://kgoldfeld.github.io/simstudy/index.html.[3] I chose simstudy for its speed, flexibility, and active development. It's built by scientists for scientists – to make simulation fast and easy.

Simstudy creates data using distributions like the two you have already seen – Poisson and beta. It adds methods for making that data have relationships of varying strengths – called correlation. The idea is that you can quickly create a data-generating process that approximates a real system you want to analyze.

## A Quick Glimpse

Before I unpack the nitty-gritty of simulation with simstudy, I want to share a simplifying function. We are going to build and then use this (somewhat familiar) function below. It creates one big table of vulnerability analysis data. It's all you need to get rolling:

```
dt <- GetSecResults()
```

If you print a small sample of the dt data table, you get the data below. Note, the table's columns wrap around due to its width. I will be walking through how to create this table. Before we begin, take a moment to look at the 17 columns and their data. I also list out a column description just below.

```
> dt
        idTeam          team nDays   id audit exposure exposure_id severity hits severity_id fix_time fix_date
   1:        1 external audit     5    1     0 external           1  extreme    1           1        6       11
   2:        1 external audit    25    2     0 external           1  extreme    1           1        8       33
   3:        1 external audit    54    3     0 external           1  extreme    1           1        7       61
   4:        1 external audit    76    4     0 external           1  extreme    1           1       11       87
   5:        1 external audit   108    5     0 external           1  extreme    1           1       13      121
  ---
1149:        6 internal no audit  347 1149     1 internal          3     high    1           3       89      436
1150:        6 internal no audit  347 1150     1 internal          3     high    1           3       96      443
1151:        6 internal no audit  347 1151     1 internal          3     high    1           3       82      429
```

```
1152:    6 internal no audit  347 1152   1 internal    3    high  1        3    91   438
1153:    6 internal no audit  354 1153   1 internal    3    high  1        3    81   435


        status first.seen  last.seen week.fseen week.lseen
   1:        0 2020-01-06 2020-01-12          1          2
   2:        0 2020-01-26 2020-02-03          4          5
   3:        0 2020-02-24 2020-03-02          8          9
   4:        0 2020-03-17 2020-03-28         12         13
   5:        0 2020-04-18 2020-05-01         16         18
   ---
1149:        1 2020-12-13 2021-03-12         50         63
1150:        1 2020-12-13 2021-03-19         50         64
1151:        0 2020-12-13 2021-03-05         50         62
1152:        0 2020-12-13 2021-03-14         50         63
1153:        0 2020-12-20 2021-03-11         51         63
```

- **idTeam:** There are six teams. They each have an id number 1–6.
- **team:** This is a team name. Each name describes risk characteristics.
- **nDays:** The day number for when the vulnerability first showed up.
- **id:** The unique id for the record/row.
- **audit:** A Boolean factor that determines if what the team creates is under audit, i.e., pci, sox, etc.
- **exposure:** This holds three types of exposure: external, partner, internal.
- **exposure_id:** An integer that represents each exposure type.
- **severity:** There are three types of severity: extreme, critical, high.
- **severity_id:** An integer that represents each severity type.
- **fix_time:** The number of days the vulnerability was open.
- **fix_date:** The day number the vulnerability was fixed on.
- **status:** A Boolean override field that determines if a vulnerability is still open despite what a date field may say.
- **first.seen:** Date stamp for when the vulnerability was first seen.
- **last.seen:** Date stamp for when the vulnerability was last seen.
- **week.fseen:** Week number for when the vulnerability was first seen.
- **week.lseen:** Week number for when the vulnerability was last seen.

In the next section, we build this data table out column by column and row by row. But to do this, we need a motivating example. I have chosen appsec-based vulnerability management.

## Modeling Vulnerability Management

Simulation is use case driven, and our use case is vulnerability management. Within vulnerability management, we will focus on appsec.

Modern software development, and hence appsec-based vulnerability management, is complex. Complexity is a function of velocity and team structure. You have many product teams composed of many services. Modern teams usually release software and platform changes daily – in some cases, hundreds if not thousands of times a day.[4]

The image below is a logical diagram that shows the relationship from product, to team, to vulnerabilities, to time.

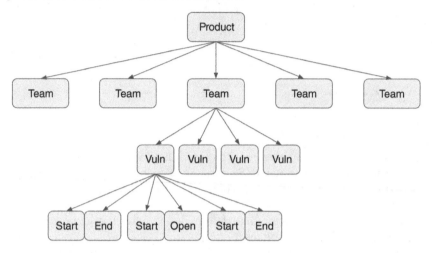

A company has many products, and a product team has many teams building services. We want to measure vulnerability arrivals and departures over time created by those teams.

Our goal is to baseline the vulnerability creation and elimination rate. Once we have a baseline, we can set targets for improvement and monitor to determine if we are accelerating or slowing in achieving targets over time.

With that model in mind, we are going to simulate a data set, beginning with the team data structure.

## The Team Data Structure

First, you will need to load a number of libraries into R. You will see those in the R file for this chapter. The three main libraries are as follows – they are also contained in the manifesto_functions.R file, which you should be using by default. If you have loaded that, then you have these libraries and all of the following code running:

```
library(data.table)
library(simstudy)
library(tidyverse)
```

Data.table is for analyzing big(ish) data. It is optimized for speed. Simstudy makes it easy to generate data using data tables. You have already met the tidyverse, an api for cleaning and querying data.

## Basic Team Structure

```
team_count <- 6
days <- 365
total <- days * team_count

team <- defData(varname = "team", dist = "nonrandom",
                formula = 0, id = "idTeam")
team <- defData(team,varname = "nDays",dist = "nonrandom",
                formula = days)
team <- genData(team_count, team)
```

defData() is used to define data structures, and genData() takes definitions and creates data. It's "Define Data," then "Generate Data." You pass data definitions to the data generator. Simple, right?

Let's look at the output, and follow with explanations:

```
> team
   idTeam team nDays
1:      1    0   365
2:      2    0   365
3:      3    0   365
4:      4    0   365
5:      5    0   365
6:      6    0   365
```

We created six rows of data, one row per team. Other than the idTeam column, the rest are placeholders.

The "dist" parameter in defData() is short for *distribution*. The distribution used here is for creating static values. That is why it is called the nonrandom distribution.

## Expand Team Rows

In the next function, we expand each team so they each have 365 rows. That is one row for each day of the year per team. The function that makes this happen is genCluster() – which is short for "generate cluster."

We pass the team data structure into genCluster(). The first variable we define is cLevelVar. It's short for "cluster-level variable." The team's id is our cLevelVar and is the parent to the vulnerabilities that will be generated. cLevelVar points to a team, which you can see in the diagram at the beginning of this section. We are going to cluster data (vulns) around team values.

numIndsVar is short for "number of individual variables," and it makes
365 rows per team. Finally there is level1ID, which is just an index:

```
> team <- genCluster(team,
                     cLevelVar = "idTeam",
                     numIndsVar = "nDays",
                     level1ID = "id")
> team
      idTeam team nDays    id
  1:       1    0   365     1
  2:       1    0   365     2
  3:       1    0   365     3
  4:       1    0   365     4
  5:       1    0   365     5
 ---
2186:       6    0   365  2186
2187:       6    0   365  2187
2188:       6    0   365  2188
2189:       6    0   365  2189
2190:       6    0   365  2190
```

We have six teams with 365 rows per team. Fairly simple.

The nDays column still has a placeholder value. We want a day number
in there. We can solve that in one line of R. See if you can figure out what
that little one-liner does. It uses the id fields and the idTeam field to do
some very simple arithmetic, one row at a time:

```
> team$nDays <- (team$id - (365*(team$idTeam - 1)))
> team
      idTeam team nDays    id
  1:       1    0     1     1
  2:       1    0     2     2
  3:       1    0     3     3
  4:       1    0     4     4
  5:       1    0     5     5
 ---
2186:       6    0   361  2186
2187:       6    0   362  2187
2188:       6    0   363  2188
2189:       6    0   364  2189
2190:       6    0   365  2190
```

## Creating the Vulnerability Data Structure

For the moment, we are going to set aside the "team" data.table to focus on
vulnerabilities. We will eventually merge the two data structures.

The vulnerability data table holds quasi randomly generated and moderately correlated vulnerabilities. There are three levels of vulnerabilities: extreme, critical, and high.

The chance of one or more vulnerabilities materializing depends on criticality. In this made-up example, we are saying that "extreme" vulnerabilities occur 5% of the time. Critical and high vulnerabilities are more frequent – 15% and 20%, respectively. The function we are creating will allow you to change this as you see fit.

For this function, I am only going to show a subset of the parameters:

```
dt <- genCorGen(n = total,
                nvars = 3,
                rho = 0.30,
                dist = "binary",
                params1 = c(0.05, 0.15, 0.20),
                cnames = "extreme_event,critical_event,high_event",
                corstr = "cs",
                wide = TRUE,
                method = "ep",
                id = "id")
```

genCorGen() creates a starter table of vulnerabilities. Just think of it as a very flexible function for creating data that tends to "wiggle" or "vary" together. Let's define each field:

- **total:** The total rows. It is equal to 365 × 6 = 2,190.
- **nvar:** The number of columns, one for each criticality level.
- **rho:** The amount of correlation.
- **dist:** The data-generating function that gets called. The binary distribution is for basic hits and misses. A "1" is a hit and a "0" is a miss. It requires input for its logic. That is next.
- **params1:** This is the input for the binary function. The first column (extreme) has a 5% chance of generating a yes for each day, 15% for the second column (critical), etc.
- **cnames:** The column names.
- **id:** The index for the table.

```
> dt
        id extreme_event critical_event high_event
   1:    1             0              0          0
   2:    2             0              0          0
   3:    3             0              1          0
   4:    4             0              0          0
   5:    5             0              0          0
   ---
```

```
2186: 2186            0              0              0
2187: 2187            0              0              0
2188: 2188            0              0              0
2189: 2189            0              0              0
2190: 2190            0              0              0
```

A "1" in a field above simply means there is one or more vulnerabilities discovered for that team, on that day, for that criticality level.

## Vulnerability Counts

The binary function in genCorGen() determines if a vulnerability event happened for each criticality level per day. The addCorGen() function below determines the count of vulnerabilities given an event happened. Notice that there is a call to addCorGen() for each event by criticality.

addCorGen() uses the Poisson distribution to do this. The Poisson distribution is set in the "dist" parameter below. We met the Poisson distribution earlier. For the moment, think of it as a semi-random count generator.

addCorGen also adds a bit of correlation to the data. The rho parameter does this. It is the same rationale as the binary function above – that is, vulnerability research and release sometimes produce vulnerabilities in bundles. In short, vulnerability arrival can be correlated.

```
dt <- addCorGen(dtOld = dt, idvar = "id", dist = "poisson", nvars = 1,
                corst = "id", param1 = "extreme_event", cnames = "extreme",
                rho= 0.40)

dt <- addCorGen(dtOld = dt, idvar = "id", dist = "poisson", nvars = 1,
                corst = "id", param1 = "critical_event",
                cnames = "critical", rho= 0.40)

dt <- addCorGen(dtOld = dt, idvar = "id", dist = "poisson", nvars = 1,
                corst = "id", param1 = "high_event", cnames = "high",
                rho= 0.40)
```

The Poisson distribution may put a zero where we previously defined that one or more events happen. I decided to override the zeros using the code below. Using extreme risk as an example, it says that where extreme_ event is set to true (1) and where extreme is 0, update extreme to equal 1.

```
#Event showed 1 but poisson returned 0 - Make it at least 1
dt$extreme[dt$extreme_event == 1 & dt$extreme == 0] <- 1
dt$critical[dt$critical_event == 1 & dt$critical == 0] <- 1
dt$high[dt$high_event == 1 & dt$high == 0] <- 1
```

This is what our vulnerability data table looks like. Rows 7 and 8 demonstrate the difference between an event and the count. The event columns have a 1 where the event is true, and the severity level columns (extreme, critical, high) hold the actual counts.

```
> head(dt,10)
    id extreme_event critical_event high_event extreme critical high
 1:  1             0              0          0       0        0    0
 2:  2             0              0          0       0        0    0
 3:  3             0              1          0       0        1    0
 4:  4             0              0          0       0        0    0
 5:  5             0              0          0       0        0    0
 6:  6             0              0          0       0        0    0
 7:  7             0              1          1       0        1    4
 8:  8             0              1          1       0        2    1
 9:  9             0              0          0       0        0    0
10: 10             0              0          1       0        0    1
```

## Merge Team and Vulnerability

Now that we have basic teams and vulnerability counts, we are going to merge them and use that new data table to go forward. The tables are joined on "id."

```
dt <- mergeData(team, dt, "id")
```

# Enriching and Tidying

Over the next several pages, we are going to add metadata to our basic structure. We will also tidy it up for ease of analysis. Here is a quick list so you know what is coming:

- **Add Risk Dimensions:** Audit and exposure risk.
- **Add Identifiers:** Create team identifiers (names) that reflect risk.
- **Tidy Data:** One vulnerability per row.
- **Remediation Timing:** Add timestamps and related metadata.
- **The Whole Function:** I bring it all together in one piece.

## Add Risk Dimensions: Audit

I decided that half the teams create applications that are NOT under audit. This was arbitrary. The one-liner below sets teams 1,2,3 to "0" and 4,5,6 to "1." So, teams 1,2,3 are getting audited. The "0" and "1" play a part in a dynamic formula below for calculating remediation times.

```
dt$audit <- if_else(dt$id > total/2,1,0)
```

## Add Risk Dimensions: Exposure Levels

I also decided that there are three levels of exposure – external, partner, and internal. There is no reason you can't have more. I wanted both text and numerical values. As you can see, I set every other team to a particular exposure level.

```
#Set Exposure Type
dt$exposure[dt$idTeam %in% c(1, 4)] <- "external"
dt$exposure[dt$idTeam %in% c(2, 5)] <- "partner"
dt$exposure[dt$idTeam %in% c(3, 6)] <- "internal"

#Add Exposure ID Field
dt$exposure_id[dt$exposure == "external"] <- 1
dt$exposure_id[dt$exposure == "partner"] <- 2
dt$exposure_id[dt$exposure == "internal"] <- 3
```

## Add Risk Dimensions: View Combination

The six teams each have an exposure type and an audit state. These values will be used in generating semi-random remediation times. Here is the combination of teams with risk:

```
> dt %>% select(idTeam,exposure, exposure_id, audit) %>% distinct()
   idTeam exposure exposure_id audit
1:      1 external           1     0
2:      2 partner           2     0
3:      3 internal          3     0
4:      4 external          1     1
5:      5 partner           2     1
6:      6 internal          3     1
```

## Add Identifiers: Create Names

Now we can take the data from our asset risk definitions to create team names. genFactor() looks at the idTeam column which holds 1,2,3,4,5,6, as seen below. In the process, it created a temporary column for the team names. I copy those over into the "team" column.

```
dt <- genFactor(dt, "idTeam",
          labels = c("external audit", "partner audit", "internal audit",
                  "external no audit", "partner no audit",
                  "internal no audit"))

#Copy the team name over and get a clean dataframe.
dt$team <- dt$fidTeam
```

This is what our data looks like now:

```
> dt
        idTeam              team nDays    id extreme_event critical_event high_event extreme critical high
   1:        1     external audit     1     1             0              1          0       0        1    0
   2:        1     external audit     2     2             0              0          0       0        0    0
   3:        1     external audit     3     3             0              0          0       0        0    0
   4:        1     external audit     4     4             0              1          1       0        1    2
   5:        1     external audit     5     5             0              1          0       0        1    0
  ---
2186:        6  internal no audit   361  2186             0              0          0       0        0    0
2187:        6  internal no audit   362  2187             0              0          0       0        0    0
2188:        6  internal no audit   363  2188             0              1          1       0        1    2
2189:        6  internal no audit   364  2189             0              0          0       0        0    0
2190:        6  internal no audit   365  2190             0              0          0       0        0    0
        audit exposure exposure_id            fidTeam
   1:        0 external           1      external audit
   2:        0 external           1      external audit
   3:        0 external           1      external audit
   4:        0 external           1      external audit
   5:        0 external           1      external audit
  ---
2186:        1 internal           3   internal no audit
2187:        1 internal           3   internal no audit
2188:        1 internal           3   internal no audit
2189:        1 internal           3   internal no audit
2190:        1 internal           3   internal no audit
```

## *Tidy Data: Melting Data*

We need to make our growing data table tidy. That means making it better suited for data analysis. To do that, we need to take our vulnerability findings and move them into a new structure. Currently, they are in three columns, one for each criticality level. We are going to convert them into a single column.

First, we will select the columns that are important to use. Then we will "melt" the vulnerability findings data into the long format.

```
dt <- dt %>% select(idTeam, team, nDays, id, extreme, critical, high,
                    audit, exposure, exposure_id)

#Need To move melt to later as it messes with defCondition
dt <- melt(dt, id.vars = c("idTeam","team","nDays","id","audit",
                           "exposure","exposure_id" ),
           measure.vars = c("extreme", "critical", "high"),
           variable.name = "severity", value.name = "hits")
```

Here is what our data looks like after putting the vulnerabilities into a single column:

```
> dt
        idTeam              team nDays    id audit exposure exposure_id severity hits
   1:        1     external audit     1     1     0 external           1  extreme    0
   2:        1     external audit     2     2     0 external           1  extreme    0
   3:        1     external audit     3     3     0 external           1  extreme    0
   4:        1     external audit     4     4     0 external           1  extreme    0
   5:        1     external audit     5     5     0 external           1  extreme    0
  ---
```

```
6566:     6 internal no audit    361 2186    1 internal         3     high   0
6567:     6 internal no audit    362 2187    1 internal         3     high   0
6568:     6 internal no audit    363 2188    1 internal         3     high   2
6569:     6 internal no audit    364 2189    1 internal         3     high   0
6570:     6 internal no audit    365 2190    1 internal         3     high   0
```

## Tidy Data: One Vulnerability per Row

We have two problems. First, we want one vulnerability per row. And second, we should get rid of the rows that have no hits (hits are set to 0). The code below does that. Unfortunately, it also creates a problem with the index on the table. So, in the process we also reset the index.

```
#Get One Vuln Per Row i.e. it drops zeros...
dt <- dt[rep(1:.N,hits)]
dt$hits <- 1

#Reset ID field
dt$id <- 1:length(dt$idTeam)
setkey(dt,id)
```

## Remediation Timing: Severity Levels

Vulnerability remediation is a function of policy. For example, extreme vulnerabilities found on exposed assets usually get priority. Assets that fall under regulatory audit will also get priority. When extreme vulnerabilities on exposed assets fall under audit, you often see the highest priority in terms of response times.

In this section we will simulate a variety of time data – based on risk profiles. Our first step is converting our vulnerability severity levels into numbers:

```
# Make numeric for formula input
 dt$severity_id[dt$severity == "extreme"] <- 1
 dt$severity_id[dt$severity == "critical"] <- 2
 dt$severity_id[dt$severity == "high"] <- 3
```

## Remediation Timing: Create Time Formulas

We are going to use a version of the Poisson distribution to help set remediation times. I have created a formula within the defDataAdd() function below that spits out the average time for each combination of severity, exposure, and audit state.

We are going to use the formula in the function below to create average values. It is generated by using data found in other columns. Let's assume we have a high-risk (critical) use case:

- Audit is true = 0 (remember, 0 is true in this case)
- Vulnerability is "extreme" = 1
- Asset is "external" = 1

Thus the formula based on the function below would be:

- ((audit * 3 + severity_id * 3 + exposure_id * 3) * (severity_id*1.43))
- ((0 * 3 + 1 * 3 + 1 *3) * (1*1.43))
- 6 * 1.43 = 8.58

```
# Set Fix Time Based On Vuln, Asset and Audit
defFix <- defDataAdd(varname = "fix_time",
        formula = "((audit * 3 + severity_id * 3 + exposure_id * 3)
                * (severity_id*1.43))",
        dist = "noZeroPoisson")

dt <- addColumns(defFix, dt)
```

The resulting process is a random value chosen from the Poisson distribution created by the mean of 8.58. The visualization below is an example of our critical use case. It will spit out a day between 0 and 20+. The higher the probability, the more likely that number will be produced. So, 6–10 is pretty likely.

```
plot(0:20,dpois(0:20,8.58), type = "h", lwd=3,
        ylab="Probability",xlab="Remediation Days")
```

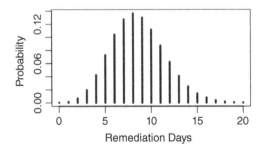

Here is what a subset of the data looks like now. Notice the far right column:

```
> dt %>% select(id, idTeam, team,audit, exposure, severity,fix_time)
         id idTeam              team audit exposure severity fix_time
   1:     1      1     external audit     0 external  extreme         9
   2:     2      1     external audit     0 external  extreme         9
   3:     3      1     external audit     0 external  extreme        10
   4:     4      1     external audit     0 external  extreme         8
   5:     5      1     external audit     0 external  extreme         8
  ---
1211: 1211      6  internal no audit     1 internal     high        82
1212: 1212      6  internal no audit     1 internal     high       103
1213: 1213      6  internal no audit     1 internal     high        85
1214: 1214      6  internal no audit     1 internal     high        84
1215: 1215      6  internal no audit     1 internal     high        83
```

## Remediation Time: Additional Time Values

There are a few more time values that need to be added in. We will capture them in one fell swoop.

- **Fix Date:** This is the number of the day the vulnerability was fixed on.
- **Status:** This is an override for the existing fix date. The chance of something not getting fixed goes up with the amount of time it is open.
- **First Seen:** This is an actual date stamp as opposed to a number.
- **Last Seen:** This too is a date stamp.
- **Week First Seen:** This is a week number for when the vulnerability was first seen.
- **Week Last Seen:** This is a week number for when the vulnerability was last seen.

```
#Fix Date: Day Number for Fix Date
defFixDate <- defDataAdd(varname = "fix_date", formula = "fix_time +
                     nDays", dist = "nonrandom")
dt <- addColumns(defFixDate, dt)

#Chance of Something NOT getting fixed goes up with more time.
defStatus <- defDataAdd(varname = "status",
                    formula = "(fix_time/1.25)/365",
                    dist = "binary")
dt <- addColumns(defStatus, dt)

#Add date stamps for first seen and last seen
dt$first.seen <- if_else(dt$nDays <= 365, as.Date(dt$nDays,
                    origin = "2020-01-01"),
                    as.Date(dt$nDays, origin = "2021-01-01"))
```

```
dt$last.seen <- if_else(dt$nDays <= 365, as.Date(dt$fix_date,
                        origin = "2020-01-01"),
                        as.Date(dt$fix_date, origin = "2021-01-01")))

#Add week number for simplicity
dt$week.fseen <- if_else(dt$nDays <= 365, week(dt$first.seen),
                        as.integer((week(dt$first.seen) + 52)))
dt$week.lseen <- if_else(year(dt$last.seen) == 2020, week(dt$last.seen),
                        as.integer(week(dt$last.seen) + 52))
```

## *The Whole Function*

Here is the complete code wrapped in a convenience function. In the examples above, I left off extraneous pieces that were distracting. This has it all.

There are three default parameters for this function. The first sets the chance of vulnerability events happening at each level of criticality. Extreme is .05, critical is .15, and high is 0.2. You can change these to whatever seems reasonable.

The event correlation is set to 0.3 – with a low count of extreme vulnerabilities, you can't go much above a 0.4.

Lastly, patch_fail can be any positive number. I usually set it between 1 and 3. But, there is no reason you can't set it to .5. The lower the number, the fewer vulns get fixed.

```
GetSecResults <- function(events = c(.05,.15,.2), event_corr = 0.3,
                        patch_fail = 1){
    #Simplify, 6 team combinations, so groups of 6
    team_count <- 6
    days <- 365
    total <- days * team_count

    # Create 6 Groups of 365 Each.
    team <- defData(varname = "team", dist = "nonrandom",
                    formula = 0, id = "idTeam")
    team <- defData(team,varname = "nDays",dist = "nonrandom",
                    formula = days)
    team <- genData(team_count, team)
    team <- genCluster(team, cLevelVar = "idTeam",
                    numIndsVar = "nDays", level1ID = "id")

    #Put days into the nDays columns
    team$nDays <- (team$id - (365*(team$idTeam - 1)))

    # Probability each day will have one or more extreme,
    # critical or high risk events.
    # Mild correlation between the variables
    dt <- genCorGen(n = total, nvars = 3, params1 = c(events[1], events[2],
                    events[3]),
                    dist = "binary", rho = event_corr,
                    corstr = "cs", wide = TRUE,
                    method = "ep",
                    cnames = "extreme_event,critical_event,high_event",
                    id = "id")
```

```
# For each day with an Ext,Crit,High events randomly draw
#  a small number of hits for each
# These are slightly more correlated.
dt <- addCorGen(dtOld = dt, idvar = "id", nvars = 1, rho = .4,
                corstr = "cs", dist = "poisson",
                param1 = "extreme_event", cnames = "extreme")
dt <- addCorGen(dtOld = dt, idvar = "id", nvars = 1, rho = .4,
                corstr = "cs", dist = "poisson",
                param1 = "critical_event", cnames = "critical")
dt <- addCorGen(dtOld = dt, idvar = "id", nvars = 1, rho = .4,
                corstr = "cs", dist = "poisson",
                param1 = "high_event", cnames = "high")

#Event showed 1 but poisson returned 0 - Make it at least 1
dt$extreme[dt$extreme_event == 1 & dt$extreme == 0] <- 1
dt$critical[dt$critical_event == 1 & dt$critical == 0] <- 1
dt$high[dt$high_event == 1 & dt$high == 0] <- 1

#Merge the Team/Days data with the hits/events data
dt <- mergeData(team, dt, "id")

#Add Exposure Categories for Audit and Exposure Type
dt$audit <- if_else(dt$id > total/2,1,0)

#Set Exposure Type
dt$exposure[dt$idTeam %in% c(1, 4)] <- "external"
dt$exposure[dt$idTeam %in% c(2, 5)] <- "partner"
dt$exposure[dt$idTeam %in% c(3, 6)] <- "internal"

#Add Exposure ID Field
dt$exposure_id[dt$exposure == "external"] <- 1
dt$exposure_id[dt$exposure == "partner"] <- 2
dt$exposure_id[dt$exposure == "internal"] <- 3

#Add Names based on audit and exposure type -
#note that this is just text, idTeam is most important.
dt <- genFactor(dt, "idTeam",
     labels = c("external audit", "partner audit", "internal audit",
                "external no audit", "partner no audit",
                "internal no audit"))

#Copy the team name over and get a clean dataframe.
dt$team <- dt$fidTeam

## Clean Table
dt <- dt %>% select(idTeam, team, nDays, id, extreme,
                    critical, high, audit, exposure, exposure_id)

#Melt data so we have one severity column
dt <- melt(dt, id.vars = c("idTeam","team","nDays","id","audit",
                           "exposure","exposure_id" ),
           measure.vars = c("extreme", "critical", "high"),
           variable.name = "severity", value.name = "hits")
```

```r
#Cache records with Zeros for Poisson
dtZeros <- dt %>% filter(hits == 0)

#Get One Vuln Per Row i.e. it drops zeros...
dt <- dt[rep(1:.N,hits)]
dt$hits <- 1

#Reset ID field
dt$id <- 1:length(dt$idTeam)
setkey(dt,id)

#####Get Remediation Times

# Make numeric for formula input
dt$severity_id[dt$severity == "extreme"] <- 1
dt$severity_id[dt$severity == "critical"] <- 2
dt$severity_id[dt$severity == "high"] <- 3

# Set Fix Time Based On Vuln, Asset and Audit
defFix <- defDataAdd(varname = "fix_time",
        formula = "((audit*3 + severity_id * 3 + exposure_id * 3) *
                    (severity_id*1.43))",
        dist = "noZeroPoisson")

dt <- addColumns(defFix, dt)

#Fix Date
defFixDate <- defDataAdd(varname = "fix_date",
                    formula = "fix_time + nDays",
                    dist = "nonrandom")
dt <- addColumns(defFixDate, dt)

#Chance of Something NOT getting fixed goes up with more time.
defStatus <- defDataAdd(varname = "status",
            formula = "(fix_time/..patch_fail)/365", dist = "binary")
dt <- addColumns(defStatus, dt)

#Add date stamps for first seen and last seen
dt$first.seen <- if_else(dt$nDays <= 365,
                    as.Date(dt$nDays, origin = "2020-01-01"),
                    as.Date(dt$nDays, origin = "2021-01-01"))

dt$last.seen <- if_else(dt$nDays <= 365,
                    as.Date(dt$fix_date, origin = "2020-01-01"),
                    as.Date(dt$fix_date, origin = "2021-01-01"))

#Add week number for simplicity
dt$week.fseen <- if_else(dt$nDays <= 365, week(dt$first.seen),
                    as.integer((week(dt$first.seen) + 52)))
dt$week.lseen <- if_else(year(dt$last.seen) == 2020,week(dt$last.seen),
                    as.integer(week(dt$last.seen) + 52))

    return(dt)
}
```

## Advanced Simulation

We have covered a lot in this chapter. You were introduced to a tool for creating large amounts of correlated data using simstudy. This tool makes it easy to imagine a data-generating process and to reasonably model in a short afternoon.

I don't expect you to master simstudy from this introductory chapter. But, I do believe you can get some mileage from what we created.

To that end, let's put our new function to work. If you look back to the hierarchical diagram toward the beginning of this chapter, you will see one product at the top with several teams below. Most companies have several large products with numerous teams. Let's create three product groups and merge them together. We can make each product group slightly different in characteristics. Again, if you manifesto_functions.R, you will have all of these functions ready to go.

```
source("manifesto_functions.R")

#Product Team With Default Settings
dtGroupOne <- GetSecResults()
dtGroupOne$group <- 1

#Product Team With Lots of Vulns, Low Remediation
dtGroupTwo <- GetSecResults(c(.10, .15, .30), .4, .5)
dtGroupTwo$group <- 2

#Product Team With Less vulns, high remediation rate
dtGroupThree <- GetSecResults(c(.05, .08, .12), .4, 3)
dtGroupThree$qroup <- 3

dt <- bind_rows(dtGroupOne, dtGroupTwo, dtGroupThree)
```

Let's quickly look at small samples of our data from a group and team perspective. As you can see, we have several groups now.

```
dt %>% select(group,idTeam,team,exposure, exposure_id, audit) %>% distinct()
      group idTeam              team exposure exposure_id audit
 1:       1      1     external audit external           1     0
 2:       1      2      partner audit  partner           2     0
 3:       1      3     internal audit internal           3     0
... ...
16:       3      4  external no audit external           1     1
17:       3      5   partner no audit  partner           2     1
18:       3      6  internal no audit internal           3     1
```

You are not limited to always having six teams. Let's say you want to eliminate all the teams in group 3 that are under audit. This is how you can easily do it. Remember, 0 means it is under audit. The "!" below means "not."

```
dt3 <- dt[!(dt$group == 3 & audit == 0)]
dt3 %>% select(group,idTeam,team,exposure, exposure_id, audit) %>%
filter(group == 3) %>% distinct()
   group idTeam              team exposure exposure_id audit
1:     3      4 external no audit external           1     1
2:     3      5  partner no audit  partner           2     1
3:     3      6 internal no audit internal           3     1
```

## Quick Data Exploration

Is what we put together jiving with our intuition about the process we
expect to model? It doesn't need to be perfect, but is it close enough?

Let's get a feel for how quickly vulnerabilities are closing. In this case,
I am just exploring the range of the data and how it is roughly distributed.

```
# Range for all closed vulnerabilities
> range(dt[dt$status == 0,fix_time])
[1]    3 113

# Quantiles for all closed vulnerabilities.
> quantile(dt[dt$status == 0,fix_time])
    0%    25%    50%    75%   100%
  3.00  28.00  50.00  69.75 113.00

# Range for most critical, exposed and under audit vulns that are closed.
> range(dt[(dt$status == 0 & exposure_id == 1 & severity_id == 1 &
         audit == 0) ,fix_time])
[1]    3 16

# Quantiles for the same as above.
> quantile(dt[(dt$status == 0 & exposure_id == 1 & severity_id == 1 &
         audit == 0) ,fix_time])
  0% 25% 50% 75% 100%
   3   6   8  10   16
```

As you may recall, 8.58 was the mean remediation rate in our data
generating function for the last use case above. Our median (50%) is close
to that number. **But before we can approve this, I have spotted a
few problems.**

First, the range of fix time is too tight. That is, 3–16 days isn't random
enough – even for extreme vulnerabilities. This, of course, is my belief
about the data-generating process. It wants more spread in my data – it's
closer to what I know as an SME about reality.

More spread means more uncertainty. I will want to inject a bit more
entropy into our data. Also, should the mean rate I start with hold for a
whole year? That really is a design decision. I would like to add an effect at
the product level that represents capability maturity. In short, something that
could have an incremental impact on improvement over time.

**These advanced features get integrated into an upgraded function called: GetAdvSecResults().** I will only cover a few aspects of it here. And note, you get this function by default if you have instantiated the manifesto_functions.R script.

## Advanced Data Generation

Remember the beta distribution from the beginning of this chapter? Remember the binomial? We are bringing them back. The beta is for shaping data and the binomial uses shapes to produce hit data. Taken together, they are called the *beta-binomial distribution*.

As you may recall, the beta function works a bit like the knobs on an Etch-A-Sketch. One knob moves data along the *x*-axis of a graph. It defines the central tendency of the data. And one knob determines how spread out things are. For simstudy, we call the spread the variance.

If the data isn't spread out much, then we would say the data is dense and pointy around the central tendency. If the data is spread out, then the data looks more like a low speed bump – full of uncertainty. The central tendency and the spread knobs become inputs to the binomial distribution. Its job is to then create hits given those knobs.

Each function below takes data (audit, severity, exposure, time_adj) from the existing data table. The function then uses that data to generate parameters (knobs) for our functions.

The betaFormula() function below spits out a central tendency – a type of average. The betaVariance() in turn spits out a variance – the spread. These are our two Etch-A-Sketch knobs that determine the shape of our beta distribution.

The binomialVariance is the spread for the binomial (hit) data. The binomial function takes the input from the betaFormula(). The beta provides the expected rate and the binomial variance provides the spread. The beta Etch-A-Sketch is input into the binomial Etch-A-Sketch. Hence the name beta-binomial.

> **Note:** I have created a new advanced function for this called getAdvSecResults() that includes all these new features. You can use either function. They exist mostly for tutorial purposes.

```
# Spits out a probability that adjust based on
# time, volume, mature, risk
betaFormula <- function(audit, severity_id, exposure_id, time_adj,
                        nDays, dev_maturity) {
```

```
    adj_val <- ((nDays*2)/365) * dev_maturity
    alpha <- (((audit*3 + severity_id * 3 + exposure_id * 3) *
           (severity_id*1.43)) * (1 + time_adj))
    mult <- if_else(alpha < 10, 2.5, if_else(alpha < 30,2,1.5))
    beta <- alpha * mult
    avg <- (alpha - adj_val)/(alpha + beta)
    return(avg)
}

# Beta variance defines spread, similar to above in terms of inputs
# Just not making it sensitive to maturity...to keep spread wide
betaVariance <- function(audit, severity_id, exposure_id, time_adj){
    alpha <- (((audit*3 + severity_id * 3 + exposure_id * 3) *
           (severity_id*1.43)) * (1 + time_adj))
    mult <- if_else(alpha < 10, 2, if_else(alpha < 30,2,1.5))
    beta <- alpha * mult
    ret <- ((alpha * beta)/(alpha + beta)^2 * (alpha + beta + 1))
    return(round(ret,4))
}

# Defines how much spread for binomial. Similar to beta variance
binomVariance <- function(audit, severity_id, exposure_id, time_adj){
    avg <- (((audit*3 + severity_id * 3 + exposure_id * 3) *
           (severity_id*1.43)) * (1 + time_adj))
    mult <- if_else(avg < 10, 4, if_else(avg < 30,3,2))
    var <- round(avg * mult)
    return(var)
}
```

Below is an example of what the betaFormula() does. It determines the central tendency of our data for determining days to fix a vulnerability. The probabilities it spits out help determine the count of days out of a possible range of days.

There are six parameters for the betaFormula() function:

1. Audit: 0 means it is audited.
2. Severity: 1 means extreme vulnerability.
3. Exposure: 1 means external exposure.
4. Time Adjustment: The sum of the hit rates for each of the three severities.
5. Day of Year: The day works with the next variable – maturity.
6. Dev Maturity Level: Level 4 is the highest level of maturity. This could be NIST CSF Tier or some form of CMM (Capability Maturity Model). 1 is weakest.

```
#High Risk, Early In Year, High Dev Maturity
> betaFormula(0,1,1,.3,5,4)
[1] 0.3235082
```

```
#High Risk, Late In Year, High Dev Maturity
> betaFormula(0,1,1,.3,300,4)
[1] 0.1368316

#High Risk, Middle Of year, High Maturity
> betaFormula(0,1,1,.3,150,4)
[1] 0.2350824

#High Risk, Early Days, Lowest Dev Maturity
> betaFormula(0,1,1,.3,5,1)
[1] 0.3325146

#High Risk, High Days, Lowest Maturity
> betaFormula(0,1,1,.3,300,1)
[1] 0.2842079

#High Risk, Medium Days, Lowest Maturity
> betaFormula(0,1,1,.3,150,1)
[1] 0.3087706
```

We will use these functions to make two new columns. One column will hold a probability that is generated by the beta distribution. The second column holds the new fix_time. Hopefully, it provides the level of wiggle that reflects our SME beliefs (me) about remediation times.

I have added one additional item that increases entropy a bit. Note the addition of "time_adj." This function uses the sum of the event rates. If your extreme, critical, and high rates were 0.05, 0.15, 0.25, respectively – then your events sum is 0.45.

That value becomes the mean of a normal distribution. That distribution will randomly select a time adjustment that's roughly between 0.25 and 0.65 in this case. But, in rare cases it could go lower or higher.

> **Note:** To save on space, I have not added all of the GetAdvSecResults() function code below. To run these snippets below in context, please reference the chapter_eleven_scripts.R file on the book's website. All code is contained within the manifesto_functions.R file.

```
#Random Time adj based on event volume. Used for Fix Time Generator
defTimeAdj <- defDataAdd(varname = "time_adj", formula = eventSum,
                         variance = .1, dist = "normal")

# Add Time adj column
dt <- addColumns(defTimeAdj, dt)
```

```
#Get Prob Associated With Time from Beta Dist
betaDef <- defDataAdd(varname = "beta_prob",
                 formula = "betaFormula(audit,severity_id,
                           exposure_id,time_adj,nDays,dev_maturity)",
                 variance = "betaVariance(audit,severity_id,
                             exposure_id,time_adj)",
                 dist = "beta")

#Add column with list of probabilities
dt <- addColumns(betaDef, dt)

# Use beta probabilities as input into binomial for time to fix
binDef <- defDataAdd(varname = "fix_time",
                 formula = "beta_prob",
                 variance = "binomVariance(audit,severity_id,
                             exposure_id,time_adj)",
                 dist = "binomial")

#Create a column for time to fix.
dt <- addColumns(binDef, dt)

#Update any time to fix zero values with a 1
dt$fix_time[dt$fix_time == 0] <- 1
```

Let's print out some sample data to see what happens:

```
> dt %>% select(group,team,audit, exposure, severity, fix_time, time_adj,
             beta_prob,fix_time)
        group        team audit exposure severity fix_time     time_adj beta_prob
   1:       1  external audit     0 external  extreme       21   0.14871359 0.4946543
   2:       1  external audit     0 external  extreme       13   0.29813911 0.4038463
   3:       1  external audit     0 external  extreme       11   0.71776858 0.2416493
   4:       1  external audit     0 external  extreme       12   0.25236490 0.3867316
   5:       1  external audit     0 external  extreme        4   0.26692077 0.1956246
 ---
3425:       3 internal no audit     1 internal     high       65  -0.16248957 0.3896098
3426:       3 internal no audit     1 internal     high       49  -0.15621278 0.3150251
3427:       3 internal no audit     1 internal     high       95   0.28505569 0.4069845
3428:       3 internal no audit     1 internal     high       51  -0.02906718 0.3110701
3429:       3 internal no audit     1 internal     high      101  -0.03116936 0.5855754
```

It already looks better, at least for the high-risk items. Let's run our quantile tests again, the one that alerted me to the issues. This time we will look at each of the three groups.

```
# 5% chance of extreme vuln per day, high dev maturity
# Median 7.5 days to remediate over 1 year. Improved from ~8.5 start
> quantile(dt[(dt$status == 0 & exposure_id == 1 & severity_id == 1 &
             audit == 0 & group == 1) ,fix_time])
    0%    25%    50%    75%   100%
  1.00   1.00   7.50  12.75  25.00

# 10% chance of extreme vuln per day, moderate dev maturity
# Median 8.5 days to remediate over 1 year. Minimal change
> quantile(dt[(dt$status == 0 & exposure_id == 1 & severity_id == 1 &
             audit == 0 & group == 2) ,fix_time])
```

```
   0%    25%    50%    75%   100%
 1.00   4.75   8.50  14.00  27.00

# 13% chance of extreme vuln per day, low dev maturity
# Median 12 days to remediate over 1 year. 3.5 day increase in time
> quantile(dt[(dt$status == 0 & exposure_id == 1 & severity_id == 1 &
              audit == 0 & group == 3) ,fix_time]))
   0%    25%    50%    75%   100%
 1.00   8.00  12.00  16.25  27.00
```

This is much closer to what I wanted in terms of spread of data and adjustment to time and capability maturity. The median and spread seem about right.

Remember, the time_adj for the most part expands time. It uses the event rate. The higher the frequency of events the more time added to remediation. It's a function of work volume, but it is a random process. Sometimes the time to fix decreases slightly, which you can see in the negative values. It is only a minor adjustment.

## *Wrapping Things Up, and What's Next*

We've created a data-generating process that is a rough model of our expectations. We have a lot of exploration yet to do.

The quick quantile analysis above was purposefully rudimentary. The point being, you can tell a lot about your data when you are the one designing the data-generating process.

I could see that the spread of the data was too tight. I know enough about the standard Poisson distribution to know it might be the problem. I also knew that the beta distribution provides some easy to use data-shaping parameters. Combining the beta distribution with the binomial distribution (beta-binomial) would allow me to make a more wiggly data generator.

In terms of testing your metrics on this data, here are some things to consider:

- Can your metrics pick up subtle changes in the data-generating process?
- Are you seeing changes that you know are there, or are they hidden in noise?
- Are the risk dimensions you defined meaningful? Or do you have useless decompositions? For example, is the partner risk dimension useless? Meaning, does it have a low information value? Maybe.

Ultimately, this is what I want to know. Are the changes I am making to security processes showing up in the data? Are differences in risk reduction or control as large as expected? Are things heading in the right direction at the right rate, or are they plateauing or slowing unexpectedly? And, is there something systematically happening that can account for that change?

The tool I just created allows me to test my metrics. And in many of the chapters we do just that. We test BOOM metrics using data simulated by this process. We also use OSINT (open source intelligence from the National Vulnerability Database) data as well as anonymized data from an actual engagement.

Simulated or "real" matters little. What matters is can you confront both types of data and generate useful metrics? The answer is yes. That is, the answer is yes if the data generating process resembles actual security processes. Does the data-generating process produce timestamps in the form of hits (arrivals) and/or processes (first seen and last seen)? If so, you can use the methods in this book to measure that process over time. You can also set KPIs. And you can determine which factors in the data seem to matter most in controlling rates of change.

## Notes

1. Albert, J. (2020). Intro to the ProbBayes Package. https://bayesball. github.io/Intro_ProbBayes.html
2. Jingchen Hu, J. A. A. (2020, July 30). *Probability and Bayesian Modeling*. Chapman and Hall/CRC Press. https://bayesball.github.io/BOOK/ probability-a-measurement-of-uncertainty.html
3. Simulation of Study Data. (2021). SimStudy. https://kgoldfeld.github. io/simstudy/index.html
4. Nelson, D. (2020b, November 20). Spotify scales its infrastructure with thousands of microservices, open source, and "fail faster" approach. *SiliconANGLE*. https://siliconangle.com/2020/11/20/spotify-scales-infrastructure-thousands-microservices-open-source-fail-faster-approach-kubecon/#:%7E:text=The%20company's%20infrastructure %20is%20supported,about%2020%2C000%20deployments%20per%20 day

# Epilogue: A Short One-for-One Substitution Guide

In *How to Measure Anything in Cybersecurity Risk,* we created a one-for-one substitution-based risk register. It was a simple way to get started with a quantitative approach to risk management. You use your existing risk register and replace high, medium, low, and other ordinal values with probabilities and financial impacts. A similar method can be accomplished using metrics.

Our one-for-one substitution takes an existing metrics list and substitutes in BOOM baselines. The list I will use is the Center for Internet Security (CIS) Critical Security Controls Measures and Metrics.[1] I will only cover a handful of these metrics. For each metric, I will reference the supporting chapters and provide a simple algorithm and data as an example.

There is one caveat before I start. Many of the CIS metrics measure security deployment capabilities for legacy environments. CIS considers how much coverage your deployed solutions have and how well they are configured. This is different from our focus. The Manifesto targets security outcomes. Here, an outcome is defined as what the deployed solution attains in terms of managing (mitigating) risk.

Caveats aside, deployment is a necessary capability. You can use BOOM baselines to help measure deployments, and we also extend those deployment metrics to include risk.

## BOOM for CIS Metrics

In this first section I will cover five CIS metrics – one for each BOOM baseline. Each BOOM example has several noteworthy fields. And each CIS metric could have many BOOM metrics associated with it as opposed to just one.

The first field of interest is for KPIs. You will want to adjust KPIs to your needs. Next is the simple equation field. Its purpose is to express the high-level mathematical function behind the metric. The data field provides the smallest amount of example input for the simple R metric that follows. The subsequent detail field provides an explanation for the metric while the optimization field considers more advanced ideas. Many of the advanced ideas will be explored over time in code and narrative at www .themetricsmanifesto.com.

**Asset Management One-for-One**

| CIS ID | Title | Description | | | | | |
|--------|-------|-------------|---|---|---|---|---|
| 1.1 | Utilize an Active Discovery Tool | Utilize an active discovery tool to identify devices connected to the organization's network and update the hardware asset inventory. | | | | | |
| **Measure** | | **L1** | **L2** | **L3** | **L4** | **L5** | **L6** |
| What percentage of the organization's networks have not recently been scanned by an active asset discovery tool? | | .69< | .31< | .07< | .06< | .02< | ~.0 |

| BOOM Title | Baseline | KPI | Simple Equation |
|------------|----------|-----|-----------------|
| Asset Update Rate | Burndown Rate Chp 4 | 95% updated every 24 hrs each quarter | Compliant/Total |
| **Description/Outcome** | | | |
| Assets must be inserted and or updated in the asset inventory system within SLA. | | | |
| **Simple Data Example** | | | |
| # 10 asset compliant/noncompliant rate over 90 days<br>compliant <- sum( 89, 89, 81, 85, 87, 86, 87, 86, 83, 88, 84)<br>noncompliant <- sum(1, 1, 9, 5, 3, 4, 3, 4, 7, 2, 6) | | | |
| **Simple R Metric** | | | |
| # 90% CI and Median: note uninformative prior of + 1<br>metric <- qbeta(c(.05, .5, .95), compliant + 1, noncompliant + 1)<br>round(metric,3)<br>[1] 0.942 0.954 0.964 | | | |

| Detail |
|---|
| If an asset is updated within 24 hours, it is marked compliant; otherwise, it is noncompliant. Within a quarter, a single asset would have some ratio of 90 compliant/total events. For example, in Q1 you have 945 compliant events (hits) and 55 noncompliant events (misses) for a handful of assets.<br><br>Above, the median is a 95.4% compliant rate for 1,000 events. The 90% credible interval (CI) on that data is 94.2% to 96.4%.<br><br>A lower bound CI of 95%, as opposed to 94.2%, would mean you have credibly beat your KPI. You can refer to Chapter 10 for a discussion on scoring scores. |
| **Optimization Considerations** |
| What is the relationship between asset update rates and patching rates? You could answer that in part with a regression model. The simplest of models would put "patch rate" as the outcome and "asset update rate" as the predictor. These rates would be per asset over a time frame.<br><br>What if there is no apparent relationship between patch rate and asset update rate? As an expert, does that match your expectations? Meaning, have you been pushing for better asset scanning and faster asset management updates with the hopes of faster patching? Or, if there is a relationship, is the relationship as strong as you are hoping (paying) for?<br><br>Models like these will be explored over time at the book's site. This model would be a standard regression model as opposed to a logistic regression model. Chapter 8 used a logistic regression model. |

### Multifactor Authentication One-for-One

| CIS ID | Title | Description | | | | | |
|---|---|---|---|---|---|---|---|
| 4.5 | Use Multifactor Authentication for All Administrative Access | Use multifactor authentication and encrypted channels for all administrative account access. | | | | | |
| **Measure** | | **L1** | **L2** | **L3** | **L4** | **L5** | **L6** |
| What percentage of the organization's hardware assets are not configured to utilize multifactor authentication and encrypted channels for all elevated account access? | | .69< | .31< | .07< | .06< | .02< | ~.0 |

| BOOM Title | | Baseline | KPI | Equation |
|---|---|---|---|---|
| Admin Non-MFA Use Rate | | Arrival Rate Chp 5 | 0% | Login/Time |
| **Description/Outcome** | | | | |
| Determine MFA coverage by measuring the admin login without mfa weekly rate. | | | | |
| **Simple Data Example** | | | | |
| # Admin non mfa logins per week over 12 weeks<br>non_mfa_logins <- c(13,14,7,14,6,8,15,9,10,9,5,11) | | | | |
| **Simple R Metric** | | | | |
| # Probability of 10 or more logins per week<br>login_risk <- 1 - ppois(10, lambda=mean(non_mfa_logins))<br>round(login_risk,2)<br>[1] 0.43 | | | | |
| **Detail** | | | | |
| We want to drive non-mfa admin logins to zero. We treat non-mfa admin logins like threats to measure and stop. There is a rate with which they happen over time across various systems be they hardware or SaaS based.<br><br>For example, in a 12-week period, assume there were 120 non-mfa based admin logins. That is a rate of 10 (120/10). This could be 120 individuals or one person logging in.<br><br>The likelihood of 10 or more non-mfa admin logis per week is 43%. The goal is to a 0% of 1 or more non-mfa logins per week. | | | | |
| **Optimization Considerations** | | | | |
| The data I used was artificial. It fits a standard Poisson model well. Assuming the data has more variance (wiggle), you would want to use a gamma-Poisson Bayesian model like we did in Chapter 5. If the data was very sparse with many zeros, then we would consider a zero-inflated Poisson model. I will touch on the zero-inflated model at the book's site. | | | | |

## DNS Filtering One-for-One

| CIS ID | Title | Description | | | | | |
|---|---|---|---|---|---|---|---|
| 7.7 & 8.7 | Use of DNS Filtering Services | Use DNS filtering services to help block access to known malicious domains. | | | | | |
| **Measure** | | **L1** | **L2** | **L3** | **L4** | **L5** | **L6** |
| What percentage of the organization's DNS servers are using DNS filtering to help block access to known malicious domains? | | .69< | .31< | .07< | .06< | .02< | ~.0 |

| BOOM Title | Baseline | KPI | Equation |
|---|---|---|---|
| Evil DNS Time to Live | Survival Analysis Chp 2 | 95% Blocked <= 24 hours | (times <= 24) / sum(times) |

**Description/Outcome**

Time to live (ttl) of evil sites from first access to block.

**Simple Data Example**

```
# Diff in days between domain access and block
diff <- c(1, 2, 5, 1, 4, 18, 4, 20, 1, 5, 8, 9, 5, 2, 1, 7, 12, 22, 1, 14)

# 1 means blocked and 0 means not blocked . . . hence censored
status <- c(1, 1, 1, 1, 1, 0, 1, 1, 1, 1, 0, 1, 1, 1, 1, 1, 1, 0, 1, 1)
tmm <- tibble(diff, status)
```

**Simple R Metric**

```
# Build survival object
res <- survfit(data = tmm, Surv(diff, status) ~ 1)

# Get basic metric where time equals 1 day
res$n.event[res$time == 1]/res$n
[1] 0.25

# Print out survival object, shows median ttl of evil urls and their conf interval.
res
    n events median 0.95LCL 0.95UCL
   20    17      5       2      14
```

**Detail**

Effective filtering reduces the time to live (ttl) of evil domains. This metric measures the ttl of evil urls where attempts to connect to the domain were made prior to getting blocked – meaning the domain was eventually put on to a "blocklist" but at least one host attempted to reach that domain.

You can query DNS history to find preblocked evil domains (assuming you are logging this information). It is a post-hoc query that happens after the domain appears on a blocklist.

You want to record the earliest attempt to reach domains on the blocklist. You also want to record the date the domain was added to the blocklist. These are your first.seen and last.seen timestamps. The difference between those dates is the count in days aka diff.

Any malicious domains that are active, yet not on the blocklist, are censored per Chp 2. Their status is marked with a 0, otherwise 1.

| Optimization Considerations |
| --- |
| Assume you want to reduce the ttl of accessed evil domains. There are capabilities you may be deploying for this. Some capabilities are threat intelligence based, some are analytics (ML) based, and others are training based. |
| Let's assume you are interested in comparing survival times between two threat feeds. Each source is numbered 1–2. You would need to know which source was responsible for the insert into the domain to the blocklist. This would require an additional variable as such: |
| source <- c(1, 1, 1, 2, 2, 1, 2, 1, 2, 1......)<br>tmm <- tibble(diff, status, source)<br>res <- survfit(data = tmm, Surv(diff, status) ~ source) |
| This would allow you to detect any differences between the sources in terms of the volume and impact in reducing the ttl of this class of residual risk. |

## Cloud Configuration One-for-One

| CIS ID | Title | Description | | | | | |
| --- | --- | --- | --- | --- | --- | --- | --- |
| 11.1 | Maintain Standard Security Configurations for Network Devices | Maintain standard, documented security configuration standards for all authorized network devices. | | | | | |
| **Measure** | | **L1** | **L2** | **L3** | **L4** | **L5** | **L6** |
| What percentage of the organization's network devices do not utilize a standard, documented security configuration standard for the device? | | .69< | .31< | .07< | .06< | .02< | ~.0 |

| BOOM Title | Baseline | KPI | Equation |
| --- | --- | --- | --- |
| Cloud Configuration Escape Rates | Escape Rates Chp 7 (Chp 4) | 5% | Escaped / Total |
| **Description/Outcome** | | | |
| CIS cloud infrastructure misconfigurations found in development that escaped into production. | | | |

| Simple Data Example |
|---|
| # 10 asset compliant/noncompliant rate over 90 days<br>dev <- sum( 110, 122, 130, 200, 210, 301, 178, 189, 333, 213)<br>prod <- sum(5, 2, 12, 5, 13, 14, 23, 24, 17, 32, 16) |

| Simple R Metric |
|---|
| # 90% CI and Median<br>metric <- 1 - qbeta(c(.05, .5, .95), dev, prod)<br>round(metric,3)<br>[1] 0.085 0.076 0.067 |

| Detail |
|---|

This is a specific sub-use case of the 11.1 CIS metric.

Cloud infrastructure is built in development using infrastructure as code (IaC). IaC files can be scanned against CIS standards using static analysis. This is "build time" scanning, similar to static analysis for software. The same "build-time" CIS standards can be applied to "run time" via dynamic scans – most modern vulnerability management providers perform these scans.

If a CIS control is found to be misconfigured in development (staging) and then later found in production, it would be marked as escaped. If it was found misconfigured in development and not in production it would be marked as fixed.

As you can see, the R model is the same as the burndown metric. It is based on the same models you used in Chapters 4 and 7.

| Optimization Considerations |
|---|

What capabilities have you deployed to reduce misconfigurations getting into production?

One capability to consider is CICD integrated policy management.[2] Policies can block misconfigurations in development prior to production. Can you measure the difference in escape rates where policies are in use? For example, is there a measurable before-and-after effect for a given product team over time? Is there a measurable difference across teams? Are the escape rate differences of the magnitude you expected?

In terms of risk, CIS controls have severities. You would want to measure how different risk levels are being treated. Higher-risk items should escape much less frequently than lower-risk items. Is there a difference in escape rates based on severity?

A logistic regression model similar to the ones used in Chapter 8 can be applied to these questions. Look to the book's site for more complete examples like these over time.

## Account Disablement One-for-One

| CIS ID | Title | Description | | | | | |
|---|---|---|---|---|---|---|---|
| 16.8 | Disable Any Unassociated Accounts | Disable any account that cannot be associated with a business process or business owner. | | | | | |
| **Measure** | | **L1** | **L2** | **L3** | **L4** | **L5** | **L6** |
| What percentage of the organization's user accounts are not disabled if they cannot be associated with a business process or owner? | | .69< | .31< | .07< | .06< | .02< | ~.0 |

| BOOM Title | Baseline | KPI | Equation |
|---|---|---|---|
| Orphaned Account Disablement Wait-Times | Wait-Times Chp 5 | 5% < 1 Week | events/ time |

**Description/Outcome**

The time between difficult to disable accounts materializing.

**Simple Data Example**

```
events <- 38
time_days <- 365
wait_time <- events / time_days
```

**Simple R Metric**

```
# Chance of a high risk disablement showing up in seven days or less.
pexp(q = 7, rate = wait_time)
[1] 0.52

# Chance for days 1 thru 7
round(pexp(q = 1:7, rate = wait_time),2)
[1] 0.10 0.19 0.27 0.34 0.41 0.46 0.52
```

**Detail**

Disabling user accounts rapidly (be it human or system based) is important. Unmanaged accounts can be vectors for attack. They should appear infrequently. When they do appear, they may create extra work to figure out who owns them and what impact there is in disablement.

The fact is, there are many queues related to IAM management. This is just one of a variety of example metrics that can be used to both understand the rate of risk as well as potential workload.

---

**Optimization Considerations**

There may be a variety of IAM related processes and technologies you put in place to reduce risk and keep up with work queues. As you roll out betterments, can you tell if they are working over time? An advanced analytic method for measuring change over time is longitudinal analysis.

Longitudinal analysis is a form of multilevel regression modeling. It is beyond the scope of this book to consider such models. They will be covered over time at the book's website.

---

## Focusing on Outcomes

A challenge in metrics design is focusing on outcomes. As stated, most metrics focus on deployment. To find and determine outcomes, I like to ask, *"What would you see occurring specifically (mathematically unambiguously) that would let you know the capability you have deployed works?"* Alternatively, you could ask, *"What would it get for you if this capability was operating perfectly?"*

Questions like these are used to determine if there is a risk outcome. You want to turn risk outcome statements into one or more metrics, which I did above in long form. You can also start simpler. Use the two questions above to rapidly define your outcomes and then map them to BOOM baselines.

Let's do some rapid outcome analysis by taking a set of five CIS metrics. We will extract metric outcomes for each of them. For each set, I ask, "If this CIS deployment metric works perfectly, how would I know that risk is being reduced?" Or simply, "What would I see occurring that would let me know risk is reducing?"

Look at the first example below. The CIS metric ask you to measure unsupported software. If you get rid of unsupported software, what would you see? For one thing, you would see software patches materializing. A leading indicator of systems falling out of support is slowing patch releases.

To increase the amount of patchable systems, you need to burn down unsupportable software. Thus, your KPI should be ~100% patchable software. To get there you will need to stay on top of burning down (removing) unsupported systems. You stay on top of that by measuring time to patch.

You can use this same approach to iterate dozens of BOOM metrics. The ones that bubble up to the top can be written up more thoroughly, as I did with the first five metrics examples above.

## CIS to BOOM Resources

| CIS | Title | Metric Outcome(s) | BOOM |
|-----|-------|-------------------|------|
| 2.2 | Ensure Software Is Supported by Vendor | **Outcome:** Keep patchable systems on the network.<br>■ Monitor time to patch/update<br>■ Removing exploitable, unsupportable software | ■ Survival: Chp 2<br>■ Burndown: Chp 4 |
| 2.10 | Segregate High Risk Assets | **Outcome:** Keep segmenting critical assets to reduce blast radius and lateral movement.<br>■ New unsegmented high-risk asset rate<br>■ TTL of unsegmented high-risk assets<br>■ % of high-risk assets that are segmented | ■ Arrival: Chp 5<br><br>■ Survival: Chp 2<br>■ Burndown: Chp 4 |
| 4.8 | Alert on Changes to Admin Group Membership | **Outcome:** Monitor and baseline rate of admin change and respond quickly to alerts.<br>■ New admin added rate<br>■ Next admin added rate<br>■ Time to respond to alerts | ■ Arrival: Chp 5<br>■ Wait-time: Chp 6<br>■ Survival: Chp 2 |
| 6.8 | Regularly Tune SIEM | **Outcome:** Respond to, and validate, true positives faster.<br>■ Time to validate true positives alerts<br>■ True positive turned false rate<br>■ False negative rate<br>■ Critical dwell time (time to discover) | ■ Survival: Chp 2<br>■ Escape: Chp 7<br>■ Arrival: Chp 5<br>■ Survival Chp 2 |
| 9.5 | Implement Application Firewalls | **Outcome:** Block escaped vulnerabilities without blocking functionality.<br>■ Successfully mitigating known vulnerabilities<br>■ Count of legit traffic that triggers WAF | ■ Burndown: Chp 4<br>■ Arrivals: Chp 5 |

This was a quick brainstorming example. It's one you can apply right now. Your first step can be confronting your deployed solutions. Ask what you would see occurring in terms of risk reduction if the capability worked perfectly. The answers should be in the form of outcome statements. You then turn outcome statements into one or more BOOM metrics. They will be some form of burndown, arrivals, interarrivals, escape, and survival.

## Next Steps

There are a small handful of security metrics books in circulation. Of the ones that I have read, they tend to follow along the same lines as the CIS metrics. This is not a problem. In fact, it's very useful. You can use that literature to perform more one-for-one metrics substitutions.

The good news is that there are other sources beyond niche books for your metrics inspiration. Personally, I like to use security frameworks. One example is The Mitre Att&ck framework.[3] It can provide a career's worth of metric wealth.

Mitre Att&ck focuses on threat actor techniques and how to mitigate/detect them. The lists of mitigations and detections are nothing more than capability deployment recommendations. So, in that regard, it is just like the CIS metrics. Again, this is not problematic. It requires you to ask confrontational questions to design outcome-based metrics.

Let's walk through one quick example. Navigate to the Mitre site https://attack.mitre.org/techniques and click on "tactics." From there, you can drill into the "initial access" tactic and then into the "external remote services" techniques. This will give you three lists. The first is a list of over 20 procedural examples. Many of these examples are nation-state-level threat actors. Just below the procedural examples is a small handful of mitigations and detections. If you look at the mitigations, you can see two we addressed above: MFA and Network Segmentation.

Hopefully, you can see how to broadly apply the one-for-one substitution approach Mitre and more. Whatever framework or list you use, your process remains the same:

- Translate a security deployment requirement into one or more measurable outcomes.
- Map your outcomes to the appropriate BOOM baseline.
- Determine the required data inputs.

Remember: Baseline data inputs are derived from timestamps. Timestamps become count of events.

I suspect that there will be a section on the book's site dedicated to Mitre Att&ck and other frameworks. That being said, nothing stops you from getting started right now. Just getting clear about outcomes is value in and of itself.

## Notes

1. https://www.cisecurity.org/white-papers/cis-controls-v7-measures-metrics/
2. https://www.openpolicyagent.org/
3. https://attack.mitre.org/

# Index

Page references in *italics* refer to figures.

# V

values, shaping, 252
Vergeltungswaffe 1 (Vengeance
　　Weapon 1) (V-1), *81*, 81
vulnerabilities, 249
　arrival, probability, *119*
　data, data table formatting, *23*
　number, *108*
　probability, contrast, *9*
　processes/events, *20*
vulnerabilities per week, *106*, *107*
vulnerability
　count, *89*, 262–263
　creation, 258
　data structure, creation, 260–262
　data table, correlated
　　vulnerabilities (presence), 261
　interarrivals, simulation, 125
　management, modeling, 257–258
　management policy
　　curve, *187*, *188*

materialization, probability, 118
rate, *132*
remediation capabilities, 229
team, merger, 263
values, simulation, 102
vulnerability business intelligence
　(vulnerability BI), 230

# W

wait-time (interarrival time),
　10, 51, 148
　forecasting, 118–119
　models, 116–120
　rates, 111
wait-time by day, 115–116
Wald, Abraham, 6
web application, 198
weekly vulnerability arrival
　rate, *96*, *98*
"what-if" scenario, 207
wrapper function, 209–211